CHARLES TEMPLETON

An Anecdotal Memoir

CHARLES TEMPLETON

An Anecdotal Memoir

McClelland and Stewart

McClelland and Stewart Limited
The Canadian Publishers
25 Hollinger Road
Toronto M4B 3G2

Canadian Cataloguing in Publication Data
Templeton, Charles, 1915-
   Charles Templeton: an anecdotal memoir

Includes index.
ISBN 0-7710-8545-1

1. Templeton, Charles, 1915-   2. Authors – Canada
– Biography.   3. Canada – Biography.   I. Title.

FC601.T45A3   971.06′092′4   C83-098534-4
F1034.3.T45A3

Printed and bound in Canada
by T. H. Best Printing Company Limited

For my children —
Deborah
Michael
Bradley
Tyrone

Books by Charles Templeton

Life Looks Up
Evangelism for Tomorrow
Jesus
Act of God
The Kidnapping of the President
The Third Temptation
Charles Templeton: An Anecdotal Memoir

The world's a scene of changes, and to be
Constant, in Nature were inconstancy

—Abraham Cowley

CONTENTS

FOREWORD

All the characters in this book are real. Any resemblance to anyone living or dead is not coincidental but is the deliberate intention of the author. The people and places referred to exist, or did exist at the time referred to, although too many of them have changed or gone.

Fact recounted is invariably fiction; any event is coloured in the perceiving and the telling. In these pages I traverse more than two-thirds of a century and recall hundreds of incidents. It may be that others will remember some things differently. If my recollection is at any point inaccurate, it is a result of the tenuousness of memory and not for want of a desire to present things as they happened. You may find some bias here, but no malice.

Many of the incidents are told in part through dialogue. My memory is acute but it is not, of course, adequate to recall the exact words spoken. Dialogue is employed as a device to enable me to convey what happened and to break what would otherwise be an overly long narrative.

This is an anecdotal memoir rather than an autobiography. Judging them to be of limited interest, I have not written about my psychic struggles or intimate relationships. My purposes are to recreate various incidents and encounters in what has been an eventful life and, having had the unique opportunity to work at the heart of most of the communications media, to tell what it is like on the inside.

Beginnings

BEGINNINGS

It is doubtless true that the child is father to the man. Nevertheless, because this book is less about me than about what happened to me, I shall little more than touch on my origins and my youth, much as a watercolourist might lay in a wash as a background. I will pass lightly over those childhood traumas which, it is argued, shape us all. I do so not only because I am not sure which events did the shaping, but because any extended attempt to identify and plumb them might be tedious.

So, briefly:

Never having climbed my family tree above the lower branches, I know only that my forebears were Irish with Scottish antecedents and a dash of French. I am not even certain that my family name is Templeton. When we were children, our father used to intrigue my three sisters, my brother and me with a story that hinted at a family scandal that had led to the changing of our name to its present form.

Knowing the propensity of the Irish to trace their ancestry to kings – there were, conveniently, a host of kings – I have wondered if his story is not apocryphal; but according to father, our great grandfather was Lord Templetown of Templeton, County Armagh, Northern Ireland. He was a prominent Roman Catholic landowner, whose predecessor had been knighted by the crown for bringing fighting men from among his tenants into the British army. One of his sons, James Bradley, fell in love with a girl by the name of Kathleen Denroche, a Protestant; through her influence he began to attend services in the Methodist chapel, where he underwent what is termed today a "born-again" experience.

Shortly thereafter, he approached his father with the two requests most likely to enrage him: might he have permission to marry the young lady; and worse, might he study for the Methodist ministry? There was a towering row and permission was refused. Moreover, young James was warned that, if he persisted in his foolishness, he would be disowned and lose his patrimony.

But he did persist, and only after months of impasse, the rift was repaired in part. During an uproarious session behind the locked doors of the library, an agreement was reached: he might retain his inheritance, but only if he left the area and changed his name. He did so, and within weeks he was married. A few years later, having completed the prescribed course of study, he was ordained the Reverend James Bradley Templeton, a minister in the Methodist Church of Ireland.

The couple produced nine sons. Most of the boys had different birthplaces because of the Methodist custom of moving its clergy to a different parish every three years. My father, William Loftus, fifth in line, was born in 1889 in Roscree, County Tipperary. At fourteen he was sent to boarding school at Methody, a denominational college, and then to Trinity College, Dublin.

At twenty, seeing no future for himself in Ireland, he followed in the way of thousands of his peers and left for the promise of Canada. In Toronto there was little work, and he was reduced to pushing a merchandise-cart at the T. Eaton Company for eight dollars a week. He got the job through a subterfuge, stating on his application that he was from Timothy Eaton's home town, Ballymena, it being well known that you were sure of a job at Eaton's "if you were a Ballymena man and could sign your name."

Not many months afterwards, he met a young lady, Marion Elizabeth Poyntz, who had, oddly enough, emigrated to Canada from Ballymena. She had been born in Belfast, the eldest of five children born to Robert James Poyntz, a draper, and Doris Elizabeth Kershaw. Though her father was, as the saying had it, "in trade," mother took particular pride in the fact that her mother's brother was Sir Louis Kershaw of Lancashire, England. The premise was a dubious one, but through our youth, we children were often admonished to "stand up straight – you have blue blood in your veins."

Mother and father were surely mismatched. She was a high-spirited, happy woman from a family that had a great love of fun, a highly developed sense of the ridiculous and an enormous zest for life. She loved to perform in public and was gifted with an excellent singing voice; she won the contralto division of the

Saskatchewan Musical Festival in 1925. Among my most vivid memories are those of my mother, dressed in a pierrot costume – a vogue at the time – singing or reciting an unabashedly sentimental bit of doggerel, "Skimpsy Was a Jockey." Ah, how the tears did flow!

Dad could not have been more different. His reserve may have stemmed from his being "a child of the manse" or from his years within the strict regimen of a Methodist boarding school. I have seen him laugh until reduced to tears, unable to finish the story he was telling, but he was more often stiff and restrained, sometimes forbiddingly so. A fastidious man in speech and dress, he preferred Loftus (with the diminutive, Loftie) to his first name, William, and only encouraged "Bill" in his later years.

Dad was a handsome man and irresistible to some women. He was a different man when there were women about: a softness and a hint of vulnerability entered his manner. And there were many women. Perhaps because he had been raised by an undemonstrative father, had no sisters, and was one of nine boys competing for his mother's attention, he had a need to be enfolded in female arms. Whatever the causes, he was loved by many women in his lifetime, even to the end of his eighty-one years.

Inevitably, this led to tension in the marriage and as inevitably to its dissolution. From the time I was fourteen, I saw my father only occasionally and rarely heard from him. When he left, he took with him something vital from mother. Her courage and resourcefulness remained, and there were flashes of the enormously zestful woman she had been in the early years of her marriage, but she was only restored to something of her former self five years later when she found solace in religion.

I was born October 7, 1915, in Grace Hospital, Toronto. I was the second of five children and was named Charles after one of my father's brothers who was languishing in a German prisoner of war camp. (He died three weeks after the armistice when, too impatient to wait for transportation home to Ireland, he set off on foot and was felled by influenza.) My three sisters were all given good Irish names: Kathleen, Mickey (her baptismal name was Doris but it was never used) and Norah. My younger brother is William, after Dad. When I was six months old, the family removed to Regina, where Dad had been named merchandise manager of the new Robert Simpson Company store.

Regina in the 1920s was a burgeoning but unprepossessing city, sprouting for no logical reason – except that the CPR had willed it – from the flat, unrelieved prairie. Today, it remains a friendly but undistinguished place: its core unexceptional, its climate often inhospitable, its small frame houses characteristically western; such beauty as it has, man-made. But to a boy growing up, it lacked nothing.

I lived in the city but could be on the open prairie within minutes. There the horizons are as distant as they are at sea, and the land is overarched by more sky than I would ever see again. There is much in landlocked Saskatchewan to conjure up the sea: the horizon is an unbroken line. The endless expanses of grasses and grainfields can be transformed by the wind into a vast ocean, with tiny ripples and broad combers moving across the surface. Towering cumulus glide majestically across the blue to the far horizon where they heap up like snow-covered mountains on the distant shoreline. Little wonder Saskatchewan men, when given the option, are disposed to the naval branch of the Armed Forces.

The wind is the dominant fact of life on the prairie. Like men of the sea, the people of the prairies live with a constant awareness of its vagaries. In the dry years it can raise great clouds of dust in a boiling miles-high wall and sweep it across the parched land; darkening mid-day, purpling the sunset, sifting through sealed windows and closed doors, suffocating the lungs and dropping its gritty load in drifts and runnels in the lee of anything that slows its progress.

But that same wind can air out the sky as a bustling housekeeper airs out a room in spring, driving rankness and dust and pollution before it until the heavens are squeaky clean. It can be capricious with whirling dust-devils or vicious with cyclone: whipping the tip of its black maw about, gobbling trees and houses and barns and spitting out the debris. I was three when a twister ran its hellish cone through the heart of Regina. Long afterwards, I heard stories of a straw being driven through an automobile tire, of stones embedded in telephone poles, of chickens plucked naked and of a prize bull being tossed fifty yards into a neighbour's field.

But it is in winter especially that the wind determines life on the prairie. In the deep-freeze of winter the thermometer may plunge to sixty below; but what matters is the wind chill. Unimpeded by grain field or woods or mountain, the wind sweeps in: howling, blustering, badgering, tyrannizing. Walking into it, you lean forward as though ascending a slope. Moving downwind, you are driven hunched and off-balance in a stumbling run. *The cold!* It whitens ears and cheeks and fingertips. It freezes the tears on your face, congeals your matted lashes and turns your eyeballs into orbs of pain. It reams your sinuses, stiffens the hair in your nostrils and paralyzes your throat and lungs. Fifty years later, you can recall the ordeal of the mile from school to home: peering through the stitching of the woollen toque, shivering like an animal in shock, whimpering as you are bullied forward only a step ahead of panic.

For all its rigours, winter also yielded joys. The cold that flayed the skin froze the flooded surface of a skating rink within minutes. The compacted snowdrifts were of just the right consistency for the hollowing out of caves and tunnels. Oiled leather shoe-packs — heavy moccasins — turned the slightest slope into a slide. There was a hockey cushion (unlikely noun!) on every second corner and the fabulous "Duke" Keats of the Regina *Pats* was your God.

There was the cold; there was also the warmth. The shivering frenzy of undressing in an unheated bedroom was followed by the ineffable, rosy glow of the hollow in which you soon lay curled, with a wool mattress below and a goose-down comforter above. (Have I ever known such exquisite warmth since?) There was the desperate, breathless run to the corner store to fetch something forgotten and the gritty horror of "taking out the ashes" in the teeth of a howling, horizontal blizzard, but afterwards there was the ruby heat of the wood stove, with bread fragrant in the oven and soup simmering on the top, and your mother singing as she set the table, and the weekend comics (saved until now) to be read lying on your stomach on the kitchen floor.

Happy, happy days.

When I was twelve we moved back to Toronto. I was fourteen when Dad, in a fit of pique, quit Simpsons' Mutual Street store and moved to Montreal to become merchandise manager of Henry Morgan's. The promise was that we would soon join him but we never did. He went from Morgan's to The Hudson's Bay Company in Saskatoon and later Edmonton, finally — after complaining in his occasional letters about the small-mindedness and internecine rivalries of the department-store business, he quit it entirely – ending in Vancouver without a job. Each move had taken him farther from home.

Dad had sworn to starve before he would work again in a department store. During the Depression years he nearly did – and so did we. Mother, with five children and no money coming in, had no choice but to rent out rooms. We were living in a great barn of a house on Beaty Avenue in the Parkdale section of the city, and the next few years were spent with strangers in the halls, seething resentments and aching kidneys over the occupancy of the one bathroom, and the worrisome sight of mother growing wan and dispirited from work and worry. And, of course, from loneliness for my father.

To survive, we took in tourists at two dollars a night during the Canadian National Exhibition. I sifted through the ashes for any unconsumed nuggets of coal. Stews were made more substantial with flour and barley, and we filled up with bread and the standard dessert, "fish-eye pudding." It seemed the relief cheque was always late. There was one twenty-four-hour period when there was nothing, not a thing, in the house to eat. How often the six of us waited hushed and motionless – like animals freezing when a predator is near – until the bill collector had gone from the door. Fifty years later, I can see mother at the kitchen table counting the coins from a china teapot and dabbing at her eyes with a handkerchief. . . .

Through the years I have earned my living by words, spoken or written, and by my ability to draw. It was my father who turned me toward both.

Words: the Irish love to talk, and exult in disputation. In my childhood, on weekends, there were invariably guests in the parlour and the house was filled with conversation. Irishmen all, recent immigrants, managers at Simpsons most of them, they came to join my father for a drink and a bout of talk. I don't recall it happening anywhere but during those early years in Regina; it may have been that these men, fresh from "the old country," hadn't yet extended their boundaries.

I would find a chair just outside the circle of men – the women went off to the kitchen – and was allowed to stay there so long as I didn't fidget or swing my feet or interrupt. Their games were played with words: throwing out opinions, challenging each other's statements and wresting, often hotly, with meanings. I recall my father announcing on one occasion that he was prepared "to prove through unassailable logic" that black was white. Which, using a sequence of carefully planned syllogisms, he proceeded to do. The achievement set off a boisterous debate but I was oblivious to it. I was puffed with pride and dizzy with the wonder of it all.

Drawing: one idle Sunday afternoon when I was twelve, I made a sketch of Felix the Cat, a popular comic-strip character, and took it to my father. It was a rash thing to do, for each Sunday afternoon he retreated to the parlour with a variety of reading materials and a package of figs, closing the French doors behind him. He did not like to be interrupted.

But this Sunday afternoon he put his book aside and looked carefully at the drawing. "Very good, Chuck. Was it done freehand?"

"Yes."

He studied the drawing, nodding approval while I vibrated with excitement. He passed the sketch back to me. "You have a talent for drawing," he said. "Keep it up."

From that day, I drew anything and everything that caught my eye. I filled up exercise books at school, indifferent to what was being taught. After Dad left home, I mailed off sketches I thought might impress him and watched the mails for a reply. He seldom wrote, but when he did, each injection of praise stimulated me for weeks.

But I was doing poorly at school. At Parkdale Collegiate I failed grade nine (we called it First Form) and was required to repeat it, failed grade ten (standing thirty-second in a class of thirty-three), and began to repeat it, switching suddenly to the newly opened Western Technical School to study art. In the midst of the first year, "drawing a bow at a venture," I sat down at the dining-room table and made three sketches; portraits of the Toronto Maple Leafs' famous "Kid Line." Overnight, my life changed direction.

Inside Sports

INSIDE SPORTS

In the summer of 1932 the four Toronto newspapers were housed only three blocks apart. The *Star* was on the north side of King Street, midway between Bay and York. The *Mail and Empire* was on the northwest corner of the intersection at Bay and King. One short block south, at Melinda, was the *Telegram,* and east on Melinda, at Yonge, was the *Globe.*

The sports department at the *Globe* was on the second floor at the end of a long row of telegraphers' stalls – the news was transmitted by Morse code; there were no teletype machines. You took the broad staircase because the elevator was an ancient, wrought-iron contraption, subject to shuddering convulsions and unpredictable enough to give pause even to the intrepid.

The sports department was, in fact, no more than a large room. Five mismatched desks lined the south wall. The sports editor's office – a narrow, rectangular cubicle, made private by dimpled glass windows, occupied most of the wall opposite. Such open space as there was was covered with a worn, green linoleum and was usually ankle-deep with that litter once common to newsrooms but now, alas, gone.

One evening in late August, a homemade portfolio under my arm, I made my way to the sports department and stood in indecision in the doorway. I was seventeen. No one so much as looked up; everyone was busy at a typewriter or editing copy. After a while, I asked the man nearest the door, "Can you tell me where I might find Mike Rodden?"

He jerked his head toward the tiny office. "In there."

I tapped tentatively on the glass and a voice roared, "Come!" I opened the door and was immediately enveloped in a miasma of pipe-tobacco smoke, exhaled rye whisky, witch hazel aftershave and body humidity. There, in a hinge-back wooden armchair before an untidy roll-top desk was the great Mike Rodden, sports editor of the *Globe*. He pounded the typewriter for another thirty seconds and then swung around to face me.

"What the hell do you want?" he asked.

Mike Rodden was extraordinary even in an era when sports writers like Lou Marsh of the *Star* and Ted Reeve of the *Telegram* were as celebrated as most of the athletes they wrote about. Mike was a round-faced Irishman of medium height and, when I knew him, tending to corpulence. He was the prototypically macho male. On a Queen's University's football team, weighing "no more than 160 pounds soaking wet," he played at the centre of the line with an animal ferocity that intimidated opposing backfields. He had been a referee in the National Hockey League and in the Ontario Hockey Association, and was often assigned games between rival mining towns in northern Ontario where there were as many fights in the stands as on the ice. Rodden called them as he saw them and was often followed to his dressing room by gangs of hard-rock miners. He would hold them off by dropping to his back in the narrow passageway, skates aloft ready to slash. Once, as the mob beat on his door, he emerged with his skates laced to his fists. It was enough to cow them.

Now, his pipe between his teeth, a nimbus of smoke about his close-cropped white head, he glared at me and growled, "What the hell do you want?"

"I wanted to show you these," I said. I dug into my portfolio and produced three drawings; portraits of Joe Primeau, Harvey "Busher" Jackson, and Chuck Conacher, the "Kid Line" of the Toronto Maple Leafs. He looked at them closely.

"Could you do a drawing of Bobby Pearce?" he asked. Bobby Pearce, an Australian, was the world's best single sculler. He was to row the following day in an invitation race at the Canadian National Exhibition waterfront.

"I could if I had a picture," I said.

He found a photograph and handed it to me. "Have it here by six tomorrow."

The following evening I was back with the drawing. Mike looked at it and tossed it onto the desk of Tommy Munns, the assistant sports editor. "Run it," he said. "Three columns."

I stayed awake all night, and before dawn ran to the corner, barefooted and naked except for trousers, to get a newspaper from the bundle. There was my drawing – faded, for I didn't yet understand how to draw for newspaper reproduction – with a cutline describing me as "a young Toronto artist." The following day, Tommy Munns telephoned to offer me a job. I would do a daily drawing and would begin with a series – a portrait of each member of the Toronto Maple Leafs. The salary would be twelve dollars a week.

I stayed at the *Globe* for four years.

Modern journalists, working in antiseptic and decorous newsrooms, may find it odd that I was initiated into the *Globe* sports department much as a college student might be welcomed to a fraternity.

I sensed nothing amiss when I arrived at the office one night to find Mike and Tommy Munns in a heated argument. "Of course I can lift five hundred pounds," Mike shouted, hammering a fist on a desk. "Christ almighty, I've done it dozens of times."

"Mike, you're out of your mind. An Olympic weightlifter your size couldn't lift five hundred pounds."

"Five bucks" – a good day's wages then – "says I can."

There was a problem: what was there about that weighed five hundred pounds? Mike resolved it. "Gordie, what do you weigh?" (Gord Walker was later public relations director for the Canadian Football League.)

"A hundred and sixty."

"Don?" (Don Cowie was the *Globe*'s horse-racing expert.)

A shrug. "One fifty."

"And you, Templeton?"

"One eighty-five."

"All together, 495 pounds." He turned to Tommy. "Close enough?"

Tommy nodded. "But how are you going to lift the three of them?"

Mike paused, frowning. "How the hell do I do this?" More furious pondering, and then, "Got it! Here, Templeton – you're the biggest. Lie down on the floor." Lamb to the slaughter, I lay on my back, self-conscious at being the centre of attention in such august company. "Good. Now stretch your arms straight out. And spread your legs. Spread 'em!

"Okay," said Mike, his ebullience mounting. "Now, Don and

Gord, you lie down on either side of him. Templeton, put your arms around their necks. Each of you take hold of his wrists. Right. Now, both of you put a scissor-hold on Templeton's legs. Here's what I'm going to do: I'll lift Templeton. When he comes up, all three of you will, and Munns can kiss his five-spot goodbye."

A sly grin stole over Mike's face and it broke on me that I'd been had. There I lay, spread-eagled, immobilized. Each arm was snubbed about a neck. Each leg was locked. The office rang with boisterous laughter. Off came my tie. My shirt was unbuttoned. Trousers and shorts were pushed down. Mike took a pot of copy-paste – in those days, a glue that hardened to the consistency of glass – and dribbled it from my throat to my groin. Sheets of copy-paper were laid on and patted into place. Another layer and I was locked in Mike's office until the glue hardened. Half an hour later, Tommy Munns opened the door, grinned at me, and said, "Welcome to the *Globe.*"

The walk to the street car was an agony. Each step, any movement pulled out hair. At home, I ran a bath, making the water as hot as I could bear and slowly lowered myself into it. But the bath was ineffective. When finally the glue and paper had been removed, a pink, hairless area ran down the front of my body.

I was very happy.

It was one of the great eras of sport. The New York Yankees, with Babe Ruth and Lou Gehrig, were close to their prime. Carl Hubbell and Dizzy Dean displayed their pitching mastery. Joe Louis, who had seemed invincible, faltered before Max Schmeling's right cross. Jimmy McLarnin was middleweight champion. Eddie Shore, Howie Morenz, Chuck Conacher and Bill and Bun Cook dominated a six-team National Hockey League. Jesse Owens won three Olympic gold medals, to Adolph Hitler's chagrin. Jack Lovelock and Glenn Cunningham set records for the mile. Fred Perry and Helen Jacobs dominated tennis courts in the United States and Europe. Bobby Jones was trying for a comeback. The forward pass had just been introduced to Canadian football. Ab Box's soaring punts led the Toronto Argonauts to a Grey Cup. Jim Londos, "The Golden Greek," packed arenas, the star of the new-style wrestling. Six-day bicycle riding, with Canada's "Torchy" Peden, was a fad at its height, and another novelty, box lacrosse, had just been introduced. The Depression was at its peak but the sports arenas were jammed and I seldom lacked subject matter.

To a boy in his late teens, it was the best of all possible worlds. I was obsessed with sport. I had won the junior track-and-field championship at Parkdale Collegiate and had quarterbacked the football team to a Toronto final at Varsity Stadium. I was captain of the basketball team and three times cross-country champion. I made halfback with Toronto's Balmy Beach Club but got into only one game, a mud bowl with the Hamilton Tiger Cats. And now here I was, at the heart of the Canadian sports world, sitting in the press box at Maple Leaf Gardens for every NHL game and on first-name terms with many of the great athletes of the time.

Beyond that, I was well paid. The drawings I did daily for the *Globe* were syndicated to eighteen Canadian newspapers. I also syndicated, through *Central Press Canadian,* a one-column feature called *Chuck Templeton's Sportraits* – a drawing and three hundred words of copy. Tommy Munns, who did publicity for the Queensbury Athletic Club, hired me regularly to do sketches of such wrestling behemoths as George Zaharias, Danno O'Mahoney "The Irish Whip" and the Four Dusek Brothers for the official program. Ed Fitkin, who now works for Jack Kent Cooke's Los Angeles Forum, and I started a newspaper, *Canadian Sporting News.* We saved engraving costs by using the zinc etchings of my drawings for the *Globe,* and between us wrote all the copy. The venture expired after four issues.

Most evenings when I arrived at the paper with my completed drawing, Mike would summon me to his office. It had begun on my second day at work.

"How old are you, Templeton?"

"Eighteen," I said, stretching it a few months.

He reached for his wallet. "Do you know where the liquor store is?"

"No, sir."

"Forget the sir. It's at Church and Lombard." He extracted a two-dollar bill and handed it to me. "Get me a mickey of rye, Hiram Walker's 16-C. There'll be eighty cents change."

I would deliver my drawing to the engraving department and then fetch the whisky. Mike, who had already had a few belts, would close the door to his office and begin to write. I would hang around, reading the out-of-town papers, helping out any way I could, absorbing the ambience, reluctant to leave. Some nights, the sound of Mike's typewriter would slow, become intermittent and finally cease. Tommy would say to me, "Check on Mike." I would tap on the door, enter to find him slumped asleep in his chair, or discover that he had slid down and was in a heap under the desk. I would gather what had been written and take it to Tommy. "We'll need a wrap-up," he'd say, or perhaps, "Give me two or three short items."

I would finish the column in Mike's office, sometimes with my feet on the man I idolized. It was the only typewriter available, and it was bolted to the desk.

With the drink in him, Mike Rodden was a tough, combative and sometimes cruel man. He would come up beside junior members of the staff, and without warning, hook a hard right to your upper arm, numbing it for half an hour. He would light his pipe and then flick the flaming wooden match at you. Once, telling one of his inexhaustible fund of stories, an extravagant gesture threw him off balance. He staggered across the office, put a hand on a desk to recover his balance and ran a copy spike through the palm and out the back of his hand. (At the time, copy spikes were fashioned in the composing room from a pointed steel wire set in a rough-cast lead base.) Rodden stared at the protruding spike, yanked it free and finished his story. He scorned suggestions that he have it seen to, spat on both sides of the hand, massaged the spittle into the wound, wrapped a handkerchief about it and went into his office to finish his column.

The grapevine sped the terrifying rumour from the news room to the sports department and through the various beverage rooms frequented by reporters: negotiations were going on between the owners of the *Globe* and the *Mail and Empire*. The *Mail* was about to swallow the *Globe* and most of us would be fired. In 1936, in the trough of the Depression, it was sobering news. A purchase of the *Globe* by the *Mail and Empire* seemed a reasonable development. The *Globe* was the oldest paper in Toronto. It had been founded eighty-three years earlier by George Brown, one of the Fathers of Confederation, and had the smallest circulation of the four Toronto papers.

Then on November 19 the exhilarating news – the *Globe* had

bought the *Mail and Empire* and our jobs were safe! More than that, we would be moving out of our gloomy, creaking Victorian building to new premises at the corner of King and York. Heaven bless William H. Wright's money and George McCullagh's entrepreneurial dash!

At the newly formed *Globe and Mail,* all was right with the world. There was a feeling of optimism and expansiveness. The paper was enlarged. More prominence was given to sport. My cartoons sometimes ran three, four, even five columns wide. When they were exceptionally newsworthy, they were carried on the front page of the bulldog edition, to catch the eye of people on their way home late at night. And I was being asked to do special assignments by the city desk. When the Moose River mine disaster gripped the interest of the nation, I prepared drawings depicting the desperate efforts of the rescuers to reach the trapped men. When Mitch Hepburn, the flamboyant premier of Ontario, visited the editorial offices, I drew his portrait and it was carried on the front page. Heady days for a youth of twenty.

On the side, I was taking advantage of the vanity of the wealthy. When I could find the time, I went to the morgue at the *Globe* and dug out the "official" photographs of prominent Torontonians. I then rendered them larger than life size, put a mat on the drawing and presented myself unannounced at the office of the Great Man. His secretary would inform me that it wasn't possible to see him without an appointment. "I only wanted to show him this," I would say ingenuously, uncovering the drawing. Invariably, the subject would see me, ask if the sketch was for sale. And if so, for how much. "Twenty-five dollars." It was more than I made in a week at the *Globe.*

I did a dozen or more such drawings. Not once did I fail to make the sale.

In 1936, a profound change entered my life, a change that would alter radically my next twenty-one years and leave an indelible mark on my psyche. I "got religion." From my present vantage point I am at a loss to understand my blind acceptance of the fundamentalists' Christian beliefs. A number of facile explanations present themselves: that I yearned for a satisfactory father figure; that I wanted very much to repay my mother for her years

of loneliness and struggle by accepting her new-found faith; that
my adolescent experiences of sex – innocent enough in retrospect – had burdened me with guilt. But enough of amateur
psychoanalysis; whatever the reasons, I went through what is
described today as a "born-again experience."

I was nineteen, and although I had been out of school and
earning a living for almost three years, I was relatively naïve. The
family had begun to attend the Church of the Nazarene, a small
denomination in the old-fashioned Methodist tradition, in Parkdale. Mother had undergone a religious experience at the church
that had made her a changed woman. She looked better, sang as
she went about her housework and seemed filled with an inner
happiness.

All of us children responded differently to the pressures that
we surrender our lives to God. I was the only holdout. When I was
importuned to go to church – as I was almost daily – I begged off
with the excuse that I was busy at the *Globe* which, happily, did
require that I work every night but Saturday. Moreover, the
family's new religiosity did not attract me; indeed, it made me
uncomfortable, restless and sometimes impatient. I was moving
away from family and home. I had been introduced to a new
world – a stimulating one when I first encountered it at seventeen – of personal independence, downing a few beers with some
of the *Globe* staff, first-name acquaintance with celebrated athletes and attaining minor celebrity status myself.

And there was a girl. Angela. She was two years older than I
but much more sophisticated. She worked hard as a photographer's model and was strikingly beautiful in a Jean Harlow,
platinum blonde, slightly tarty way. She lived alone in a rooming
house on Carlton Street across from Maple Leaf Gardens and it
was convenient to drop in on her before or after covering events
there. I learned a lot from Angela, none of it available in books at
that time.

I took Angela to a Parkdale Collegiate Fourth Form dance at
the Canoe Club. I had left school three years earlier but wanted to
see the old gang, the fellows I'd played football and explored my
early teens with – partly because I missed them and partly
because I wanted to show off my new maturity. It was a mistake.
When I picked up Angela, she was wearing a floor-length white
satin dress and a necklace. The dress was unornamented by
ruffles or furbelows, and fitted as if it had been painted on. I

wanted to remonstrate; "Hey, this is a high-school dance!" but didn't have the courage.

At the Canoe Club we were the focus of all eyes and many low and unidentifiable wolf-whistles. I was distinguished by the pinkness of my skin and the rivulets of sweat on my brow. I was cut in on whenever we got ten feet onto the dance floor. Nobody asked me about my glamorous career as a newspaper cartoonist; everyone asked where I'd found Angela.

I took Angela to a New Year's Eve celebration. She arranged the reservations. When I picked her up it was evident that she'd gotten an early start on the evening. I was appalled to find that she'd booked a table for the New Year's Eve Gala at a hotel on Jarvis Street at Gerrard, now gone. Early on, getting into the spirit of the evening, she shouted, "Whee!" and flipped a spoon high in the air. It broke a wine glass two tables away, inflicting a slight cut on the hand of a woman seated there. We were asked to leave by a man with very wide shoulders and a club-fighter's nose. It was 9:30 New Year's Eve and there was nothing to do but go back to Angela's place.

So it went for the better part of a year, with Angela beginning to hint broadly of marriage.

One morning, I returned home at 3:00 a.m. after a party. For no obvious reason I was heavy with depression. There was a mirror in the entrance hall of our home, and I paused before it for perhaps a minute. I didn't like the man I saw there. I went softly down the hall, not wanting to awaken mother, but she heard me and called out, and I went to sit on the side of her bed.

She began to talk about God, about the happiness her faith had brought her, and about how she longed to see me with the other children in church. I heard little of what she was saying; my mind was doing an inventory of my life. Suddenly, it seemed empty and wasted and sordid. I said, "I'm going to my room."

As I went down the hall, I was forming a prayer in my head, but as I knelt by my bed in the darkness, my mind was strangely vacant; thoughts and words wouldn't come to focus. After a moment, it was as though a black blanket had been draped over me. A sense of enormous guilt descended and invaded every part of me. I was unclean.

Involuntarily, I began to pray, my face upturned, tears streaming. The only words I could find were, "Lord, come down. Come down. Come down. . . ."

It may have been minutes later or much longer – there was no sense of time – but I found myself, my head in my hands, crouched small on the floor at the centre of a vast emptiness. The agonizing was past. It had left me numb, speechless, immobilized, alone, tense with a sense of expectancy. In a moment, a weight began to lift, a weight as heavy as I. It passed through my thighs, my belly, my chest, my arms, my shoulders and lifted off entirely. I could have leaped over a wall. An ineffable warmth began to suffuse every corpuscle. It seemed that a light had turned on in my chest and its refining fire had cleansed me. I hardly dared breathe, fearing that I might end or alter the moment. I heard myself whispering softly, over and over, "Thank you, Lord. Thank you. Thank you. . . ."

After a while I went to mother's room. She saw my face, said, "Oh, Chuck . . !" and burst into tears. We talked for an hour.

When I went back to my bedroom, dawn was just breaking. I undressed, drew the shade, climbed into bed, and lay motionless in the diminishing darkness, bathed in a radiant, overwhelming happiness. Outside, the birds began their first tentative singing and I began to laugh, softly, out of an indescribable sense of well-being at the centre of an exultant, all-encompassing joy.

As might be supposed, the announcement was not greeted with shouts of "Hallelujah" in the *Globe* sports department.

With astonishing ingenuousness, I related to my associates what had happened and saw polite incredulity enter their eyes. That soon gave way to good-natured barbs and off-colour kidding. All the preacher-and-the-choir-girl jokes were dusted off. Raunchiness reached new heights. But for all the irreverent fun and the attempts to act as if nothing had changed, it became apparent I had distanced myself from them, and we were no longer at ease with each other.

I began to spend less time at the paper. I would deliver my drawing, ask if there was anything wanted of me, and leave. Mike began to send Gord Walker for his mickey of rye. I didn't try to press my faith on them, but friendship and the easy camaraderie cooled, and when the time came to tell Tommy Munns that I was leaving the paper to go into the ministry, there was relief on both sides. Tommy shook my hand, smiled his shy, off-centre smile and said, "Good luck, Chuck. I think you're nuts, but good luck."

Inside Evangelism

INSIDE EVANGELISM

I

Driving north on Avenue Road in Toronto in the summer of 1941, an unlikely sign caught my eye. It was affixed to an imposing limestone church, gothic in style and surmounted by a massive stone bell-tower. The sign read:

FOR SALE OR RENT
Auditorium or
Meeting Rooms
INQUIRE: 243 Avenue Rd.

I was in Toronto for a brief visit with my family after three years on the evangelistic trail. I had travelled most of Michigan, had ranged across northern New York State to parts of Indiana and Illinois, even dipped to the Deep South, preaching to congregations of as few as five and as many as five hundred. I owned two suits, one sufficiently presentable to preach in, a 1935 Ford Victoria with no window on the driver's side – the crumpled left door was fastened by a trousers' belt to the steering column – and six hundred dollars in savings.

During my travels I had met and married Constance Orosco, a beautiful Californian of Mexican extraction. She was a "licenced song-evangelist" in the Church of the Nazarene and had a superb soprano voice. Three years earlier, she had been awarded a starlet contract by Metro-Goldwyn-Mayer, but having been raised in a deeply religious family, she had sought release from it, choosing to sing in evangelistic campaigns. We met in Grand Rapids, Michigan, where she was the singer and I was the evangelist, and were married six weeks later.

I pulled over to the curb, pointed to the sign and said to Connie, "Let's take a look."

I learned from the rental office across the street that the

building had been vacant since the formation of the United Church of Canada in 1927, when its congregation amalgamated with the membership of the St. Paul's Methodist church down the road. The interior was forbidding. The sanctuary smelled of must and neglect. Many of the lights were burned out and the walls were streaked and peeling. I trailed my fingers through the dust on the pews.

But I was intrigued by the possibilities. The ceiling reared high in graceful Gothic arches. The great windows were of leaded glass. On the platform there was a solid oak pulpit and three massive chairs, and behind them a choir loft and an impressive bank of organ pipes. For all the dinginess, for all the peeling paint and the dust and debris, it was a soaring cathedral compared to the conse-crated shacks I'd been preaching in. Could I bring this echoing sanctuary to life again? On the spot I decided to try.

"The rent's a hundred dollars a month," I told Connie. "It will take all our savings. Are you game to try it?"

She nodded, smiling, happy at the prospect. She had come to love Toronto on our visits home and wanted very much to live in one place for longer than the customary fifteen days of a cam-paign. I signed a six-month lease, paid six hundred dollars, closing out our bank account, crossed the street and removed the sign.

Three years as an evangelist had profoundly tested my new-found faith and had introduced me to an entirely different way of life. I had been converted through the Church of the Nazarene, which did not require high academic standards of its clergy. I was ordained after reading half a dozen books and submitting to an oral examination by a group of local preachers. They seemed more interested in my orthodoxy than in my intellect, and one summed it all up: "You'll do fine, Chuck. What you lack in lightnin' you make up for in thunder."

I learned to preach by preaching and by aping others. In those early years, I traded on my ability to draw, doing swift, dramatic sketches – "chalk talks," they were called – before audiences composed mostly of young people. In the circumscribed world of the Church of the Nazarene, my background as a newspaper cartoonist made me something of a celebrity, and soon invitations to speak came from farther afield. I began my career as an evangelist by crossing the American border with a bus ticket to Lowville, New York and $1.67 in my pocket. The immigration officer was loath to let me pass. "We got plenty of unemployed here already," he said. It was 1936.

I preached in tarpaper shacks and concrete-block basements, on street corners, and at out-of-doors "camp meetings"; in hamlets marked only by a cluster of buildings at the intersection of two highways and in grubby, storefront churches in the dying cores of great cities. I preached in 110-degree heat in Paris, Kentucky, and in a tiny frame church in northern Ontario, where the only heat came from a pot-bellied stove at the centre of the meeting hall and a haze rose from the bundled bodies of the congregation. When we sang an up-tempo hymn, the exhalations suggested a steam calliope.

I preached from a wrestling ring parked in a softball stadium in Sudbury, Ontario; in an outdoor "tabernacle" in Clarksville, Tennessee, where the summer insects attracted by the platform lights were sometimes inhaled; in a church basement in Lapeer, Michigan, where the pastor and his family lived in quarters back of the platform and you could smell what they'd had for dinner each night; in an unfinished shed in Carbondale, Illinois, where all the young mothers sat in the front row breast-feeding their babies; in Tullahoma, Tennessee, where my bed swarmed with bedbugs and the chicken I saw expiring in the driveway when I arrived was served for dinner that evening; in Pontiac, Michigan, where the church building was adjacent to the shunting-yard of the railway terminus and I lost my voice competing with it; and I preached on the subject of "God's Perfect Love" in Minden, Louisiana, as a tornado touched down, disintegrating the segregated African Methodist church across the street and killing eight members of the congregation, including the pastor. . . .

There was a notion in the 1930s that the skies would soon be filled with light aircraft, that we would fly as casually as we drove a car. I decided that, as I was living on the road, I should learn to fly. Conducting a campaign in Chicago, I went to a flying school in Harvey, Illinois, a suburb south of the city. The airport was no more than a mown pasture. The hangar was a refurbished barn. Navigation aids were limited to a tattered windsock and a single flag at each end of what served as a runway. The Harvey Flying

School equipment consisted of one early Piper Cub with a sixty-horsepower Lycoming engine.

The instructor was a gargantuan man who ate pistachio nuts and spat shells. He wore khaki coveralls and a Chicago Cubs baseball cap and cursed with an incredible inventiveness. I decided not to tell him that I was a preacher – if I was doing something foolish at the controls, I wanted to be told so in language that would brand it on my brain.

"How much to learn to fly?" I asked.

"Ten dollars an hour. If you're any good, you'll solo after eight hours, and that's the minimum."

The first seven and a half hours were without incident. I did all the mandatory manoeuvres – circuits, landings and takeoffs, power-on and power-off stalls, figure eights on pylons (trees), forward-slips and side-slips and two hours of cross-country. On occasion, he cursed me fervently: "Pile her in if you like, you stupid bugger; she's insured. But not with my ass aboard, for Chrissake!"

The day I was scheduled to solo there were strong, gusting winds. "I don't know," he said, frowning, hesitant, standing at the middle of the field, his coveralls flapping, "it's pretty roller-coaster up there."

I was apprehensive, but said, "Look, I leave for Charleston, West Virginia, tomorrow. It's mountain country, and if I don't solo with you, it'll cost me twenty bucks to get checked out down there."

He got in and we did a couple of circuits. It was very bumpy. As he heaved his bulk out of the front seat, he said, "Okay. Go around once. But take it easy."

I taxied into position, did a cockpit-check (there were precious few instruments to check), and gave the engine full throttle. To my horror, the tiny plane was airborne almost immediately. The nose came up and I was climbing at what seemed a dangerous speed. The first lesson drummed into a fledgling's head is not to climb too swiftly after takeoff. When the aircraft has only passed landing speed, raising the nose puts the plane in immediate danger of a stall and a certain crash.

I was gaining altitude at a frightening rate. The nose of the aircraft wanted to come up and I had to push forward hard on the stick. The plane still insisted on climbing. I shouted above the roar of the engine, "Think! You know what to do. *Do* it! *Think!*"

It broke on me: I had become airborne quickly because, without my instructor, the aircraft was three hundred pounds lighter. And there was a stiff wind, producing lift. The nose was rearing because my instructor hadn't reminded me to trim the aircraft to compensate for his weight. I reached down beside the seat, cranked the trim-handle, made a left-hand turn, made a circuit fighting the gusts, and bounced into a landing.

He came out to meet me. "*I'm* the dumb sonofabitch this time," he said. "Go 'round again."

I logged thirty-four hours before I quit for lack of money. And it was beginning to be obvious that the day when everyone owned his own auto-plane was far off.

I temporarily lost my faith in a hamlet in Michigan. It was no more than a cluster of houses and stores at a crossroads, yet it had three competing churches. There was little to do during the day, and it was impossible to establish a relationship with the pastor. He was a neurotically shy, shrivel-souled, skinny little man, a secret smoker who reeked of tobacco and whose fingers had a mahogany hue. When anyone spoke to him his face would flush and the acne he was cursed with would flame. But he had an extensive and eclectic library. It lined the walls of what he called his study but was actually the dining room. I spent most of my days in it, reading omnivorously.

I had read widely since childhood, but seldom any textbooks and always to my own taste. When a biography of Kemal Ataturk, Turkey's astounding dictator (the only man to my knowledge who, having total power, voluntarily surrendered it) engrossed me, I went on a binge with the library's biographies. For a time, George Bernard Shaw fascinated me – especially the prefaces to his plays – and I read them all, skimming the plays themselves. Then it was everything I could find by or about Gandhi, who remains a major influence in my life.

I have always been subject to my enthusiasms.

In this dreary Michigan town, I picked up Thomas Paine's *The Age of Reason*. In a few hours, nearly everything I knew or believed about the Christian religion was challenged and in large part demolished. My unsophisticated mind had no defences against the thrust of his logic or his devastating arguments. In the next ten days I read François Voltaire's *The Bible Explained at Last*, Bertrand Russell's *Why I am Not a Christian*, the speeches of the great

American atheist, Robert Ingersoll, including his *The Mistakes of Moses,* and dipped into David Hume and Thomas Huxley. I read through the days and into the early morning hours. Each night, I stumbled lamely through my sermon, drenched in perspiration, desolate of spirit.

By the end of the two weeks my course seemed obvious: my faith was disintegrating, I couldn't remain in the ministry, couldn't possibly continue to preach. I couldn't even pray. I cancelled the few meetings I had scheduled and returned to Toronto, utterly at a loss. There, I wandered in the wilderness of my mind for six weeks, fending off the questions of family and friends, trying to get some bearings. To earn some money, I sold four political cartoons to the editorial page of the Toronto *Telegram.* I was like a boxer who has been stunned and is out on his feet. Then, slowly, I began to emerge from the grey befuddlement. Only half believing, I tried again to pray. In hope, I turned again to the New Testament. . . .

The way back was tortuous and slow.

Now, a year later, there I was tearing down the "for rent" sign on a disused church. Connie and I were about to try to give it new life. The prospects were not encouraging. In subsequent months I would say many times: "We had a sanctuary but no members, pews but no people, aisles but no ushers, an organ but no organist, a choir loft but no choir and collection plates but no money." But we did have an unquenchable optimism and a conviction that we had been called by God to revive this dead church.

My family and Connie and I and a few friends went to work. We swept and vacuumed the floors. We polished the pews. We washed the walls as far as ladders could reach. Mother made a curtain for the altar rail. I bought a dozen pie tins, painted them brown and glued green felt to the bottoms – they would be our collection plates. There was a pile of dog-eared song books in a corner of one of the Sunday School rooms; they would serve as our hymn books.

For three weeks in advance of the opening Sunday we ran two-column advertisements in the church pages of the *Telegram* and *Star*:

COMING SOON!
Toronto's New
Centre of Evangelism

The advertisement was followed with others: "Two weeks to go!" "Next week!" "*Tomorrow!*" An organist, Fred Payne, telephoned to offer his services and a musician, Bill McCall, volunteered to direct the choir – when and if we had a choir. On the eve of the opening, a basket of flowers arrived anonymously. A nearby hardware merchant donated three dozen light bulbs. The lessee of the service station across the road offered his premises for free parking. We were as ready as we could be.

I had decided to hold the opening service on a Sunday night on the assumption that most churchgoers would attend their own services in the morning. At six-thirty, half an hour before the first service, our little band knelt at the front pew to ask God to bless this new venture and to – please! – send someone through the doors.

One hundred and twelve came. In a sanctuary seating twelve hundred, they seemed a pitiful few. Strangers, ill at ease, not knowing what to expect, they sat in the back pews and left a great gulf between themselves and the pulpit. The congregational singing was ragged. Connie's songs and my preaching echoed sepulchrally. The offering was sixty-seven cents short of the week's rent. There was nothing for the preacher, but because we were living at my mother's house, I did not need anything. The following Sunday morning there were only twenty-seven present. I preached as though the world were on fire, knowing that if these few didn't return the venture would be dead in the water.

But they did return, and others with them. Within six months it was impossible to find a seat in the Sunday-night service unless you were on hand by 6:45. Each week people were turned away at the doors. Soon there were the beginnings of a Sunday school and Wednesday prayer meetings and a Saturday-night meeting for young people. Within months we had a white-robed choir and hymn books and proper collection plates; even a Board of Elders, some so young as to be almost beardless. There were two services each Sunday night: one at 7:00 and a second, called Songfest, at 9:15. It was a happy, buoyant afterservice designed especially for young people, and they came from across the city to jam the sanctuary. I had set my salary at eighteen dollars a week. After six months, the church board raised it to forty dollars.

Three years later, I proposed to the board that we enlarge the church by building a gallery on three sides of the sanctuary. We had bought the church with a down payment of $4,000 and a mortgage of $27,000, and there were faint hearts who drew back from the additional debt that would have to be assumed. I prodded, I pleaded, I cajoled, but found myself faced with a contre-temps. Finally, I made it clear that, if they were prepared to rest at ease after so short a battle, I would not be their leader. The issue was resolved, an architect was hired and the work was begun. For the next seven weeks we would hold our services in the Masonic Temple at Yonge Street and Davenport.

It is the custom among evangelicals to pray for the sick. Jesus' three years of ministry were filled with healings, and when he commissioned the apostles he commanded them to heal. In the New Testament book of James there is this injunction:

> Is any sick among you? Let him call for the elders of the church and let them pray over him, annointing him with oil in the name of the Lord, and the prayer of faith shall save the sick, and the Lord shall raise him up.

I had, when requested, prayed for the sick many times, never effectually. I never preached on faith healing, seldom referred to it and was publicly critical of evangelists who majored in it. I regarded it as peripheral and, in the hands of charlatans, danger-ous.

Nevertheless, one Sunday afternoon, I went to one of those small, boxlike frame houses common to Toronto's east end at the request of a woman who attended the church. Her infant daugh-ter had been born deformed. The large muscle on the right side of the neck was attached to the left collar-bone, binding the baby's head to the left. As I understood it, there was some conjunction of the muscle and the jugular vein that made it impossible to correct the problem surgically. Once a week the woman took the infant to the Hospital For Sick Children for muscular rehabilitation. The baby's head was repeatedly twisted to the right, to stretch the muscle so that, in later years, she would be able more or less to face the front. The mother was required to repeat the therapy for ten minutes each day despite the baby's screams. Finding it unen-durable, she importuned me to come and pray that the infant be healed.

I went reluctantly, feeling like a mountebank. The baby was in the bedroom in its crib. I put some olive oil on my fingers, kneeled with the mother, put my hands on the infant and prayed. I had no expectation that the child would be healed. With the glib words on my tongue, I was thinking about the woman – about her pain, and about how disheartened she would be when the baby was unchanged and months of agonizing therapy lay ahead.

At the close, we rose to our feet and returned to the living room. I was questing in my mind for sentiments with which to buoy up her courage and ease her disappointment. We sat for a few minutes, talking, I in a chair and she on the chesterfield opposite, the baby on her lap. As we talked, I looked at the baby. Confused, I asked, "Wasn't the baby's head bound to the left?" The baby was looking to the right and then turned to face me. The woman let out a small exhalation and fainted. She was a large woman, and as she began to slide to the floor, I caught the baby and placed it on the chesterfield. When the woman revived, she was near hysterics. I told her to report what had happened to the hospital.

Four years later, *New World,* a Canadian imitation of *Life* magazine, came to me looking for a story idea. They planned to do a feature in their Easter edition under the heading, "What My Faith Means To Me." I sent them to the woman and to the Sick Children's Hospital. They ran the story and a full-page picture of the mother and child, now a young girl and manifestly normal.

Not long afterwards, I encountered another instance of instantaneous healing. My aunt, Ada Poyntz, a graduate nurse and my mother's youngest sister, was terminally ill with what was described to me as stomach cancer. Exploratory surgery had discovered that the malignancy was inoperable. She suffered greatly from adhesions and was bedridden. There was little point in her remaining in hospital, and, in those days before medicare, the costs would have been prohibitive. She was sent home to live out the rest of her days with my mother.

Mother insisted that I come to the house and pray for Ada. I went, again with reluctance and that sense of embarrassment I invariably felt when asked to pray for healing. I had investigated many claims of faith healing over the years and had never seen any instance that seemed to me authentic. I couldn't account for what had happened to the baby's neck but was by no means convinced that it was as a result of divine intervention.

I placed my hands on my aunt's body and began to pray. The moment was intensely emotional. My mother was praying and weeping. My aunt was gasping in an agony of hope, "Oh God!

Please! Please God!" As I was praying, I felt something akin to an electrical charge flow through my arms and out my fingers. I remembered the incident in which the woman "suffering from an issue of blood" touched the hem of Jesus' garment and was healed. Jesus stopped and said, "Who touched me?" Peter remonstrated with him: "What do you mean, who touched you? There's a crowd pressing us, jostling us." "No," Jesus said, "somebody touched me; I felt power go out of me!" I wondered if what I was feeling was what Jesus had spoken of.

Afterwards, there was the usual mutual encouragement, the "trying to have faith." When I returned home, the telephone was ringing. It was my aunt, who had not been out of bed for weeks. "Chuck," she said, half laughing, half in tears but far from hysteria, "I've been healed. I really have." Mother came on the phone. "It's absolutely incredible. She's been walking around. She's been up and down the stairs. Chuck, she's healed. There's no doubt about it."

There was no return of the malignancy. The adhesions ended. She outlived the rest of her brothers and sisters and died forty-two years later at the age of eighty-seven.

How do I account for these two instances of apparently instantaneous healing? I cannot. They certainly didn't happen because of my faith. Nor do I believe they resulted from divine intervention. Having investigated faith healing over many years I have no doubt that, occasionally, men and women are healed of actual illnesses. I am not speaking of those illnesses that are hysteric in nature, symptoms of an underlying psychological problem. Nor of those "healings" that are undoubtedly remissions; the temporary subsidence of symptoms or pain. Nor again, am I referring to the so-called healings seen on television when the ailing victim is anaesthetized by the intensity of the moment and becomes able, if only for a brief period, to bend a painful back or walk on a crippled limb.

I am opposed to the public healing services of contemporary evangelism. Occasionally, a form of cure may be effected, but the good done is minuscule compared to the harm. Television healing evangelism is a fraud. The "healers" are often simpletons or rogues or both, living off the avails of medical bunkum. They knowingly mislead, leaving behind them emotional wreckage and illnesses often worsened by neglect. Despite all this, I am convinced that what may loosely be called faith healing is an area of medicine with unrealized potential.

The contractor had been busy; only seven weeks had passed and the new gallery of the church was completed. On Saturday night, March 7, 1944, some fifty people, most of them young, gathered with brooms and mops and dusting cloths to ready the refurbished sanctuary for the reopening service. It was an hour for elation. At 10:30 I climbed to the topmost seat in the gallery and sat for a few minutes contemplating the scene, seeing in my memory that afternoon not many months before when I had walked tentatively into the gloomy, dust-mantled auditorium. Below, I could see the workers, resting from their labour, clapping their hands and singing a Negro spiritual.

Everything was ready. We would rededicate the church the following evening with the mayor present and some sixteen hundred people in the pews. (In truth, there were no pews in the gallery. We couldn't afford them and had temporarily substituted wooden kitchen chairs.) When the last of the volunteers had gone, I locked the doors and went wearily but happily home. I called Connie, who was in Detroit on a singing engagement, arranged to meet her at the airport the following afternoon, and went to bed.

I was awakened by the persistent ringing of the telephone. It was 3:15 a.m. A woman's voice shouted, "Mr. Templeton, you'd better come. Your church is on fire."

Nearing the crest of the hill on Avenue Road south of St. Clair, I saw the flames roaring into the night sky a hundred feet above the church, streamers of sparks racing even higher. As I pulled up by a welter of hoses and fire-fighting equipment, the roof of the main sanctuary collapsed in a roiling fury of flame. I had left a new suit, purchased for the opening service, in my office and ventured a dash to rescue it. Coming out, I was collared by a policeman who took me for a looter.

Now, in every section of the building, the roof was ablaze. Windows sagged and crumpled as the leaded glass melted. A slate shingle skimmed down and gashed a fireman's face. Water poured in torrents from the open doorways, cascading in a series of waterfalls down the stone steps. Mocking me was the sign at the front of the church: GREAT REOPENING SERVICE – Sunday 7 p.m.

When we bought the building, we had assumed a mortgage of

$27,000. Fortunately, it had been protected with an insurance policy. But we still had to settle with the contractor who had built the gallery, and all that would be left would be the walls and a heap of smoking debris. We would have no place to worship, debts and no funds. Some members of the board arrived and, as dawn broke, we repaired to an apartment across the street. I drafted an advertisement on the spot and delivered it personally to both the *Star* and the *Telegram,* talking them into opening the church pages so that it could be included:

OUR BEAUTIFUL CHURCH IS BURNED
BUT!
"All things work together for good
to them that love God."
Hear the story of the fire.
SUNDAY 7 P.M. – THE MASONIC TEMPLE

The temperature dropped overnight. When I returned to the church later that day to appraise the damage, the debris had frozen into a solid mass. Every part of the building had been destroyed or damaged. The basement was untouched by fire, but the ceiling was dripping everywhere. Hundreds of icicles suggested stalactites in a low, dark cave. The floor was inches deep in water; the surface covered with a skim of ice. A photographer from one of the newspapers took a picture of me standing in what remained of the pulpit, surrounded by a surreal tangle of charred beams and rafters, the snow falling around me inside the church. . . .

Then, an astounding reversal of our fortunes. Hundreds were turned away from the Masonic Temple. In place of a sermon, I recounted the brief history of the church, told of the dreams we'd had and then described the disaster. I put before them our financial dilemma and our intention to persevere and asked for pledges. Seventeen thousand dollars was committed.

J.V. McAree, the respected columnist for the *Globe and Mail,* wrote a column the Monday following the fire.

THIS CHURCH MUST NOT DIE

If we know anything about the spirit which forms the Avenue Road Church of the Nazarene, the devastating fire will be no more than a goad to stronger effort and a milestone on the way to still greater accomplishment. What has happened there in the last couple of years since the church was taken over by Charles B. Templeton might be regarded as a miracle.

The minister and his young wife, whom many might regard as no more than boy and girl, have built up a congregation which for earnestness and determination to live the Christian life is not surpassed anywhere, even by churches that can trace a continuous existence for more than a century. In fact, it has set an example that had amazed many much more fashionable and prosperous churches; and, as we have predicted, its recovery from the fire may amaze them still more.

An advertising agency owned by my uncle, Alford Poyntz, reprinted the McAree column in quarter-page display ads in the three Toronto papers. Included was a candid photograph of me watching the fire, dismay on my face, the top of my pyjamas peeking through my upturned overcoat collar. In response, contributions came in the mail from a number of cities.

I had announced on the Sunday that, granted a thaw, we would begin the clean-up the following Friday night. Strangers came from all over the city, some with dump trucks, others with shovels and axes and wheelbarrows. There were almost too many to organize. We backed the trucks to the doors of the church and set the men to work in gangs. Some pried and ripped apart the debris. Others filled barrows and trundled them on a path of planks to the trucks. The trucks rumbled off and returned. Soon we were black as coal miners. We up-ended the organ pipes and spilled out the ice that filled them. A great mound of icicles, each the exact shape of one of the pipes, was stacked in a bizarre heap. But it was a vain task; all the pipe seams had split as the water froze.

That evening, when the debris was gone, I went alone to the shell of the building and walked about, assessing the damage. The walls remained but the windows were gone. The girders that had borne the roof were twisted and bent. The internal structure of the gallery remained intact but the surfaces were burned and disfigured. The floors were scorched and scarred but still solid — although many of the boards would warp. The pews beneath the gallery were salvagable, although we would have to repair and paint them. The organ appeared to be a write-off. (It would finally cost $102,000 to rebuild the church.) After my tour of inspection, I went into a corner and sat with my back to the wall. The

enormity of the task before us finally broke on me, and my head
went down.

The first five months of that summer we held all our services in
the basement of the church. We opened up the area until we could
seat about five hundred on rented kitchen-type chairs. There was
one worrisome problem: there was no roof over our heads, only
the ceiling. For weeks, the sanctuary above was open to the
weather. When it rained the water poured through the ceiling and
continued to drip long after the rain had ended.

We advertised our basement auditorium as "Toronto's Sub-
marine Centre" and held two services each Sunday night, one at
6:30 and a second at 8:00. There was a pervasive smell of mildew,
and sometimes a background sound of water dripping. The choir
put on their robes in what had been the kitchen, and walked
precariously on planks laid on the floor to keep their feet dry. I
stood on a platform so that I was visible to the congregation, my
head a few inches from the ceiling. Fortunately, it was summer
and there was no need for heat. But in the more than two months
before the sanctuary received its new roof, it didn't rain on a
weekend and we didn't miss a service. We read this as the goodness of God.

I was notified by the Fire Marshall's office that the church fire had
been deliberately started. "Arson," was the verdict. "Someone
stood at the top of the stairs and poured a quantity of a flammable
substance, probably gasoline, down the stairs, lighted it and left.
Whoever did it knew the layout: the fire was started at the one
place that would cause it to spread to both wings of the building."

Some weeks later, as I returned from an out-of-town engagement
I was given a message to call the police at the old Number 5
Division at Davenport Road at Belmont. A sergeant came to see
me and told me a disturbing story. During the regular Saturday
night young people's meeting in the basement auditorium of the
church, one of our group, an eighteen-year-old I will call Eddie
Miller, heard a sound from above and slipped out of the meeting to
investigate. Moments later, the young people heard the sound of
running feet, a crash and then silence. They found Eddie on the

floor, unconscious, and called the police. The sergeant now told me that, when he arrived, Eddie was conscious but still stunned. Eddie told him that when he went up to the auditorium he saw a man. The intruder was tall, he said, wearing a topcoat and had his hat pulled low over his face. The man ran, and as he went, picked up a piece of scrap two-by-four and threw it, striking Eddie on the head. Nonetheless, he grappled with the man but was knocked unconscious by a blow to the solar plexus.

As the officer finished the story, I said, "You seem a little dubious."

"I'm not sure why," he said. "But there was something odd about the whole business."

"Are you saying that Eddie was lying?"

"No. He's got a lump on his head where he was hit by the two-by-four. It's just there's more to the story than he's telling. I keep wondering if it could be connected with the fire."

I visited Eddie at his home. He was a good-looking boy with wide-set, clear blue eyes and blonde hair. He had joined the church some six months earlier. I'd heard that he had been part of a teen-age gang in the east end of the city but had quit when he was converted. Since then he'd been trying to live an exemplary life. He was an officer in the youth group and a member of the choir.

He was wearing a Band-aid on his brow over an angry red abrasion. As he told me the story he'd told the policeman, one thing struck me as odd: he had been knocked unconscious, he said, not by the blow to the head but by a punch to the solar plexus. I knew that such a blow could knock a man down, even incapacitate him, but not knock him out. Why was he lying? Was it possible that he knew the intruder? Perhaps there was some connection to the fire.

"Eddie," I said, "did you know the man?"

"No, Mr. Templeton. I never saw him before."

"But how do you know? It was around 9:30. It was dark."

"Yes it was. But not that dark."

I was vaguely disquieted but put it out of my mind.

Three weeks later, early on a Sunday morning, I received a telephone call from a Constable Ross at the East York police station. Did I know a young man by the name of Eddie Miller? The constable then explained that, the previous night, Eddie had been beaten up by a gang of young hoodlums. He hadn't been seriously injured — mostly bumps and bruises — and had been driven home by the police. Constable Ross told me that Eddie was worried about attending church Sunday morning, bandaged, and had asked him to call me to explain what had happened.

Eddie arrived with a Band-aid on one cheek. His left arm was in a sling. He opened his shirt to show me broad strips of tape on his chest; two ribs had been cracked, he said. The bandages seemed awkwardly applied. The doctor had done them too tightly, he explained, and he had loosened them. He bore the pain well and drew a lot of sympathy from his friends.

The incident nagged at my mind. That afternoon it occurred to me that Eddie might be in more trouble than he was admitting to. Was it possible that he hadn't been able to break clear of the gang and that that was why he had been beaten up? Could it be that, angered by his leaving and by his commitment to the church, they had set the fire? The questions wouldn't rest.

I called the East York police station. The duty officer didn't know of a Constable Ross; there was no one on staff by that name. Nor did he have a report about a young man being beaten up the previous evening. Nor had he heard of Eddie Miller.

I hung up, my mind racing. Eddie or a friend must have made the call to me, impersonating the officer. Eddie hadn't been beaten up. The bandages were loose because he had applied them himself. But why? My mind went back to the incident at the young people's meeting and I remembered my doubts about his being knocked unconscious by a blow to the solar plexus. I called the sergeant who had investigated the incident.

"I thought I might be hearing from you again," he said.

A course of action was decided on. I called Eddie. "You and I need to have a talk. I don't want to disturb your family by coming to your house, so I'll drive by this afternoon at four and blow my horn."

He was immediately tentative. "I can't do that. I . . . ."

"Eddie," I said, "don't make me come to your house; there'll be a policeman in the car with me. He wants to ask you some questions. You come out to the car."

There were, as it turned out, two policemen in the back seat of my car as I blew the horn. Eddie got in the front seat beside me. I drove slowly about the area.

"Eddie," I said, "I need some straight answers. You weren't beaten up last night. You weren't taken to the East York station. You've been lying to me."

He protested earnestly. "Mr. Templeton, I'm not lying. I *was* beaten up. I'm telling you the truth."

"You also lied to me about being knocked out at the church. Why, Eddie? Are you in trouble?"

One of the officers spoke sharply from the back seat. "Why did you burn down the church, Eddie?"

"Burn down the church . . . !"

"Why'd you do it, Eddie?"

"Me burn down the church? Are you kidding?"

"I'll ask the questions – why'd you burn down the church?"

Eddie appealed to me. "Mr. Templeton, you know how much I love our church. Tell them."

"The officer cut me off. "We'll handle this. Now, Miller, let's have no more lying. I'll give you one more chance. Tell the truth or we'll take you down to the station and book you. Why'd you burn down the church?"

Eddie was silent, his head down. Then he slumped sideways on the seat and put his head in my lap, sobbing.*

That night, after the service, I drove home by way of Davenport Road and paused outside the station where Eddie was lodged in a cell. It had begun to rain and the night was dark.

The new church was beautiful: brightly lit, modern, the acoustics greatly improved. The choir-loft accommodated sixty. The seating capacity of the sanctuary was close to sixteen hundred. On the night of the reopening, we put the overflow in the Sunday school auditorium and turned away hundreds. During the next four years, winter and summer, it was necessary to arrive by 6:30 to be sure of a seat. Policemen were assigned each Sunday to direct traffic.

II

Billy Graham at thirty was a thin, gangling six-foot-two with a thatch of blonde wavy hair (he wore a baseball cap in private to

---

* Eddie at first pleaded guilty but then changed his mind. At the trial, he was found guilty and served time. But he never revealed his motive.

keep it from mounding too high). He had a lean, angular face, a wide mouth, a square jaw, and jutting eyebrows above a hawk nose. The denim-blue eyes seemed more intense for being surrounded by dark circles. He was not as handsome as he would be with the addition of a dozen years. On a platform, despite an impression of immaturity, he had a commanding presence and a strong, flexible voice. Oddly, he was tone deaf, and to stand beside him during congregational singing dizzied the brain.

Nor was he physically well coordinated, compensating for it by mentioning often – the wish being father to the thought – an aborted career in semi-professional baseball. It was surprising when, in a game of pick-up softball at a summer conference at Canadian Keswick, he came to the plate holding his bat crosshand.

Billy and I became friends on first meeting. That friendship deepened and has endured, although it has sometimes been strained by the different paths we have chosen. We met in the spring of 1945, backstage at the Chicago Stadium. I was there at the invitation of a man I'd never met, Torrey Johnston, the pastor of an evangelical church in Chicago. Torrey had begun holding Saturday-night youth rallies for servicemen and others; attendance mushroomed. Similar rallies sprang up in New York City, Detroit, St. Louis and Los Angeles. Torrey's invitation to attend a young people's rally in, of all unlikely places, the Chicago Stadium intrigued me and I arranged to go. Now, backstage, he clapped Billy Graham and me on the back and introduced us, saying, "You guys have a lot in common."

Billy had a small church in Western Springs, a suburb of Chicago, and a popular late-night radio program, "Songs in the Night." On the platform, as he was being introduced, he leaned toward me and said, "Pray for me. I'm scared to death."

Little wonder. Twenty thousand young people jammed all the seats in the vast sports arena, including the ice area. A one-thousand-voice choir ranged behind a massive platform. Above our heads a banner trumpeted:

CHICAGOLAND YOUTH FOR CHRIST
"Anchored to the Rock but Geared to the Times!"

Billy betrayed none of his fear. He spoke for twenty minutes and then gave an invitation for would-be converts to come forward. Hundreds responded. I was impressed.

In my hotel room afterwards, I couldn't sleep. In the morning,

I called Toronto and arranged to hire Massey Hall every Saturday night for the next six months. It didn't occur to me that we might fail.

Youth for Christ was a phenomenon of the 1940s. Across the United States and Canada – and later, Europe – Saturday-night rallies of young people sprang up independent of the churches. The war had much to do with it. The major cities were filled with servicemen, many of them far from home and at loose ends on a Saturday night. The meetings were fun with a serious purpose. Most were held in secular auditoriums, and the emphasis was on informality. The music was more like community singing; rather than hymns, rhythmic gospel tunes and Negro spirituals were sung. Musical groups performed and, at the end, a youthful preacher gave a brief "sermon" that was really a religious talk in contemporary language. The thrust was evangelical and the emphasis was pietistic but the atmosphere was derivative more of show business than church.

From its beginning, Toronto Youth for Christ was the largest of the more than one thousand weekly rallies in North America. Massey Hall was not available the first few weeks and we had to hold our meetings in the Old Elm Street church, but from our first week in the Hall, young people, 2600 strong, flocked to the rallies every Saturday night. We had little support from other churches for it was presumed, not unreasonably, that the meetings would increase attendance at Avenue Road Church. To minimize that, I sought out the Christian Businessman's Committee, an interdenominational laymen's organization, and put all financial matters in their hands. I took nothing for my services.

The music was professional. On a visit to London, Ontario, I had discovered a shy, reed-thin sixteen-year-old pianist, Tedd Smith. I put him in charge of the music. He was extraordinarily gifted (in later years he joined Billy Graham's team, and, still later composed a rock opera) and he formed a number of musical groups: a youth choir, a vocal trio and a group of nine girls — chosen as much for their beauty as for their voices – called inappropriately, The Youth for Christ Octette. The first cornetist in the Toronto Symphony formed a trumpet trio, and we featured frequent guests. A favourite was Tommy Ambrose, who became a well-known singer and composer of advertising jingles. His brother, Gus, led the singing and shepherded Tommy about, for he was only four when I first lifted him onto a chair so that he could reach the microphone. He belted out Negro spirituals with infallible pitch and an innate sense of rhythm; each time he sang, he brought the house down.

CJBC, the key station of the Canadian Broadcasting Corporation's Trans-Canada network, put us on the air, broadcasting one hour of the rally, live from Massey Hall, every Saturday night. It was a great opportunity but it led to a serious problem.

Bob Keston, the station manager at CJBC, was a "take charge" sort of man, fast-talking and ebullient. I met him only once, not long after the inauguration of our weekly broadcast. One Saturday evening, at the close of the rally, the CBC technician who produced the program from Massey Hall told me that Keston wanted me to telephone him the following Monday. In his office at the Corporation's headquarters on Jarvis Street, Keston congratulated me on the rally and, after a brief conversation, asked if I would be interested in extending the broadcast coast to coast.

I could hardly credit what I was hearing. The network would enable us to extend the reach of Youth for Christ across Canada and, in the days before television, would provide an audience of millions.

"The entire network?" I asked, not yet believing it.

"From eight to nine Saturday nights, coast to coast."

"But what would it cost?"

"Nothing. Not a dime."

"No control over programming?"

"Of course not. Look, it's a good show and it's great radio. I want the country to hear it."

But there was a catch. As he walked me to the door, he said, "There *is* one thing. I'm sure you can understand that doing the broadcast will require the expenditure of a lot of time and energy by the producer and the engineer – they'll both be working on their day off, and so on. Can you see your way clear to spending twenty-five dollars a broadcast, not as a payment of course, but as a gesture of appreciation for the time and trouble necessary to make the broadcast perfect?"

I told him I didn't have any money.

He looked at me. "Charles, Charles. . . . Do you have any idea what the time would cost if you had to buy it?"

I shook my head.

"Then think about it. Think of the mail the program will pull. Coast to coast, remember."

As we shook hands at the door, he added, "You understand, of course, that our little arrangement will have to be off the record. Just put the money in a sealed envelope and give it to the producer before the show."

I left his office, stunned. As much as I wanted the increased audience, as much as I wanted to extend the influence of the rally, I couldn't accept his proposition. As I was leaving the building to drive to the airport (I had a speaking engagement in Los Angeles the following day), I ran into Don Sims. Sims was a staff announcer at the CBC, an adherent of Avenue Road Church, and would one day be named Ontario's film censor. I told him what had happened. He was almost disbelieving.

"There's only one thing to do," he said. "You've got to go right to Bush" (Ernest Bushnell, then Director General of the CBC). "He won't stand for that kind of hanky-panky for a minute."

But I decided to think it over during my absence from the city. I had no idea what the repercussions might be. And I was worried that I might end up losing the local broadcast. Back in Toronto, I asked Sims to arrange for me to speak to Reed Forsee, a senior producer. Forsee was visibly shaken. He questioned me at length and asked my permission to take it up with his seniors. Nothing further was said to me, but not long afterwards, Keston resigned. We never did get the network.

Billy Graham came to Toronto to speak at our Youth for Christ rally and at the Avenue Road Church the following day. A movement was afoot to form Youth for Christ International and to send representatives to Europe to found the movement there. Billy wanted the job of full-time employee for the new organization and asked me to help him get it. The following week at a founding convention at Winona Lake, a Christian campground in Wisconsin, I was elected one of three international vice-presidents and immediately moved that we hire Billy as our evangelist at large. The motion was carried unanimously. A team was selected to carry the message to Europe. Torrey Johnston, as president, would lead the group. Billy and I would alternate as preachers, and a robust baritone named Stratton Shufelt would supply the music.

The movement was attracting fascinated attention from the

news media. *Life* assigned a reporter and a photographer to follow us during the preparation for the trip. He took literally hundreds of pictures. William Randolph Hearst instructed his newspapers to give full coverage to our activities. There were articles in *Time* and *Newsweek* and by all the wire services. In Canada, there were major stories in *Maclean's* and most of the newspapers. Journalists from England and the continent interviewed us.

The Saturday prior to our departure, I invited Graham to Toronto for a "farewell rally." A thousand young people followed us from Massey Hall to Union Station, jamming the concourse, cheering and singing in a high-spirited mêlée. Billy and I had to climb onto the marble balustrades to speak to them.

At Chicago's O'Hare airport, hundreds of young people came by bus to see us off. A dozen reporters and photographers surrounded us on the way to the plane. Torrey suggested a prayer of dedication and, self-consciously, we all kneeled on the tarmac. It was Alice in Wonderland: Torrey on his feet, face upraised, bawling at God; the cameramen scuttling about or crouching low, seeking the best angles and shouting, "Keep prayin' fellas! That's it — hold it! Just one more prayer!" In the photographs it can be seen that Billy and I are having trouble restraining our laughter.

So, off to carry the gospel to benighted Europe.

The beginning was not auspicious. The plane, a DC-6, made a scheduled stop at Gander, Newfoundland, then a U.S. army base. The weather closed in and we were forced to stay overnight, quartered in the officers' barracks. Torrey disappeared and returned electric with excitement to announce that we had been invited to conduct a special service for the troops at the base activities centre, a large Quonset structure used mainly as a movie theatre. We were elated at the news, not knowing that we would be appearing under false pretences.

Torrey Johnston was a born entrepreneur. He had a cherub's face with rosy kewpie-bow lips. His hair parted in the centre and fell in tight, dark waves. Torrey was a great talker, though not much of a preacher, and was as shrewd as a Yankee horse trader. I've never known him when he wasn't involved in some grand project or "deal," as he often called them. And he made most of them work. Shortly after our arrival at Gander, he had been invited by the Commanding Officer to his quarters and questioned about our group. (The C.O. was not unaware that we were accompanied by a Hearst reporter.) Torrey's answers were ambiguous and the C.O. took it, perhaps from our flashy clothes, that we were entertainers. Nor did Torrey disabuse him.

"Are you with the USO?" he asked.

"Something like that," Torrey conceded.

Billy and I, knowing nothing of the subterfuge, went for a walk under a lowering sky, grateful for the unexpected opportunity, which we saw as an indication of God's blessing on our European enterprise. Returning to the camp, we saw long lines forming outside the theatre and heard announcements about the meeting on the public-address system.

In a quick conference backstage it was agreed that I would act as master of ceremonies. Stratt Shufelt would sing a secular and then a religious song. Torrey would explain Youth for Christ's mission and Billy would preach.

Dressed in a sports jacket and slacks and wearing a bow tie, I made an entrance onto the stage. The applause was deafening and laced with cheers and whistles. All the seats were taken; servicemen lined the walls, sat in the aisles and crowded on the floor below the stage. I told a few quick jokes and was cheered to the echo. I introduced Stratt. He did an up-tempo version of the Jacques Wolfe tune, "Short'nin' Bread," to enthusiastic approval. I returned, told another couple of jokes, to somewhat diminished applause, and then introduced "Dr. Torrey Johnston, president of Youth for Christ International! Let's hear it for Torrey . . . !"

Torrey walked out to face a puzzled audience. Trying to establish some rapport, he announced that he was from Chicago. "Anyone here from the Windy City?" A ragged show of hands. "Any Canadians?" he asked, identifying me as the Canadian. Silence. "Anyone from New York City?"

The booing began, interspersed with cries of, "Bring on the girls!" After a minute or two, Torrey abandoned whatever he had in mind, made his exit, and I was back on stage. Shouting over the chaos, I brought on Stratt for his second song, "The Old Rugged Cross." Even with the microphone he was inaudible in the din. The crowd had turned ugly and was shouting and booing. Backstage, Torrey was saying, "Hey! – we're doing great. Go out there Chuck and introduce Billy." I refused, but having no option, again faced the hooting mob. Billy gave it a valiant try but it was a lost battle.

The C.O. stormed into the dressing room, his face paper white, and summoned Torrey to his office. Billy and I went for another long walk. As we went, we prayed, asking forgiveness for our egotism and our presumptuousness. We returned to find that we had narrowly escaped being thrown in the stockade. Only the importunities of the Hearst man, with his promise not to file the story, deflected the commandant's wrath.

In London we were booked into the Dorchester. It was and is one of the most expensive hotels in the city, frequented by wealthy foreigners, senior diplomats and second-echelon royalty. The committee of ministers and laymen who had invited us were shocked – British clergy are notoriously underpaid – as they had been by our casual attire and general informality. Billy and I were led by a bellman to a suite that seemed as big as a football field. We looked at each other, eyebrows raised, and began a tour of the rooms. Billy called out from the bathroom, "Chuck, come here." He was examining the bidet, turning the faucets, looping the spray. "What is this thing?" he asked.

Billy at twenty-eight was not far removed from the southern country boy he had been raised, and it was my conceit, at thirty, to think myself more sophisticated. I didn't confess my ignorance but offered what seemed a logical guess: "It's a foot bath." The telephone rang. It was Torrey. "What's the extra thing in the bathroom?"

Billy replied with the lofty superiority of an initiate. "It's for washing your feet. What'd you think?"

We held meetings in London, York and Manchester, in Glasgow, Aberdeen and Edinburgh, and across the Irish sea, in Dublin and Belfast. Everywhere we were greeted by overflowing churches and attentive audiences. Billy and I alternated as preachers. During the day, we met with committees and went sightseeing. Among a people spent by the long war, we were a curiosity and, I may say, a tonic. In loud-patterned sports jackets, slacks and bow ties, Billy, Torrey and I – six feet tall or better and imbued with overabundant energy – intrigued both the clergy and the people. In retrospect, I'm embarrassed at the thought of how brash we must have appeared, but our hosts welcomed it.

I remember only one negative note: Billy and I were on the street, walking to Edinburgh Castle. As we passed a sweet shop, we decided to buy some candy. It was a tiny shop. The proprietor was an aging Scot with a craggy face, great, thrusting eyebrows and a ruddy, seamed skin. "Where's your ration coupons?" he asked.

"Sorry," I said. "I didn't know we needed them. I'm from Canada. My friend here is from the United States."

He glared at us fiercely from beneath his brows and then passed a candy bar to me. "Weel," he said blunty, "I've one for you, but none for your friend. I wouldn'a gie a Yank a pinch o' salt."

On the continent we preached through interpreters, but it made no difference to our audiences — nor to us once we got the hang of it. In Stockholm, the crowds were in the thousands. At one meeting the Crown Prince sat at my side on the platform — an aging man in a business suit, unpretentious and kind — and when I finished preaching, asked for my Bible. On the first page he inscribed in a shaky hand: *O. Bernadotte.*

Billy and I had taken two days off in Copenhagen and were scheduled to join the others in Paris. We arrived a day early and wandered the streets, grateful that the city had not been pulverized as London had. Paris was thronging with Allied soldiers on leave and seemed a city of prostitutes. They paraded the main thoroughfares, soliciting openly. In civilian clothes, we were particular targets. On a daylight walk down the Champs Elysées from the Arc de Triomphe to our hotel we were accosted at least fifty times. The girls stood in front of us, impeding our progress, or fell in stride, linking their arms in ours, touching, fondling, whispering. One threw open her fur coat to reveal that she was wearing nothing but a garter belt and stockings. Billy's face was grim. "Chuck," he said, "we've got to get out of here." We set off at a half trot, literally shoving the girls aside.

Inside the hotel lobby, laughing and breathless, I turned to Billy and said, saying it for both of us, "My *Lord!*"

That evening we went looking for a restaurant. We chanced upon an attractive and "very French" place. It had a fairly large room with a bar to one side, the tables arranged around a postage-stamp-size dance floor. A trio of blacks were playing American blues. We ordered Cokes and looked about. I'd told Billy not to worry about the menu; my high-school French would suffice. In fact, I was immediately at a loss when the waitress began to respond to my questions.

Two girls stopped at our table, and before we were quite aware of what was happening, joined us and ordered drinks. They were very young, not yet in their twenties, and quite beautiful. Neither spoke English. I tried to carry on a conversation but was soon at sea. Attempting a compliment, I said to one of them, *"Vous avez très beaux chevaux rouge."* When they burst into laughter I realized that I had told her she had beautiful red horses, rather than beautiful red *cheveux,* hair.

Our meal came and we proceeded to eat it, two simultaneous conversations going on; Billy and I in English and the girls in French. As we paid the check, it became clear that they were planning to leave with us. I tried to make excuses but each had taken an arm and, as we emerged into the street, clutched tightly. My girl was pointing toward a massive apartment block across the street, Billy's was pulling him away. Over a shoulder, he gave me a despairing look. I grimaced and said, "Guess we'll have to walk them home." In truth, we didn't know how to extricate ourselves.

Inside the apartment building, a broad staircase led to the second floor. As we mounted the stairs – wanting to get out of my predicament but not sure how to – I spied a W.C. on the landing. I pointed and said, *"Excusez."* It occurred to me that I had wandered into danger and was at risk of being mugged. In the W.C. I looked for a place to hide my wallet; in it was all my money and identification. I stood on the toilet bowl, reached up and stashed it on top of the water chamber. As I emerged the girl was talking to a rough-looking man who turned and went quickly down the hall. She called out to me, *"Viens ici."* I shook my head, said, *"Non, Non,"* and went down the stairs three at a time. Outside, I watched until I saw her come out and cross the street to the restaurant. I went back up the stairs, retrieved my wallet and returned to our hotel.

At the hotel, no Billy. An hour passed. When two hours had gone, I began to worry. I considered calling the police but realized that there was little I could tell them; I had no idea where he might be. Close to midnight, he burst through the door, panting, his face shining with perspiration, his hair dishevelled, his tie in a pocket, the collar of his shirt open.

He threw himself on the bed, breathing heavily. "Chuck, you have no idea what's happened to me. I thought I was going to walk the girl home and then leave her, but she hailed a cab. We drove and drove and drove. Somewhere outside the city in a dark little suburb, the cabby stopped. He didn't speak any English, neither did she, and I couldn't understand what he was saying about the fare. I took the money from my wallet and held it out, expecting him to do what the London cabbies do – take what was his and leave the rest. He took it all.

"The girl had me by the arm and she led me toward this place where she lived. It was a dump. We got inside and she closed the door. I was trying to think of something I could say or do to let her know I was leaving. She went over to the bed, and without a word, unbuttoned her dress, tossed it aside and fell back on the bed. And Chuck, she was stark naked!

"I turned, opened the door and got out of there. In the street, I started to run. I don't know how far I ran; it could have been a mile or two. When finally I stopped, I looked around. I had no idea where I was. I was going to hail a cab, and then realized I didn't have any money. I asked some people the way to the downtown area but they just looked at me or rattled on in French. So I started to walk. I walked and walked and walked until I saw the Eiffel Tower in the distance. Then I knew where I was. . . ."

Ever since, whenever I see Billy, especially when he is with others, I grin at him and say, "Hello Bill. How's the Midnight Runner?"

In North America, Youth for Christ was growing at an almost explosive rate. Our Toronto rally and my responsibilities at Avenue Road Church kept me close to home, but I broke away for special occasions. One such occasion led to an almost comedic debacle.

Torrey Johnston had organized a Soldier Field rally in Chicago. Delegations from every city within three hundred miles were invited. The objective of filling the stands wasn't realized but some twenty-five thousand people were on hand on a blue-sky summer day. I was invited for two reasons: to report on the European tour, and to present a midfield extravaganza.

The concept was this: As the memory of the war was fresh, and the consciousness of the atomic bomb acute, I would place a representation of an enormous open Bible at midfield, and at an appropriate moment during some special narration, would detonate a large quantity of flash powder, producing a great, white mushroom cloud. Coincidentally, a hundred white doves would be released from beneath the open Bible. They would rise, circle and fly off in all directions, "carrying the message of hope rather than destruction to all the world."

Problems arose. I wasn't able to travel to Chicago until the day of the rally, so I had to make the arrangements on the telephone. I was reassured by the manner of the man assigned to carry out my plan; he was an enthusiast and seemed industrious. However, on arriving to check the arrangements at Soldier Field only a few hours before the crowd would gather, I discovered to my dismay that there were flaws in the preparations. First, the representation of the open Bible was much smaller than specified and it looked minuscule at the centre of the stadium. Second, my lieutenant hadn't been able to get one hundred white doves and had settled for fifty variegated pigeons. Further, he hadn't tracked down any flash powder and had settled for – I couldn't believe it! – a Very pistol.

There was no option but to go ahead. Not now trusting my aide, I hid myself beneath the Bible with a young lad I had dragooned. His responsibility was to open the crates full of pigeons. Torrey introduced the spectacle with ringing words. A one-thousand-voice choir and a fifty-piece orchestra began the background music that would culminate in the "Hallelujah" chorus, while I, microphone to my lips, my voice booming in the vast stadium, began the narration.

Came the climactic moment. The music mounted. I intoned: "Even as the Doomsday detonation of the Bomb sounds its message of horror and destruction around the world. . . ." I fired the Very pistol, which made a pathetic pop and descended in a thin trail of smoke. ". . . the Christian church sends its message of faith . . . and hope . . . and peace to every corner of the globe. . . !"

I had impressed on the lad who was to release the pigeons that it was essential they emerge together from beneath the open Bible. But when he threw open the tops of the crates, they didn't move. "Get them *out*, for God's sake!" I shouted, forgetting to turn off my microphone. The boy, in his zeal to do his job well, began to dip into the crates, literally hurling handfuls of birds into the air. A cloud of feathers emerged from beneath the Bible, followed by puffs of pigeons. A pitiful few flew off in various directions. Many wouldn't fly or couldn't fly, but landed on the grass and staggered about, dazed and half naked. The choir sang, *Hallelujah! Hallelujah!*

There were other mass meetings. I flew to California to speak to fifty thousand at an Easter Sunrise service in the Rose Bowl, to Detroit for a rally at the Olympia, to Los Angeles at the Shrine Temple, to the St. Louis Auditorium and elsewhere. In the meantime, we were planning our first Maple Leaf Gardens rally.

I will confess to a moment of doubt when I went to confirm the arrangements in the arena in which I had covered so many sports events. I stood at centre ice and pivoted on a heel, looking up at the banks of empty seats knowing we would have to fill them all, and felt a tremor of trepidation. In retrospect, I'm astonished that we dared to venture so foolhardily. In truth, I never really doubted that we could do whatever we set our minds to. Part of that confidence was a conviction that God was with us; it was also the reckless, uncontemplating daring of youth.

Much of what we did was, of course, show business. Spectacle. The thousand-voice choir was dressed in white except for a specified number in black forming a cross at the centre. There were five grand pianos, an international pageant in full costume, vocal soloists, our trumpet trio, the Octette and to climax it all, Connie's "The Lord's Prayer." Five-year-old Tommy Ambrose – so tiny at the heart of that vast assemblage – piped "Dem bones, dem bones, dem dry bones." The platform party, which included Mayor Robert Saunders, entered the pitch-dark arena in a blaze of spotlights. There were congratulatory telegrams from various parts of the world, a floral cross nine feet high and free souvenir programs. The speaker was Charles E. Fuller, a sixty-year-old radio preacher from California, who seemed oddly anachronistic.

We held a second Gardens rally the following year. The speakers were Torrey Johnston and Billy Graham, who was not yet well known. For Christian young people, the Gardens rallies were pop extravaganzas; they were participating in something larger than life. Surrounded by thousands of their fellows, all holding a common faith, they found a tangible justification of their religious commitment.

An invitation came from William Randolph Hearst to spend a weekend with him at his private and fabled Xanadu at San Simeon, California. It was very tempting. Hearst was one of the great buccaneers of American journalism. His nationwide chain of newspapers not only reported the news, but manipulated, and if necessary, fabricated it. The Hearst press and the term "yellow journalism" were synonymous.

It is not surprising that Hearst decided to take Youth for Christ under his wing. It was his ideal subject: it was American, conservative, the religion of the common people and, in some expressions, anti-communist.

I went to Seattle, Washington, for a Saturday-night rally. There were no more than twelve hundred present and nothing exceptional happened. But a Hearst photographer prowled backstage, in the wings and in the theatre, shooting picture after picture. After the meeting, I spent an hour with two reporters. The following morning the *Post Intelligencer* gave the meeting three pages of coverage: pictures, interviews and colour stories.

Hearst was seventy-nine at the time, somewhat enfeebled and grown reclusive. He spent most of his time at his retreat on a mountain by the coast, surrounded by tons of European and other antiquities. The idea of spending a weekend amid that baroque extravagance as the guest of one of the most notorious of press lords had us squirming with delight. But we knew we dare not go. It would become known and even if we rejected any offer of support, we would be suspected of being his creatures.

Some years later, Hearst made another gesture: Billy had gone, on his own, apart from Youth for Christ, to conduct a campaign in a great circus tent in Los Angeles. On the closing Sunday, as he later recounted, "I suddenly saw reporters and cameramen crawling all over the place." He caught the eye of one of the reporters and asked what was happening. He was told that an edict had come down from Hearst: "Puff Graham." The following day, Billy was front-page news in all the Hearst papers. The legend is that Hearst acted after one of his housemaids enthused about what was happening in the big tent.

Seizing the opportunity, the Los Angeles committee extended the meeting for one week and then for another. Various celebrities began to attend; some were converted. Crowds overflowed the site. Other media added their voices and, before the campaign ended, Billy Graham and his message were being heralded from coast to coast and beyond.

In the months following our return from Europe, I had been

fighting a losing battle with my faith. I had been so frenetically busy that there had been little time to take stock. But in the occasional quiet moments, questions and doubts surfaced. There was a shallowness in what we were doing in Youth for Christ, a tendency to equate success with numbers. There seemed to be little concern with what happened to the youngsters who responded to our appeals? If the afterservice dragged on, we tended to get impatient, wanting to wrap things up and get back to the hotel or to a restaurant for our nightly steak and shop talk. Billy, too, was troubled by it, and we talked about it many times. It undoubtedly contributed to his move from Youth for Christ to conduct his own campaigns.

But my dilemma was of a different kind. I was discovering that I could no longer accept many of the fundamental tenets of the Christian faith. I had been converted as an incredibly green youth of nineteen. I had only a grade-nine education and hadn't the intellectual equipment to challenge the concepts advanced by my friends and mentors. I *wanted* very much to believe: there was in me then as there remains now an intense, inchoate longing for a relationship with God. In the beginning, I accepted the beliefs of the people around me, but I read widely in every spare minute: on planes and trains and in bed. Slowly – against my will – for I could perceive the jeopardy – my mind had begun to challenge and rebut the things I believed.

It may be useful to set down what fundamentalists believe. There is some variance, of course but, by and large, theirs is a simple world of certainties in which the church is centre and circumference. For most, the King James version of the Bible is the rock on which all of life and history is built. It is God's Word, without error and accepted without question. It teaches fundamentalists that, in approximately 4000 B.C., God created the world in five days. On the sixth day, he created Adam and Eve and placed them in a paradise called the Garden of Eden. They sinned (the sin is commonly believed to be of a sexual nature), and as a consequence, God cursed them and their descendants so that all people are "born in sin."

The Devil is a real enemy, and is everywhere present, "seeking whom he may devour." Fundamentalists believe that God destroyed the world, saving only Noah and his family and two (or seven) of each species; that He personally delivered the Ten Commandments to Moses, that Jonah was swallowed by a great fish and that Gideon made the sun "stand still in the heavens."

They believe that Jesus of Nazareth is Almighty God and the third person of the Trinity; that a virgin was impregnated by the Holy Ghost and thus brought him to birth; that all his miracles are fact; that having been executed by the Romans and buried, he rose from the grave and ascended to heaven; that he will return to earth "in clouds of glory" to rule the world for a thousand years; that the wicked (those who have not been "born again" including all Roman Catholics, most members of conventional churches and all the millions who follow other religions) will be banished to "outer darkness," a place of endless mental and physical anguish where there will be "weeping and wailing and gnashing of teeth." "Born-again" Christians will live an eternal life of unalloyed bliss, ruling with Christ on earth for a thousand years, and forever in a heaven where the streets are paved with gold.

I never believed all of this (the Genesis account of creation, for instance, or the monstrous evil of an endless hell), but I did accept most of these doctrines and lived by them fervently. And now the entire fabric was coming apart.

Canon Arthur Chote of the Anglican church in Toronto is one of the finest human beings I know. I met him in the early days of Youth for Christ and, one Saturday night, I asked him to speak briefly to the young people about his faith. A very tall, good-looking man, he instructed pilots at the Hagersville airport under the Commonwealth Air Training Plan and was impressive in his uniform. We became friends, especially after the woman he later married was moved by a sermon I preached at a tiny mission hall on Broadview Avenue to become a committed Christian. Art reciprocated by visiting the sick and aged in my congregation, refusing to accept any remuneration.

In the early spring of 1948 he was studying for the ministry at Wycliffe College. He came to see me in my study and, in his quiet direct way, startled me by saying that, if I wanted to continue to be useful in the ministry, I should quit preaching and return to school. I listened in disbelief. I was thirty-three and had only grade nine; how could I possibly go back to school? What would happen to the church and Youth for Christ and the dozen other projects I was involved in? Suppose I did return to school, what assurance was there that, even after years of study, I would ever again be as useful?

I remained alone for hours – brooding, appraising, praying. I knew what Art had only sensed: that my faith was disintegrating. I realized that I lacked the intellectual training to deal with the questions that were beleaguering and debilitating me. If I continued as I was going I would soon be a hollow shell, a hypocrite mouthing what I no longer believed. Late in the evening I decided that, for all the dislocation it might cause, I must return to school.

At the suggestion of Jim Mutchmor, the former head of the Department of Evangelism and Social Service in the United Church, I applied for admittance to Princeton Theological Seminary. The seminary, an historic institution, is located in Princeton, New Jersey and is part of an academic community that includes Princeton University and the renowned Institute for Advanced Study. Back came a letter from the dean, pointing out that the seminary was a graduate school and that among the requirements for admittance was a bachelor degree from an accredited university. If I would complete my high-school work and earn a B.A. he would be happy to consider my application.

I wrote him, asking if I might present my case to the president. The meeting would have been in vain had it not happened that, on the day I arrived, the speaker at morning chapel was Dr. George Pidgeon, then Moderator of the United Church of Canada. After the service, Dr. John Mackay, the president of the seminary, mentioned that a young man from Toronto by the name of Templeton was coming to see him later that morning, seeking to be admitted. Pidgeon expressed surprise but said, "I know Templeton, or rather, I know his work. If he wants to return to school, do what you can to help him."

I met with Dr. Mackay for an hour. He asked me a number of theological questions and ended by saying drily, "Much room for thinking there." He then informed me that I would be admitted as a "special student"; I would be required to do the three years' work for a Th.B. and to write all the examinations, but would not be granted the degree as I did not have the prerequisites.

I returned to Toronto and notified the church that I was leaving. It was a sad and teary time. On my final Sunday night, when everyone else had gone, I returned to the sanctuary. It was dark except for the shifting patterns of light from the street and silent except for the muted sound of traffic. I stood in the pulpit for the last time. Seven years had passed since I first stood there. A hundred memories flitted before my eyes. I knew that I was standing at a watershed.

In late August 1948, just before I enrolled at Princeton, I flew to Montreat, North Carolina, to speak at a conference and to spend a day with Billy and Ruth Graham. Theirs is a marvellous house. It is secluded on the slope of a heavily treed mountain at the end of a winding road built by the governor as a tribute from the state. The house is constructed of great adze-hewn timbers salvaged from old barns in the area. The ceilings are high; the rooms are spacious and bright with sunlight. The stone fireplace in the living room is large enough to walk into.

Billy and I talked long about my leaving Youth for Christ. Both of us knew that, for all our avowed intentions to keep our friendship alive, our feet were set on different paths. He was as distressed as I was. We both knew that I was not simply giving up Youth for Christ, I was leaving fundamentalism.

We had often discussed our beliefs, meeting from time to time to talk and share experiences. Once, we spent two days closeted in a hotel room in New York City, exchanging experiences, discussing the Bible and theology, and praying together.

Our backgrounds were radically different. Billy was a country boy, raised on a farm in the American South in a deeply religious household. He had been converted and called to the ministry in his teens and had studied in fundamentalist schools: at Bob Jones College and at Wheaton, where he had earned a B.A. in anthropology. All our differences came to a head in a discussion which, better than anything I know, "explains" Billy Graham.

I had said, "But Billy, it's not possible any longer to believe the biblical account of creation. The world wasn't created; it has evolved over millions of years. It's not a matter of speculation, it's demonstrable fact."

"I don't accept that," he said. "And there are reputable scholars who don't."

"Who are they?" I said. "Men in conservative Christian colleges?"

"Most of them, yes. But that's not the point. I believe in the Genesis account of creation simply because it's in the Bible. I've discovered something in my ministry: when I take the Bible literally, when I proclaim it as God's Word, I have power. When I stand before the people and say, 'God says,' or 'The Bible says,' the Holy Spirit uses me. There are results. People respond. Wiser men than you or I have been arguing questions like this for centuries. I don't have the time or the intellect to examine all sides of each theological dispute, so I've decided, once and for all, to stop questioning and to accept the Bible as God's Word."

"But Billy," I protested, "you can't do that. You don't dare stop thinking. Do it and you begin to die. It's intellectual suicide."

"I don't know about anybody else," he said, "but I've decided that that's the path for me."

We talked about my going to Princeton and I pressed him to go with me. "Bill," I said, "face it: we've been successful in large part because of our abilities on the platform. Part of that stems from our energy, from our conviction, from our youth. But we won't always be young. We need to grow, to develop some intellectual sinew. Come with me to Princeton."

"I can't go to a university here in the States," he said. "I'm president of a Bible college, for goodness sake!" He was – Northwestern Bible College, a small fundamentalist school in Minneapolis.

"Resign," I said. "That's not what you're best fitted for. Come with me to Princeton."

There was an extended silence. Then, suddenly, he said, "Chuck, I can't go to a college here in the States, but I can and I will do this: if we can get accepted at a university outside the country, maybe in England – Oxford, for instance – I'll go with you."

He stood in front of me, his face serious, his hand outstretched. I know Billy enough to know that, had I taken his hand, he would have kept his word. But I couldn't do it. I had been accepted at Princeton. The fall term was not three weeks away. It was too late.

Not many months later, Billy travelled to Los Angeles to begin the campaign that would catapult him overnight into international prominence. I have often pondered what might have happened if I had taken his hand that day and we had gone off to school together. I am certain of this: he would not be the Billy

Graham he has become, and the history of mass evangelism would be different than it is.

In the spring of 1957, just prior to my leaving the ministry and returning to Canada, Billy Graham came to New York City for his first Madison Square Garden crusade. I was still living in Manhattan, and on a whim, telephoned Billy, simply to say hello. He insisted that I come to his hotel room so that we could talk. We spent two or three hours together, remembering good times, bringing each other up to date on what had been happening.

By late afternoon he had to prepare for the evening meeting. He let me leave only after he had exacted a promise that I would attend the service that night and sit with him on the platform.

"Bill," I said, "I don't think that would be wise. I've just left the ministry. I'm an agnostic."

But he wouldn't let me beg off. "What harm can it do?"

That evening, I went to the Garden and made my way backstage. Again, I tried to back out, but Billy hooked an arm in mine and we went out on the platform before the twenty thousand people gathered there.

Early in each service, it is Billy's practice to say a few preliminary words, to welcome special delegations, perhaps to comment on the campaign's financial needs. This night, in the course of his remarks, he suddenly made reference to me. While his associates squirmed, he told the congregation how pleased he was to have with him on the platform one of his dearest friends. He spoke of our first meeting in Chicago, of our campaigning together and of our long association. Then, to my alarm and dismay, he concluded by saying, "If you'll bow your heads, I'm going to ask my old friend, Charles Templeton, to lead us in prayer."

I knew what he was doing. He is a warm and loving man, and there is about him an astonishing naïveté. He hoped and half believed that if I attended the meeting and sat on the platform I would be stirred by profound and pleasant memories and nudged toward God by the familiar ambience. I rose and walked to the pulpit, my mind in tumult. What should I do? I could not embarrass Billy and everyone present with a stuffy explanation as to why I couldn't lead them in prayer, but neither could I involve myself in a charade.

As the audience bowed their heads, I raised mine, eyes wide, and extemporized a brief homily on the need to come to terms with one's self and on the importance of trying to understand the motives, attitudes and actions of others. I returned to my seat amid a pall of silence. I had not mentioned God nor concluded with Amen. All those thousands of people knew that a wrong note had been struck.

Stephen Olford, an English member of the Graham team, was there. He was later quoted in a book on Graham: "Billy and Chuck spent several hours talking in a hotel room. It left Billy so rattled and shaken he could barely preach that night. He literally had to struggle through his message. I think it was because he knew Chuck was there."

As was inevitable, Billy and I drifted apart. We talked on the telephone and got together from time to time, but with the years, the occasions became fewer. I was managing editor of the *Star* when, one afternoon, he called to say he was in the city and would like to have dinner at my home; he wanted to meet my wife and children, and to spend a long evening talking.

My four children, who have never quite accommodated themselves to the fact that their father was once an evangelist, found Billy a curiosity. I have always encouraged them to challenge ideas, to question, to express their own views. Bradley, the second of my three sons, was about ten at the time and precocious. He had just been admitted to full membership in the Royal Astronomical Society and was full of data and theory about the nature of the universe. With characteristic directness he broke into the dinner-table conversation.

"Mr. Graham, you're a preacher – right?"

"Yes," Billy said, smiling, "that's right."

"Therefore you believe that God created the world in six days?"

Billy's smile broadened. "Well now, Bradley, many preachers don't believe that, but as a matter of fact, I do."

Bradley fixed him with a scornful eye and said, "But how can you possibly do that? We *know* how the earth was formed — by the mutual attraction and cohesion of galactic dust millions of years ago. How can you possibly believe – "

"Bradley!" I said sharply. He subsided, shaking his head in exaggerated astonishment.

After dinner, Billy talked at length about Richard Nixon, with whom he had become friends. Billy has always been given to enthusiasms – as have I – but this was a greater one than usual. He emphasized that Nixon had come to the presidency better prepared than any of his predecessors. That argument can be made, and he made it cogently, but after the first few minutes it didn't interest me. My attitude to Nixon had been jaundiced from the time of his "Checkers speech," in which he defended himself against charges of misusing campaign funds and made cloying references to his dog, Checkers, and to his wife's "Republican cloth coat."

Billy's recital of Nixon's virtues – understandable, as he had just come from an overnight stay at the White House – began to irritate me. I wanted to take issue with some of his assertions but didn't want to cool his zeal or fall into confrontation. It was obvious as the evening wore on that the years had taken us to almost diametrically opposed viewpoints on many things. We saw world events, books, manners, morals and other subjects for conversation so differently that there was little ground for concurrence.

When the evening ended – earlier than we had planned – and I drove him downtown to his hotel, the conversation became desultory. I was very sad on the way back to Mississauga.

Marshall Frady in his book, *Billy Graham,* quotes Billy as saying:

> "I love Chuck to this very day. He's one of the few men I've ever loved in my life. He and I had been so close. But then, all of a sudden, our paths were parting. He began to be a little cool to me then. I think —" and he pauses, and then offers with a faint little smile "— I think that Chuck was always sorry for me."*

Of course that wasn't and isn't true; we had simply become different men. I think Billy is what he has to be. I disagree with him profoundly on his view of Christianity and think that much of what he says in the pulpit is puerile nonsense. But there is no feigning in him: he believes what he believes with an invincible innocence. He is the only mass evangelist I would trust. And I miss him.

---

*   I am unhappy quoting Frady. His massive book on Graham is often misleading and erroneous. In those parts of the narrative about which I have personal knowledge, the facts are frequently distorted and altered.

III

Connie asked, "Chuck, are you sure this is the way Dwight L. Moody* started?"

I was on tiptoes on a chair hanging the paper drapes she and I had bought at Woolworth's in downtown Princeton. We were in the process of moving into "the Marrieds' Dorm" and she was seated on the side of the bed resting from her labours. There hadn't been all that much to move: the house we'd left in Toronto had been rented and furnished by the church, so we had few possessions. Our students' quarters comprised a sitting-room with furniture that had been used and abused by a long line of predecessors, but didn't include so much as a kettle or a hot-plate; plus a Lilliputian bedroom with a double bed jammed into the far corner and hardly space for passage. The common bathrooms were at the far end of the hall.

We were doing a bit of mutual commiserating, Connie with her invariable good humour. It had not been without a wrench that we had left family and friends and all our pleasant associations in Toronto. We were without any assurance of income. Evangelicals were, quite properly, suspicious of my orthodoxy, and the old-line churches hadn't yet taken a reading. Any romantic notions I might have had about the superior charity of candidates for the Presbyterian ministry had been disabused earlier that day when I was invited to join a game of touch football between returning students and "the new guys." The word had been passed, "Get the Youth for Christer," and the game quickly became a contact sport. This was fine with me; I had played senior football and none of them had. What did jolt me was the fact that I had been judged *a priori*.

I won't dwell on my three years at Princeton except to say that they were among the happiest in my life. I began the first semester filled with trepidation. I was thirty-three, ten years older than most of my fellows, and hadn't done any formal study in fifteen years. Would I be able to handle the discipline? Could I meet the requirements? First-year subjects included Greek, hermeneutics,

---

* Dwight L. Moody, a nineteenth-century Boston layman, was the most famous of mass evangelists until Graham.

exegesis, homiletics, church history and ecumenics. Happily, after the first term I found little difficulty.

I was fascinated by the faculty, as diverse a mixture of insecure and eccentric characters as I had ever encountered. I became friends with a Scot who taught church history. He was a very short man with a large head and a bird's quick fidgetiness. He began class by waiting impatiently until the last student was in place. He would then say, "Promptness is the politeness of kings," and begin. I was invited often to his home, a one hundred-year-old, three-storey barn of a place with heaven knows how many rooms, in which he and his wife lived alone. He would offer a tiny glass of sherry or a cup of tea and reel off a series of witty and fascinating stories. He seemed addicted to light, and moved like the wind about the house on little short legs, turning on three-hundred-watt bulbs as he entered each room. He taught me the most valuable thing I learned at Princeton: "The world of learning isn't in the classroom; it's in the library."

There was a German who taught New Testament, a near-genius in his field; but he spoke such gutteral English that he could barely be understood. There was a professor of Hebrew who lowered his face into his dog-eared and crumbling notes and read from them for forty minutes without a break, closing the book with a snap and leaving the room without a word. There was a teaching-fellow in introductory Greek who fancied himself a comic. He studded his lectures with one-liners, but invariably got the timing wrong, as invariably drawing groans from his class. There was a Frenchman, a theatrical sort, with a habit of shaking his great mane of grey hair, chin thrust out. Unfortunately in doing so, he would sometimes lose the thread of his discourse and needed to be reminded of what he'd been saying. As his name was Cailliet, the students naturally nicknamed him, "Yippee-ay-oh."

Albert Einstein lived in Princeton during the three years I was there, teaching at the Institute For Advanced Study. His home was three houses removed from the seminary campus so I saw him on the street many times. I saw him first one cold, bright fall morning.

I was on my way into town and saw what I took to be an old bag-lady shuffling along the wide sidewalk in front of me. She was wearing a shapeless grey overcoat. Her trousers sagged over broken shoes. A wool toque was pulled low over her head, and from beneath it, rusty platinum-coloured hair pushed out untidily. As I overtook her, she stopped, stepped off the sidewalk, pulled off her hat and bowed in a courtly, old-world way. I was so taken aback at recognizing the great nuclear physicist that I hardly returned his "Guten morgen." We often passed on the street, and he was unfailingly courteous. Robert Oppenheimer, the so-called "father of the atomic bomb," was also a familiar sight. No one in the town appeared to pay either of them particular attention and all were careful not to intrude on their privacy.

Einstein was a sartorial spectacle. His unlaced shoes sometimes flapped as he walked. He wore no socks. His baggy trousers were secured with a knotted rope. He usually wore a thick sweater over a flannel shirt and, in cooler weather, a woolen toque. When an interviewer asked why he wore no socks, he replied that socks got holes in them. When asked why he removed his hat in the rain, he said that it was easier to dry his hair than his hat.

In our first year at Princeton I had very little income (only occasionally serving as a supply preacher in small churches) and it was necessary for Connie to get a job – "working on her P.H.T. degree" (Putting Hubby Through), as the working wives of students called it. She was hired by the exclusive Chapin school, to teach English and music. One day, a child defended not doing her homework by admitting she didn't understand how to multiply or divide. Her exasperated teacher replied, "Well, if you can't understand me, you'd better get Mr. Einstein to explain it to you." Being his neighbour, the child did just that. Einstein invited the child in and, lying on his stomach on the living-room floor, taught her her "numbers." Afterwards, he signed the homework. Framed, it hangs in the school, a prized possession.

I had gone to Princeton hoping to resolve some of the questions that were eroding my faith. Paramount among them was the question: Who was Jesus of Nazareth? Was he a moral and spiritual genius or was he, as the Christian church has always held, "very God of very God"?

The classroom work, especially a course in Christology, was useful, as were conversations with some of the professors, but more valuable was the library, where there were stacks of relevant material. For all that, I knew that faith is more a matter of the spirit than of the mind, and in my second year, in imitation of Mohandas Gandhi – who remains one of the formative influences on my life – I decided to fast each Wednesday, eating nothing and drinking only water. Seven nights a week, in all kinds of weather, I went walking on the golf course between the seminary and the Institute for Advanced Study, not to pray so much as to open my spirit to whatever is. I would walk in the solitary darkness, head up, eyes open, sometimes silent, sometimes trying to articulate the almost intolerable yearning I was feeling, sometimes simply focussing all my faculties on the infinite; straining to grasp what theologians like to call the "mysterium tremendum."

One night I went to the golf course rather late. I had attended a movie and something in the film had set to vibrating an obscure chord in my consciousness. Standing with my face to the heavens, tears streaming, I heard a dog bark off in the distance and, from somewhere, faintly, eerily, a baby crying. Suddenly I was caught up in a transport. It seemed that the whole of creation – trees, flowers, clouds, the skies, the very heavens, all of time and space and God Himself – was weeping. I knew somehow that they were weeping for mankind: for our obduracy, our hatreds, our ten thousand cruelties, our love of war and violence. And at the heart of this eternal sorrow I saw the shadow of a cross, with the silhouetted figure on it . . . weeping.

When I became conscious of my surroundings again, I was lying on the wet grass, convulsed by sobs. I had been outside myself and didn't know for how long. Later, I couldn't sleep and trembled as though with a fever at the thought that I had caught a glimpse through the veil.

For the next few weeks I sought to repeat the experience. It never recurred. I recognized it to be a mystical experience, and in the library pored through books on the subject. The literature is not extensive but I learned that what had happened to me was not unusual: it has been a commonplace at various times in the history of the church. More important, I learned that it was of no special significance. Mystical experience has added no insight to our knowledge of God or to Christian doctrine. Indeed, the experience is not uniquely religious: the poet Henry Wadsworth Longfellow could go into a transport at will merely by repeating his name aloud.

Nevertheless, I continued fasting and my nightly hour on the golf course. During the day, I spent my spare time in the library or in conversation, questing, searching. The foundation of Christianity is the person of Jesus. If he was a man, however gifted, he could be no more than a superlative teacher and a soaring example. If I was going to continue in the ministry, I would need to know that Jesus Christ was God.

By the end of my third year at Princeton I had found a measure of certainty, not through enlightenment but through a conscious act of commitment. It was enough.

In my last two years in Princeton I acted as interim preacher, first at the Bala-Cynwood Presbyterian church in the Main Line section of Philadelphia and, in 1951, at the Ewing Presbyterian church in Trenton, New Jersey. Ewing was an idyll. The old, ivy-covered stone church is on the outskirts of the city and is an historic parish. George Washington's army crossed the Delaware nearby and, in 1776, defeated the British on the site. The church cemetery is filled with the graves of British and American soldiers. Connie and I lived in the manse, a large, old-fashioned comfortable place surrounded by enormous oaks and elms and maples. In the spring, the walls and fences hung heavy with wisteria, great magnolia trees burgeoned with pink blooms and the lawn glowed with the mauve of a million violets.

As my final year ended, both the Presbyterian church and the National Council of the Churches of Christ approached me; the Presbyterians offered to ordain me and the National Council offered a job. I had already been ordained by the Church of the Nazarene; but that was not sufficient for the Presbyterians, who require that their clergy have a B.A. and a graduate theological degree. Princeton hadn't granted me a degree, since I didn't have the prerequisites, but the Philadelphia Presbytery moved to waive the academic-qualifications rule. Shortly thereafter, Lafayette College conferred on me an honorary Doctor of Divinity degree — "in recognition of his contribution to a balanced, intellectually sound and theogically based evangelism."

The offer from the National Council surprised and pleased me. The NCC represents most of the "standard-brand" American churches: the Episcopalians, Methodists, Presbyterians, Lutherans and others. It had never had anyone on staff with responsibility for running evangelistic campaigns. Their offer to me was that

I conduct, under their auspices, what they preferred to call "preaching missions." I accepted, specifying three conditions: that there be no interference in what I would say, that four months of each year be spent preaching in my native Canada, and that my remuneration be a salary of $150 per week.

I specified that I receive a salary in order to remove from my campaigns the scandal of what is called the "love offering." Traditionally, the evangelist is given all the money collected on the closing night of a campaign, when the largest crowd is in attendance, after a special plea is made on his behalf. There might be anywhere between 5000 and 25,000 people present on the final night, and the love offering has made many evangelists wealthy. The practice has led to the saying: "The reverend is more interested in the dollar sign than in the sign of the cross." Connie's and my salary was fixed at $7500 dollars a year, less than we might normally receive in a single two-week campaign.

The announcement of the appointment made news. *Time* magazine carried a feature story and used the opportunity to shaft Billy Graham. He had just completed a campaign in Atlanta, and *Time* ran a picture of him. Over his shoulder was a mail-sack bulging with the love offering presented to him on the closing night. Billy, to his credit, immediately put himself on salary at $15,000 a year.

There were many fundamental differences in Billy's and my campaigns. Billy is an "old-fashioned" evangelist with a heavy emphasis on the judgmental aspects of the gospel. He speaks much about heaven and hell, rewards and punishments, and ends each sermon with an appeal for converts to come forward. I seldom spoke about heaven, never preached on hell, and eschewed the traditional "altar call." At the end of the sermon, deliberately avoiding any emotional pressure, I would announce that an after-service would be held for any who wanted to make a commitment, and would dismiss the meeting. Those who wanted to remain had to move against the flow of the thousands leaving. Each night, hundreds chose to stay.

There was another difference between Billy's and my campaigns south of the Mason-Dixon line: his were segregated, mine were not.

In my early years preaching in the southern United States — the 1930s and 1940s — I was shaken by the prejudice against blacks. In Paris, Kentucky, where I first encountered it (and did little about it) there were park benches in the town square with bold lettering:

CAUCASIANS ONLY
ETHIOPIANS KEEP OFF!

There were segregated drinking fountains and public urinals. Restaurants and places of amusement were segregated, as were trains and buses. I hired a black teenager to wash, clean and wax my car. It took most of a steamingly hot day. When I asked him the charge, he wondered if two dollars would be too much. I paid him ten, less than it would have cost me in Toronto. When I mentioned it to the pastor of the church, he said crossly, "You've ruined that nigger."

I take pride in the fact that I conducted the first integrated public meeting south of the Mason-Dixon line. The year was 1953. A letter came from the Ministerial Association of Richmond, Virginia, inviting me to conduct a city-wide campaign. Richmond is a lovely and cultivated city; during the American Civil War it was the capital of the Confederacy. I accepted immediately, making mention in my reply that the services would, of course, have to be unsegregated.

There was an immediate response: the Ministerial Association very much regretted that this was impossible; the city by-laws forbade it. I replied, saying that, surely if they, the most prominent and influential clergymen in the city, were to ask that the by-law be set aside on this occasion they would not be refused. They responded that it was not possible to do this. I wrote that, under the circumstances, I would have to withdraw my acceptance.

Shortly thereafter I received a letter stating that, after pressure had been brought to bear, the city council had granted permission.

On the opening night of the campaign the tension in the Agoga Temple was palpable. The ushers had been instructed not to show people to their seats but simply to hand them a songbook. A few blacks arrived, and unsure of the situation, climbed the stairs to the balcony. I called the head usher and the chairman of the ministerial committee backstage. "Usher the people to their seats," I said. "Whites *and* blacks. Otherwise they will segregate themselves." The head usher was not prepared to do this and was told, gently but firmly, that if he didn't, someone would replace him.

But the battle was not yet won. Few blacks attended. I asked for a meeting of all the black clergy and their senior officials and specified that I be the only white man there. They filled the auditorium of one of the larger African Methodist churches.

I spoke bluntly. I reminded them that we had fought to have an integrated campaign and that an historic first had been achieved. "But now," I said, "after years of being segregated, you are segregating me. That's your right. If you are free to attend, you are also free to stay away. Now that the white man is prepared to say, after years of excluding you, 'Come on in,' it is perfectly reasonable and understandable if you say, 'Thanks, but no thanks.' But in doing so, realize that you are perpetuating the system you hate."

I then told them a story about Mohandas Gandhi. Addressing a meeting of blacks in South Africa, Gandhi had said, "One of our problems as coloured people is that we act as though we are a minority. The fact is," he said, "that the coloured peoples of the world are a great majority. When we use the terms 'whites' and 'coloured,' we demonstrate inferiority feelings. We should speak instead of coloured people and *colourless* people."

The church rocked with shouts of "Amen" and "Hallelujah!" When silence returned, I said, "As a member of a minority group, the colourless people of the world, I want to plead with you to help me in this campaign."

There was an immediate increase in the number of blacks in attendance. They sat in every part of the auditorium, sang in the choir, worked as ushers and as personal workers. There was not a single untoward incident.

Connie and I moved across the United States, conducting preaching missions. We began in Evansville, Indiana, where the largest auditorium in the city was filled on the opening Sunday night; fifteen days later, on the closing Sunday, we had to hold identical afternoon and evening services, and turned away hundreds from each. It was a similar story in Youngstown, Ohio. In Canton, Ohio, the crowds were even larger: the total attendance for the two weeks was 91,000. In each city the problem was the same – to find accommodation large enough to house the thousands who crowded at the doors.

I was experimenting with something new. In addition to the evening meetings, I conducted a noontime service, Monday through Friday, in the largest downtown movie theatre. The meeting ran from 12:10 to 12:50. There were no preliminaries; I would speak for thirty-five minutes on practical problems of ethics and human relationships. Business people at every level came from their offices, eating their lunch as they listened. Many had predicted failure: "People won't listen to a preacher for forty minutes on a weekday on their lunch hour." But they did. Within two or three days, the theatre in each city would be filled, and the doors would have to be closed to meet fire regulations. I continued the practice through my years as an evangelist.

To Canton, Ohio, to Johnstown, Pennsylvania, to Cincinnati, Ohio, to Mobile, Alabama, to Des Moines, Iowa. . . .

In Texas I saw something of the unique lifestyle of that state.

I was in Dallas to conduct Holy Week services at Highland Park Presbyterian, a magnificent stone church in the wealthiest section of Dallas. The pastor of the church, Dr. William Elliott, Jr., invited me to play an early morning round of golf with him, and as we were returning to the clubhouse, a man in a golf cart hailed us and my partner went to talk to him. I saw paper change hands. Later, as we were having lunch in the clubhouse, the minister removed something from an envelope and passed it to me across the table. It was a cheque for one million dollars made out to the Highland Park Presbyterian church of Dallas.

The explanation was simple. The man who had stopped us on the golf course was a member of the church (I'd seen him each night at the meeting) and believed in "tithing" – giving 10 per cent of your harvest or your income to God. So, having just completed an oil deal in which he had made a profit of ten million dollars, he gave one-tenth of it to the church.

More high-rolling, Texas-style:

I was invited to speak to the Dallas Millionaires Club, a luncheon club where a condition of membership is a personal worth of more than a million dollars. The club was exclusively male and the members were all Texas-gregarious. Afterwards, my host, who was also a member of Highland Park, showed me about the downtown section of the city. At one point we entered an exclusive men's tailoring shop. I was introduced to the owner, who showed me some of his most luxurious fabrics. Before I quite knew what was happening, I found my measurements being taken. I asked what was happening. My host said in his best aw-shucks manner, "I thought maybe as a goin' away present I'd like to give you half a dozen suits." I thanked him but told him I couldn't accept such a gift. He reacted to my refusal with a bemused shrug.

But he wasn't through. Down the street he led me into a store specializing in Texas boots. "Now," he said, "I can figure why you won't take the suits, but surely there's nothin' wrong with you takin' home a souvenir of Texas." I agreed, and was fitted with a magnificent pair of ornamented Texas cowboy boots. He tried to put a ten-gallon Stetson on my head but I managed to limit him to the boots.

On the Monday morning he was with the group that came to the Dallas-Fort Worth airport to see me off. As we said our goodbyes, I saw the porter who was handling our bags put a new sixteen-millimetre Bolex movie camera and a matching RCA sound-projector aboard the plane.

Each year, I spent four months holding missions in Canada. On the closing night in Charlottetown, which then had a population of fourteen thousand, there were some six thousand either in the hockey arena or listening to loudspeakers in the streets. In the Sydney arena there were as many outside as within. In two weeks, ten thousand attended; the population was thirty thousand. The meeting in Fredericton was held in winter weather. The congregation huddled in coats and hats and scarves; one night I preached wearing a topcoat. Portable furnaces were rigged to push heat through vents cut in the arena walls. Regardless of the inconvenience, every seat was filled each night and the ice area was crammed with people huddled on improvised seating. In each city, all-time attendance records were set for any event, secular or religious.

I began to have a problem with my health. I was thirty-five and thought myself to be in perfect physical condition, but I began to suffer frequent pains in the chest. Oddly, the pain never troubled me while preaching, but mornings I would find myself short of breath, with a tightness in my chest and a numbness radiating to my forearms and hands. One morning in Cincinnati, I finally gave in and went to see a doctor. Every test was applied; there was no evidence of a problem with my heart.

But the symptoms didn't go away. Indeed, they were exacerbated by difficulties I was having with my faith. The old doubts were resurfacing. I would cover them over with prayer and activity but soon there would be a wisp of smoke and a flicker of flame and then a firestorm of doubt. I would banish them again only to have them return. Part of the problem was that there was no one to talk to: how does a man who, each night, tells five to ten thousand people how to find faith confess that he is struggling with his own?

Ironically, at the very moment I was trying to shore up my sagging faith, there was a sudden flurry of interest by the media in me and in my campaigns. Even as I wrestled with my doubts, I was reading about the certitude with which I preached. People who had found strength or faith in the services shook my hand and looked at me with shining eyes. Their gratitude added to my sense of unworthiness but there was nothing I could do about it. It was not that I disbelieved; it was simply that my mind was at war with my spirit.

Stories about my campaigns were appearing in every quarter. We were cutting a new trail through the tangled underbrush of mass evangelism and it was noted in magazine articles and in wide coverage in the newspapers. The *Globe and Mail Magazine, Maclean's, Time,* the Chicago Sunday *Tribune* and others carried features. NBC invited me to do a series of four half-hour television programs from Chicago. In an article in *American* magazine entitled "Religion's Super Salesman," Edward Boyd wrote:

> I have just seen the man who's giving religion a brand-new look; a young Canadian by the name of Charles B. Templeton. Passing up the old-style hellfire-and-damnation oratorical fireworks, he uses instead a persuasive, attractive approach that presents religion as a commodity as necessary to life as salt, and in the doing, has set a new standard for evangelism.
>
> Dispensing with such props as "the sawdust trail," "the mourner's bench," and other tricks from the old-time evangelist's repertoire, he is winning converts at an average of 150 a night, and — what is something new in modern evangelism — they stay converted. At a recent two week stay in Evansville,

Indiana, for example, a count showed that Templeton had drawn a total attendance of 91,000 out of a population of 128,000. A survey taken six months later showed that church attendance was 17 per cent higher than it had been before he'd come.

He is booked two years ahead, a situation that the biggest Broadway hit can't boast, and the demands for his service are ten times greater than can be met. Moreover, observers who have closely followed his progress say that Templeton has not yet begun to hit his stride . . .

I read the article after a long night in which I had debated with myself whether I should quit the ministry.

The tempo of the work accelerated: in Winnipeg, we overflowed both sections of the Auditorium twice on the closing Sunday. In Calgary, the new Corral wasn't large enough. In Vancouver, Exhibition Stadium was jammed each night, as was the Grand theatre at noonday. At the closing, we overflowed the Stadium and the building next to it, with another fifteen hundred on the lawns outside. In Edmonton, neither the hockey arena nor the historic Macdonald church (at noon) were large enough, even though the campaign had been virtually boycotted by the *Journal*.

On the closing night, having expressed my thank-yous, I added:

> In the fifteen days we've been here, an unprecedented thing has happened. Your monopoly newspaper has not carried a single story on the campaign. I ask you: is it not news that, for the past two weeks, the people of this community, of all churches and of none, have been flocking to this building for a series of religious services? Never in the history of your city have so many people attended a similar event. And yet, the *Journal*, secure in its monopoly, has in its arbitrary and crochety way, decided to take no notice of it. Leaving Edmonton tonight, I leave you with one wish: that you get a second newspaper.

Six months later we were in Harrisburg, the capital of Pennsylvania, for what would be the greatest meeting we had yet seen. The days were filled with excitement and enthusiasm, but my nights were bedevilled by fear, by sudden sweats and by a pounding of my heart that shook the bed. Mornings I endured the now familiar pains in my chest and arms. In desperation I sought out the man reputed to be the best coronary specialist in the state. He had attended the campaign and took particular care in his examination.

I expected to hear the counsel I'd been given in Cincinnati: "Ease up. Take a vacation in the sun. Don't kill yourself." Instead, he said, "There is nothing wrong with your heart. Nothing. The pains you get – let me put it in layman's language – are the result of what I'll call heart spasm. But the trouble isn't in your heart, it's in your head. There is something in your life that is bothering you. Some conflict. Some unresolved problem. Whatever it is, deal with it. Otherwise, you will probably continue to suffer the symptoms you have described to me and will likely see other manifestations."

I knew what the problem was but couldn't discuss it with him. It was my old nemesis – doubt. And the increasing success of our campaigns was exacerbating the difficulty. I realized that soon I would be *unable* to quit. I was becoming more skilled with time, and the evidence of it was in our services. On my feet, preaching, I would be carried on the tide of the moment (it has been said that everyone preaches to the right of his or her beliefs); afterwards, that certainty would pass and I would call myself a hypocrite.

After the closing service – with what was described in the press as "the greatest crowd ever to gather in the history of Harrisburg" – Connie and I drove home to New York City. On the way, I told her part of the truth. "I've decided to leave evangelism. All I'm doing is skimming the surface. I deal in over-simplification. I feel like an ecclesiastical mountain goat; leaping from one peak to another and never getting down on the slopes or in the valleys where life is lived."

The Presbyterian Church USA had been pressing me to take over its Department of Evangelism, not to preach so much as to lead the denomination toward a program of responsible evangelism. I had rejected their overtures, but now I accepted and, as Director of Evangelism, took over a suite of offices at Presbyterian headquarters on Fifth Avenue in New York City.

For almost three years, I trained ministers and laymen, lectured in theological seminaries and universities, wrote two books and did a weekly television show on the CBS network. I continued to preach, but mostly on Sundays as a guest, most frequently at Fifth Avenue Presbyterian.

And I struggled with my faith.

It is an annual custom at Yale University to bring in a prominent preacher for a week of religious services. The guest speaks each weekday morning in chapel and makes himself available through the day for interviews with students. In the spring of 1956, I was invited. Each morning, I donned a black gown and my Doctor of Divinity hood to preach from the ornate pulpit. Students filled the pews, and stood in the aisles and doorways. I enjoyed myself: the audience was sharp and missed no nuance. The afternoon interviews were interesting.

The committee of students assigned to help me – most of them members of the Student Christian Movement – came to me late in the week in great excitement. The outstanding man in the senior class had asked for an appointment. He was an honours student in political science, captain of the Yale debating team and, since his sophomore year, had been quarterback of the football team. The students were excited because, should he declare himself a Christian, his influence would be considerable.

We met in the office assigned to me. I liked him immediately. As we began our discussion, he said, "Before we start, may we establish some ground rules? Otherwise we'll go around in circles."

"Of course," I said.

"Then let me suggest that, if at any time you say something I disagree with, I be permitted to interrupt you without seeming to be discourteous. My reason is this: if in making your argument you presume something I hold to be wrong and I let it pass – and you then go on to build on that position – it makes it difficult later on to take issue without going back to the beginning. A lot of time is wasted and a lot of confusion arises."

"I entirely agree," I said, "so long as the rule works both ways."

"Great," he said. "Now, let me tell you why I'm here. I guess the place to begin is to tell you that, although I was raised a Christian, it didn't take. If you ask me what I am today, I'd have to say I'm an atheist. I'm interested in religion but I don't find its propositions credible. I've read a lot and I've asked around, but I haven't been able to get satisfactory answers to my questions. I've been listening to you this week and you seem to come at the whole business differently. Tell me why I shouldn't be an atheist and I'll tell you why I should."

We talked for an hour, fencing at first, each of us trying to score debating points, then we grew serious. He was a resourceful debater, but it was not difficult to rebut his arguments; theology was my discipline and I'd heard most of the points he made dozens of times.

At the end of the allotted time, he rose to go. "I want to thank you," he said. "You make a hell of a good case. I won't say you've convinced me, but at least what you say makes sense." He put out his hand. "Thanks again. I promise you I'll think about it."

When the door closed behind him, my first reaction was one of elation – I'd beaten the captain of the Yale debating team. I'd made my arguments with a facility acquired in hundreds of such confrontations – not least, in confrontations with myself. They were reasonable, intellectually respectable arguments, but arguments that no longer convinced me. In the heat of discussion I believed them, but now, alone, I knew that I had been rôle-playing.

The elation was replaced by self-reproach. The student had seemed half convinced: he was searching for meaning in his life and it was entirely possible that he might go from our meeting to pray, perhaps even to commit himself. It was possible that he might do as I had done when I was about his age, as a result of which the entire direction of my life had been changed. What right did I have to meddle in his life? What right did I have to stand before the student body or the thousands of people I had been preaching to nightly for years, using all my persuasive skills to win them to something I was no longer convinced of myself? It was a reprehensible thing to do and I must stop it.

Not long afterwards I gave up the ministry. The New York Presbytery, to which I belonged, urged me to reconsider and moved not to accept my resignation for a year. To add to the dilemma, representatives from the Fifth Avenue Presbyterian church approached me about becoming their senior minister. The weekly television show I was doing on the CBS network was renewed and I was asked to continue as host. It seemed that, having made the decision to go, I was being tempted to stay.

Then, suddenly, it was impossible to leave. Mother had been ill for months and now the word came that she was dying of cancer. I flew to Toronto. As I sat by her bed, shaken by the changes in her appearance and hearing her talk about how close she felt to God, I felt unworthy. Mother's faith was as natural as breathing. I knew that if I were to tell her that I was about to leave the ministry she would be crushed. She drew strength from the reports of my missions; she saved clippings and articles. If, in her declining months, she had known that her eldest son had turned from the God she so fervently worshipped, she might not have struggled as long as she did with the pain and the despair. In the end, I didn't have the courage to tell her the truth, and let her die ignorant of it.

Connie and I had agreed to divorce. It was an amiable, even an affectionate parting, and across the years we have remained friends. We hadn't been able to have children together and very much wanted them. We were both young enough to begin families, and in the years ahead, each of us would. Moreover, her faith remained strong and she wanted to continue to express it in the church. Our separating was an added sadness, I was losing a dear friend.

It seemed that all of life was showing me its nether side. My faith was gone, my marriage was dead, my mother was dying. I was cutting myself off from the hundreds of friends I had made during nineteen years in the church. I was abandoning people who looked to me, including thirty-six men and women who were in the ministry or on mission fields because of my work. I felt like a betrayer.

But there was no real choice. I could stay in the ministry, paper over my doubts and daily live a lie, or I could make the break. I packed my few possessions in a rented trailer and started on the road back to Toronto.

IV

I didn't realize it when I left the ministry in 1957, but itinerant mass evangelism was about to die, done in by television. The only survivor is Billy Graham, the last of the great evangelists.

The mass evangelist was essentially an American phenomenon, although his progenitors can be traced to England. In the early eighteenth century, John Wesley and George Whitefield organized groups of itinerant preachers to carry the gospel throughout the British Isles. Almost simultaneously, the Great Awakening began in New England and soon the number of revivalists was legion. They multiplied in the austere soil of New England and in the Bible Belt of the South and proliferated as the population moved west.

A few rose from among the ruck, most of them eccentric, flamboyant characters who preached hellfire-and-damnation and "shook sinners over the middle kittles of hell." The most effective were Charles G. Finney, a New York lawyer, who eschewed emotionalism even as he engendered it, and that towering figure, Dwight L. Moody, a Boston shoe salesman who, with little education and no artifice, spoke to enormous audiences in the United States and Britain over a period of twenty-five years. Later and more notorious were Billy Sunday, a converted major-league baseball player, and the Canadian-born Aimee Semple McPherson, the first internationally known faith healer.

I knew many itinerant evangelists in my years in the ministry. They were as varied as other people. Among them were rogues and saints, charlatans and do-gooders. Most were simple men; strong on passion and deficient in education. Some were selfless, avoiding "worldliness" and wealth with a zeal that approached masochism. Others were dominated by avarice, consumed by pride and sexually randy. There were few outright Elmer Gantrys.

In his circumscribed world, the mass evangelist was a celebrity. In smaller communities, the annual revival meeting he conducted was the event of the year. His coming was advertised in the newspapers and proclaimed on banners and signs. During a campaign he was housed, fed, transported and feted. He was commonly praised as a great preacher – and some could indeed "bring the heavens down" – but was usually little more than a leather-lunged exhorter whose yellowed and spittle-stained sermon notes had been preached from hundreds of times. Compared to his more sedentary peers he was disproportionately rewarded for his work, receiving a love offering rather than a salary. Some grew expert at increasing the take and provided envelopes for the collection, the face of each bearing a blank cheque made out to the evangelist and lacking only the amount and a signature.

You can catch something of the ambience of an old-fashioned

revival meeting in a Billy Graham crusade. In its time, there was nothing like it. The atmosphere at the "meeting" vibrated with a special kind of excitement – an emotional compost of curiosity, anticipation, reverence, aspiration and latent guilt feelings. The sceptics were there with the zealots. Entire families assembled, from octogenarians to nursing infants. Some went to learn, others to confirm their biases. The sick went in hope of touching the hem of the garment, the weary and heavy laden in hope of finding rest.

Lives were changed – let it not be denied – some so radically as to seem new. Marriages were repaired or shattered. An alcoholic might come to sobriety. The young might have their feet set on paths of service that would lead them to the ends of the earth or might be saddled with a guilt that would weigh on them to the end of their days. But these were the exceptions; most of the time all that happened was that indifferent church-goers got a booster-shot.

When the magic left town, the prosaic moved to retake the lost ground. Studies showed that a year later little had changed. Vows were forgotten. Few were added to the church rolls. For most, the light burned lower and for some the darkness was deeper. Often, in the aftermath, congregations fell into schism as the newly annointed insisted that everyone march to their drummer's beat. In the end, things were better, things were worse, things were much the same.

Today, the itinerant evangelist is gone. In his place we have the television evangelist. Nor is he merely new; he has a new message. His gospel is a pious pablum offered in a form that renders the teachings of Jesus unrecognizable; part superstition, part pious claptrap and as unlike New Testament Christianity as a newspaper horoscope. Jesus said, "Take up your cross," and promised persecution and ostracism. The man of God in the $500 suit says, "Only believe," and promises that God will make life easy.

The electronic evangelist bears little resemblance to his pre-television predecessors. Because Christians will no longer attend church weeknights, his sanctuary is your TV set. His pulpit is a television screen. Your pew is the easy chair in your living room. You make contact by putting your hands on the set while the frequency-modulated voice of the two-dimensional man of God offers forgiveness of sins, answers to prayers, instant happiness, financial security and miracles of instant healing that would astound the Mayo Clinic.

The itinerant evangelist pounded the pulpit and shouted himself hoarse; the electronic evangelist seldom raises his voice. In lieu of sermons he delivers brief chats, and wouldn't dream of preaching on hell – it's bad for ratings. Some don't preach at all, but sit behind a Johnny Carson desk and ramble on about God in a manner that reduces the mysterium tremendum to little more than a Mr. Fixit in the sky. Prayer is a chummy conversation conducted in terms of buddy-buddy intimacy in which the evangelist informs the deity about what's going on in this wicked old world and presents a shopping list. The hymns tend to be trendy, mostly country and western – God's-country and western, of course.

Television Christianity is an undemanding faith; a media-postacy that tells listeners that, to become a Christian, all they have to do is "believe." Standards of membership are so low that some so-called "television ministries" are prepared to enroll as a believer anyone willing to say no more than, "Thank God it quit raining."

In one particular area, however, the traditional evangelist has been surpassed by his electronic successor – in taking an offering. The former made a plea, said a prayer and passed the plate. The latter offers "free gifts" and flashes a mailing address on the screen. The respondent is automatically enrolled as a full-fledged member in good standing of a mailing list, and immediately becomes the recipient of computer-personalized mail surpassing in its volume and entreaties the most energetic of book clubs. These mailings are the television equivalent of the collection plate, which, having been passed, is passed forever and ever, Amen.

The offerings, mulcted mostly from the poor, the elderly and lonely women, amount to millions of dollars annually. Few of these dollars are used to give succour to the needy, to put food in empty bellies or to help the helpless and dispossessed. Seldom is any of the money returned to the community from which it came. Most of it is used to provide generous salaries and expensive perks, to buy more broadcast time, to build larger broadcast studios, to modernize the mailing system and to perpetuate the evangelist's name in a variety of institutions.

There are, among the host of television evangelists, exceptions to those I have described, but they are a minority and most of these preach a bastardized version of the gospel. Some are not content merely to build their "ministry," but lust for temporal power. Jesus rejected a move to make him king ("My kingdom is not of this world") but the minority that presumptuously describes itself as the "Moral Majority" covets power, political power, here and now. They seek to influence presidents. They pressure legislators. And if they can't achieve their goals through intimidation, they have made it clear they will themselves seek to ascend to the seats of the mighty.

These are dangerous men, for they are intolerant of those who don't accept their premises. They claim to get their orders from God; thus, to oppose them is to oppose Him. They do not believe in freedom and, were they in positions of power, would undoubtedly forbid others the right to follow their convictions. History bears record that the church in power tends to be a tyrannizing institution.

I have had some experience with evangelists. Most of them, although not all, are relatively ignorant men with narrow minds and narrow interests. They know almost nothing of the human psyche and little of the effects of guilt on the human spirit. But that doesn't deter most of these self-appointed spokesmen for the Almighty. They are like the old-fashioned medicine men; they live off people's fears. They are quacks practising spiritual medicine without a licence, offering remedies they neither understand nor have bothered to examine. They are not evil men in the usual sense, not men of ill-will, not malicious – indeed, they may be eminently personable – but in their zeal to "do good" they often do great and lasting harm. They exploit guilt and fear. They warp the mind. They may sometimes do good – at least temporarily – but it usually happens by chance. On balance, I think the contemporary television evangelist is deleterious to society.

Inside Television

INSIDE TELEVISION

I

My first job in television was as host of my own weekly series on the CBS network. The year was 1953 and I was living in Manhattan, where I was Director of Evangelism for the Presbyterian Church USA. The new medium of television was just getting established, and programming was in living black and white. The big names were Milton Berle, Jackie Gleason, Ed Sullivan, Arthur Godfrey, Jack Paar, Dave Garroway, and that most unlikely television star, a Roman Catholic priest, Monsignor (soon to be bishop) Fulton J. Sheen. Berle was "Mr. Television" then, and it seemed pointless to mount an expensive show in opposition to him, so the Bishop was dumped into the 8:00 p.m. Sunday time-slot. He became the sleeper of the year and was soon challenging "Uncle Milty" in the ratings.

The National Council of Churches, while not unhappy that religion was prime-time television, was anxious to snatch a piece of the pie for Protestantism. With the active cooperation of CBS, it was decided to present a religious program aimed at a secular audience, and a search was begun for a host. I had demonstrated an ability to attract large audiences, so they settled on me. But churches (and television networks) are not given to risk-taking, so it was decided to try out the show Sunday mornings at 10:30. In this slot — chosen because the religious would be in church or on their way — the program's appeal to secular listeners could be tested and it might develop a form that would justify a move to prime-time.

The name of the show was *Look Up and Live*, and the concept was simple: make the target audience "unchurched" young people, eschew the look of religion, let the music be contemporary, bring in "name" entertainers as guests and let the sermon be rather a brief talk: conversational in manner, modern in its allusions and addressed to the mind and the will of the listener rather than to the emotions.

They put under contract a beautiful blonde pop-singer, Betty Cox. She had subbed for Jan Murray during her frequent absences from the *Arthur Godfrey Show* and had been featured in a network series, *Broadway to Hollywood*. A vocal quartet was formed and named The Foursome: two black and two white to make the point of racial integration. On each program, show business celebrities were featured: artists such as Sidney Poitier, Maria Tallchief, Ethel Waters, Shepperd Strudwick, the actor, George Shearing, the Dave Brubeck Quartet and others. They danced or sang or played a brief scene, after which I would interview them. At the end of the program in a simulated study, I perched on the edge of a desk or worked at an easel while I delivered a six-minute sermon.

Variety reviewed the program in typical style: " *Look Up and Live* shapes up as a natural facet of religious programming and should win plaudits all around. Everything about the show smacks of smart programming from the tele (sic) and from the religious standpoint. . . ." The New York *Daily News* carried a feature under the heading, TV TO FIGHT JD: "A Protestant pastor has gone before the cameras to battle juvenile delinquency in a quiet but effective way. He's Charles Templeton, a former football player and syndicated sports cartoonist, whose approach is far removed from the hellfire-and-brimstone school of preaching. . . ."

The show proved to be a success (twenty-five years later it was still running) but didn't cause Berle or Bishop Sheen to lose sleep.

The transition from the public platform to the television studio wasn't easy. At the first rehearsal for the initial show, I took a cue and began my talk; thirty seconds into it the director broke in on the studio intercom: "Ten minutes, everybody. Mr. Templeton, I'd like a word with you. I'll be right down."

On the set he said, "How many people do you think will be listening to you?"

"I'm told two to three million."

He shook his head. "No."

"A million?"

"No."

"I give up. How many?"

"One."

"One?"

"You're used to speaking to crowds," he said, "but television is an intimate medium. The audience may be in the millions but nobody hears as a crowd. Each person hears you as an individual. Talk to that one person."

It was the best advice a neophyte could receive.

I did the show for three years. In my last season I was joined by Merv Griffin as co-host. Merv was at the time a band singer who wanted to expand his opportunities and add to his versatility. He was easy to work with, amiable, no camera hog, and quickly became a witty and skilful interviewer. My most vivid memory is of the two of us perched on high stools bantering until we broke up in laughter – neither of us able to remember the name of the guest we were supposed to introduce.

As 1957 dawned I faced a dilemma. I had made the decision to leave the ministry and, in doing so, to quit *Look Up and Live,* but I didn't know how I might support myself. When I left the *Globe and Mail* I knew where I was going – into the ministry – but now I had no idea how I would make a living. I knew I wanted to return to Canada, but what would I do there? Who would hire a forty-two-year-old former evangelist?

By chance I read on the front page of *Variety* that Jackie Gleason, one of the biggest stars in television and then at the height of his popularity, was looking for a story for his first venture into motion pictures. He had been reading scripts for months, the story said, but hadn't found the right vehicle. Gleason made no secret of his plans: he would make a big-budget technicolour film specifically designed to establish him as a major motion-picture star. I decided at that moment – without considering how improbable it was – that I would write a motion-picture outline for Gleason.

Over the next three weeks I drafted a twelve-page outline, giving it the title *King.* It was the story of a successful television comedian, a mercurial man, restless in his job of making people laugh. One night he interjects a note of political comment into his monologue and, by luck, touches a national nerve. The response is phenomenal. In subsequent weeks he makes political comment a part of his shows. His influence mushrooms and he begins to dream grandiose dreams. In a series of swift developments he becomes the focus of a people's revolt against the traditional political parties and, in a bold move, tries to take over the leadership of one of them, only to be publicly humiliated. Blinded by ambition, he is driven to acts of near madness, and it is only his responsibility for the accidental death of his estranged son that restores him to rationality and to the realization that he should return to being what he is . . . a comedian.

I had an acquaintance who was a sometime theatrical agent. He assured me that he knew Gleason and would get my outline to him. Six weeks passed and nothing happened: the manuscript had been resting, undelivered, in a desk drawer. Apologizing, he said, "Why don't you get Merv Griffin to get it to Gleason? They both have the same manager, a guy by the name of 'Bullets' Durgom." I asked Merv if he would read the outline, and if he felt comfortable about doing so, pass it to Durgom. His response was an immediate yes.

A few days later I was entering an auditorium in Columbus, Ohio, for a speaking engagement, when I was called to the telephone. "It's urgent. A Mr. Durgom calling from New York City."

On the telephone he offered me five thousand dollars for the outline. I hesitated, knowing that if I accepted the money, that would probably be the end of it. I reasoned that, if Gleason liked the outline enough to buy it, he might let me try my hand at writing the screenplay. I told Durgom that I would be in New York City the following Monday and would prefer to discuss the matter then.

My instructions were to be at the Park Sheraton hotel on Broadway at 56th Street at 11:00 sharp on Monday morning. Gleason lived in and his entourage occupied the entire penthouse floor and most of the floor below. A receptionist told me to wait. I sat in the anteroom for better than half an hour, my nervousness growing with each minute, while cronies came and went and red-jacketed waiters passed through carrying trays laden with Bloody Marys. Finally, Durgom ushered me into his tiny, cluttered office.

He was an intense, skinny man, balding, stooped and wearing a harassed look. I learned later that he earned the sobriquet "Bullets" in a Brooklyn schoolyard, where he seemed always to be ricocheting from one point to another. He treated me with courtesy – bemused that I was a clergyman – talked about Merv with affection, and then turned to business. He had taken my reluctance on the telephone as a bargaining tactic and opened the discussion by offering to pay me ten thousand dollars for all rights to the outline. I was tempted but demurred, saying that I would like to try my hand at writing the screenplay.

"Have you ever written a screenplay?" he asked.

"No," I said. "But then I'd never written an outline before, either."

He sighed wearily. A buzzer interrupted and we went in to meet The Great Man.

Gleason was in his shirtsleeves, seated behind a massive desk, a Bloody Mary in one hand, a cigarette in the other. He looked more youthful than his image on black-and-white television. He put down his drink to shake hands, and without any feigning or caution, told me that he was "nuts" about the outline. Durgom sighed wearily. For five minutes Gleason talked about the plot with unrestrained enthusiasm; it was, he said, exactly the story he'd been looking for. Then, suddenly, he turned to Durgom. "Have you worked out a deal?" Durgom, obviously intimidated by Gleason, assured him that everything was under control. "Chuck's guy and I are going to get together in the next couple of days and work out the details."

"Well, get on it right away," Jackie said. "I don't give a damn what it costs, get it."

The only agent I knew was the man in whose desk drawer the outline had rested for some six weeks. When I told him what had happened, he chuckled and said, "We're gonna want fifty thou for the outline." I told him that I wanted to write the screenplay (visions of Hollywood danced in my head) but that Durgom had asked me first to expand the outline, which I did.

The agent and Durgom had a number of meetings over the next few weeks without resolving the matter. Durgom finally offered a flat thirty thousand dollars for the expanded outline. Counselled by my agent, but with much trepidation, I turned it down. I was working twelve to fourteen hours a day on the screenplay, basing the style and shooting instructions on some borrowed scenarios.

By June, Durgom was due to depart for a vacation on a tramp steamer; he would be out of touch for two months. Gleason was leaving for Poughkeepsie, New York, where he would spend the summer. His lawyers were tied up in negotiating a ten-year contract with CBS and Buick. Durgom made a proposal: he would pay me three thousand dollars for right-of-first-refusal on the property and we would conclude our negotiations in the fall. I had just delivered the screenplay and was anxious to return to Canada for the summer, so I agreed.

In mid-August a major motion picture was released. It was called *A Face in the Crowd,* directed by Elia Kazan, and was based on a story by Bud Schulberg. It starred a newcomer to films, Andy Griffith, who would go on to television stardom. I read the reviews with growing concern. While the plot and the principal characters were unlike mine, the protagonist was an entertainer who gets involved in politics. In late August I received a letter from Durgom notifying me that, for precisely these reasons, Jackie would not be exercising his option.

I retained the three thousand dollars, of course, but lost the thirty thousand. More important, I lost an opportunity. My brief dream of Hollywood faded.

Look Up and Live had many unlikely fans. One of them was Harvey Schwartz, vice-president of the music publishing firm, Bregman, Vocco and Conn. He called the studio and asked me to come and see him, but wouldn't tell me why.

His office was in the Brill Building, a scruffy ten-storey office building on Broadway at 49th Street. There was little evidence that this was now the locale of the fabled "Tin Pan Alley" and the heart of the popular-music business except for the knots of musicians hanging about on the street outside the entrance and the sounds of music filtering from behind many of the office doors.

Schwartz was a man in his middle years, conservatively dressed in a dark blue pin-stripe suit. He greeted me cordially, told me that he watched *Look Up and Live* each Sunday, and was convinced that I should write song lyrics. Had I ever tried it? Would I like to?

It was 1956 and the music hit of the year was the so-called inspirational song, "I Believe." I accepted Schwartz's invitation and, over the next few weeks, wrote a dozen or more lyrics, taking to him what I judged the best. He liked one especially, a song titled "True Happiness," a sentimental thing about God and marriage and children for which I had written both words and music. He suggested a few changes and agreed to publish it.

Schwartz was convinced that he had a potential hit and put his organization to work. One of his arrangers prepared it for publication in sheet-music. A "demo" was cut, with Stuart Foster doing the vocal, backed by a full orchestra. Promotion materials were prepared, and Bregman, Vocco and Conn's song-pluggers went to work.

There was a high-voltage flurry of excitement when Perry Como's A and R (Artist and Repertoire) man, the scout responsible for recommending new songs, became interested. The excitement peaked when Como, his A and R man and Schwartz made an early Saturday morning golf date to discuss the song. But no commitments were made, and that was the end of it.

I had been required to join ASCAP, the American Society of Composers, Authors and Publishers, and at the end of the year I received a royalty payment from them. As I recall it, my first cheque was for seventy-eight dollars, and the royalty was smaller each year. However, I learned an interesting thing about ASCAP: it is a real brotherhood. The tiny royalties I received each year, for a period of years, didn't reflect the earning of my one published song – which, so far as I know, earned nothing after the first year. ASCAP has a "pool" into which a portion of the earnings of all its members are put, and then disbursed to each member using certain criteria that do not necessarily reflect that member's output and earnings. The seventeen dollars I received in 1960, for instance, included a share of the earnings of such men as Irving Berlin, Hoagy Carmichael and Burt Bacharach.

After returning to Canada I transferred to CAPAC, the Composers, Authors and Publishers Association of Canada, in which I continue as a member. Over the years I have written dozens of lyrics but have done nothing with them.

I spent the summer writing television plays, living in a two-room log cabin on Georgian Bay near Lafontaine. The late fifties was television drama's best period; fine writing being done by Paddy Chayefsky, Tad Morgan and others. Spurred on by the apparent success of the Gleason venture I'd decided that I would try to make television and screenwriting my new vocation.

In three and a half months I wrote five plays; in mid-September, I drove to Toronto to submit them to the script department at the CBC. They bought three of them: *Absentee Murderer*, a half-hour suspense thriller that was directed by

Robert Christie and starred Joseph Furst, Barbara Hamilton, Peggi Loder and James Doohan (who later came to fame in *Star Trek*) and *A Matter of Principle*, a one-hour play superbly acted by John Drainie, Lloyd Bochner and Kathryn Blake and directed by Charles Jarrot. The third play, the title of which now eludes me, endured many script changes but finally went unproduced. Both of the others were subsequently shown on the BBC in England and on the Australian Broadcasting Corporation.

Garfield Weston, one of Canada's great entrepreneurs and head of the multifaceted Weston's Limited, had decided to confront his opponents and enhance his own fortunes in a single bold stroke. To do so, he needed a documentary film made almost overnight. He handed the problem to the head of his Canadian supermarket operation, George Metcalf, president of Loblaws Limited; Metcalf hired a Toronto film company, Meridian, and they hired me.

Weston had not long before introduced North American style supermarkets to Britain. The venture had been widely attacked, most vigorously by the tens of thousands of greengrocers whose small neighbourhood stores were threatened. The supermarkets bought in carload lots, sold with small mark-ups and depended on volume for profit. No corner grocer could compete with that.

With typical daring, Weston asked to be invited to address the greengrocers at their annual convention, aware that he would face an angry audience and might be booed from the platform. There, he would spring his surprise. He would offer the greengrocers the opportunity to compete with his supermarkets by introducing to the United Kingdom a Canadian innovation, the co-op. To make his presentation graphic he needed a film that would show how Canadian independent grocers had made themselves viable by pooling their purchasing power. It was Garfield's plan to sell to the new U.K. co-op.

But time was short. I would have to produce a shooting-script over a three-day weekend. Two of Weston's vice-presidents would fly to Toronto on the Monday to approve the script and to authorize the start of production. Knowing it would mean three days with little or no sleep, I demanded a high fee. Early Monday morning I delivered the script to Meridian and went to bed.

That afternoon at 1:30 I sat in the downstairs reception room at Loblaws with the two vice-presidents awaiting the summons from Metcalf's office. An hour passed, two and then three. The vice-presidents were becoming increasingly nervous, interpreting the delay as bad news. As the time passed their faces grew grey with fear. Coffee cups rattled on saucers. Ash-trays filled with butts. Curious, I asked if Weston was a demanding taskmaster, and was told a series of stories.

When Weston was a young man, he was fired from a job. Not many years later he bought the company from which he had been discharged, hiding his identity through proxies. On the day the deal was consummated, he walked into the president's office, brushed past his secretary, went to a corner, undid his fly and urinated against the wall. Then he turned to the man who had fired him and ordered him out of the office, not permitting him so much as to empty his desk.

A Weston subsidiary in the English midlands was consistently losing money. Head-office personnel and various experts were dispatched to correct the problem, but the company continued in the red. Out of patience, Weston stated that he would turn the company around within six months and went personally to visit it. Accompanied by the personnel manager carrying a clipboard, he went on a walking tour of the plant. When he saw an employee idle or involved in casual conversation, he had the name listed. Regardless of the employee's ability or length of service, he was fired. Within six months, I was told, the company moved to the black.

By five o'clock the only word from Metcalf's office was that he had been on the telephone to London for extended periods. The tension in the waiting room was palpable. I looked at the manifestations of fear around me and suddenly decided that I would have no part of it. I announced that I had a dinner engagement, which was true, although the appointment was not until seven. It was unthinkable they said. I couldn't just leave. What if there was a problem with the script?

It was no act of courage. I was reacting to the rudeness that had kept us sitting there for three and a half hours without any word. Beyond that, I refused to be a part of the abject vassalage I was witnessing. No job, no fee was worth that. If the script needed reworking, I would stay up all night if necessary. If that wouldn't do, to hell with it.

As it happened, the film went forward without a hitch and was delivered on time.

In early September, 1957, I was leaving the CBC building on Jarvis Street, when I was intercepted by a tall, somewhat awkward young man with a round face, heavy horn-rimmed glasses and a mound of wavy hair. In a verbally fastidious way he introduced himself as Ross McLean, told me that he was the producer of a program called *Tabloid*, and asked about a book of mine that had just been published in New York. (I was surprised that he would know of it; it was a series of lectures on evangelism, The Stone Lectures, I had given at Richmond Theological Seminary in Virginia.) McLean had lost a guest on that evening's *Tabloid* and wondered if I would be willing to appear and be interviewed by Percy Saltzman. A taxi was sent for a copy of the book, and I scribbled some questions for Percy.

After the show, Ross followed me into the hallway and finally onto a staircase, where we held an extended conversation. That fall, he informed me, he would be producing a program called *Close-up*, a Sunday-night prime-time public-affairs show: he offered me a job as one of two interviewers on the show. (Pierre Berton, whom I hadn't met, would be the other.) I affected some reluctance, as playwriting held a greater attraction for me, but called him back in almost unseemly haste the following day to accept the job.

Close-up was a new and exciting venture by the CBC. It was the first important public-affairs show and blazed a trail for *This Hour Has Seven Days*, *The Way It Is* and *Sunday*. Frank Willis was host. Patrick Watson was associate producer and Douglas Leiterman story editor. From time to time, Joyce Davidson, a protégée of Ross's, came over from *Tabloid* for a particular segment. The show sought to entertain as it informed, mostly through interviews and mini-documentaries, and to break from the self-consciously serious and sometimes pompous patterns of the past. The first interview I did was with George Chuvalo, a then-young boxer who went on to hold the Canadian heavyweight title and fight, among others, Muhammad Ali. During the entire interview, Ross had Chuvalo skip rope. In the end, I joined him, and ended up breathless.

Berton and I ranged much of the world for stories. He was at the time the featured columnist on the Toronto *Star* and was not as free to travel as I; as a consequence I got most of the plum assignments.

The world of public-affairs network television into which I had been so suddenly precipitated was a sweat-box of fearsome tension. The medium was new in Canada and the people in charge, despite a brave air of *savoir faire*, were pioneering. There were few precedents and no rules. Except for some brief filmed segments, programs such as *Close-up* were assembled as they were broadcast, interviews were done "live to air" and mistakes were irrevocable.

On the night of the show, after a rough run-through, Ross McLean might inform you that, "You have 8.47 for your item." In those few minutes you were required to get the issue before the viewer, extract the relevant information from your guest, keep him or her from wandering or fudging, put questions designed to elicit interesting and pertinent replies and, even more importantly, devise ways to get your guest to reveal something of him or herself. All the while, there is frantic and often unrelated activity in other parts of the studio, cameras swinging into and out of position, the floor-manager signalling for you to speed up or stretch until his final countdown – "Thirty seconds . . . fifteen . . . ten, nine, eight, seven, six, five, four, three, two, one," and a motion of his hand as though slitting his throat.

It was a peculiarly threatening time for me because I had been away from Canada for ten years and was out of touch with what had been happening. How many times, on *Court of Opinions* or *Close-up*, did my ignorance rear like a spectre behind my chair threatening to expose itself before the nation.

A more fundamental problem was that I didn't know who I was. I had lost an identity and had not yet found a new one. In the ministry, I moved in familiar surroundings, comfortable with the people, the language, the customs. Now, suddenly, I was in unfamiliar territory. The natives were friendly but foreign. I didn't speak their language nor they mine. I had, overnight, to learn how to join easily in casual conversation (sometimes punctuated with obscenities); to go out on dates, to order a drink, to dance. Seeking protective colouration, I began to smoke, and it was a dozen years before I was able to quit. It was as though I had been returned to my teens. I was in a twilight world, a creature of neither the sun nor the night. It was almost two years before I walked with any assurance.

Early on, I was sent with a crew to Europe for a series of interviews, one of the first being with novelist Evelyn Waugh. Waugh was notoriously difficult; he specified in his acidulous way that the fee would be five hundred dollars for the first thirty minutes, an additional five hundred if we went one minute beyond the half hour and five hundred more if we went one minute beyond the hour. We had hoped to record the interview at his home, but he quickly scotched that: "A BBC crew was here last week," he said. "They trampled the flower beds, mucked about on the lawns and left the premises like a pigsty." It would be done at our hotel, he said, or not at all, and at a time of his choosing. All his demands were hastily agreed to – anything to get Evelyn Waugh.

I prepared for the interview carefully and with much trepidation. I'd read four of his books; I bought another three in paperback and holed up in my hotel room. In the course of my preparation, someone told me a story about Waugh's irascibility, thinking that it would provide insights into the man. It only added to my uneasiness.

The story had it that Waugh was on the executive of a London literary society that had decided to honour a writer with whom Waugh had clashed and whom he detested. Waugh asked to be excused from the head table but acquiesced when it was pressed on him as a duty. On the night of the tribute, he arrived carrying a large copper ear trumpet. As the business of the evening began, he put the trumpet to his ear, and listened through it during all the preliminary speeches. When his hated rival was introduced and rose to respond, Waugh, with elaborate deliberateness, removed the trumpet from his ear, placed it on the table before him, crossed his arms, closed his eyes and, with a beatific expression on his face, sat back in his chair.

He arrived for the interview punctually, dressed in impeccable Saville Row style. He was shorter than I'd expected and a bit corpulent. He had the face of a kewpie-doll, the rosy nose of a drinker and round, robin's-egg-blue eyes. He moved immediately to introduce himself; first, to Bob Crone and his wife, Vi, our camera crew. Bob, an amiable fellow, when asked what his job was, said he was a cameraman. Then, reaching for some contact with the author of *The Loved One*, he added that he had once been an undertaker's helper. "Ah," said Waugh. "Capital. Undertaker's helper – surely you mean mortician's assistant?" Crone nodded vigorously, eager to please. "Why, then," Waugh continued, "having done such important work, have you descended to working as a journalist?"

I was by my chair, at a table, microphone attached, waiting for him. He ignored my outstretched hand, said nothing, sat down and didn't so much as look at me. The lights were turned on, the sound man called out, "Speed," someone banged the clapper and read the data on the slate, the director said, "Action," and I, my voice a trifle unsure, began.

Waugh responded to my opening questions with only a word or two, and seemed in no mood to expand on them. After we'd been going a few minutes, he fixed me with his cold, unblinking blue eyes and asked, "Mr. Templeton, have you read any of my books?" I said that I had and continued my questioning. A few minutes later, he said again, "Are you *sure* you've read my books?" Yes, I said, mentioning some of the titles. He shook his head as though puzzled and said, "Very well, then. Continue." In posing a question, I referred to his being a satirist. He stopped me short. "*I,* a satirist? Whatever would give you that idea? Are you *certain*, Mr. Templeton, you have actually read my books?" At one point I asked him about his children. He responded by saying that "Once a day I allow them into my presence for ten minutes. Just after tea."

So it went, a protracted agony. By the end of the interview I was in a rage that led me to refuse his proffered hand. Doubtless that pleased him.

It appeared at first that the day would end as badly as it had begun. After the Waugh ordeal we went backstage at the Haymarket Theatre in London to interview Ralph Richardson. Sir Ralph is one of the most eminent of English actors, famed equally for his roles in film and on stage, and knighted for his contributions to the theatre. I expected arrogance, but found instead an astounding insecurity. He came from the stage and went with hardly a word into the shower. Ten minutes later he was back in a white terrycloth robe begging off. He paced the small confines of the dressing room, cluttered with our lights and cameras, wringing his hands. "Look, chaps, you really don't want to interview me. I'm a dull stick. I have nothing to say. Can't we just forget the whole thing? I'd much rather not go through with this." This celebrated, gifted man was, quite obviously, nervous and frightened. After perhaps ten minutes of entreaty, he assented. He proved a fascinating subject.

From London, we went off to the Riviera for an interview with novelist Somerset Maugham. Maugham lived with his male secretary-companion on a magnificent estate at Cap Ferrat, near Antibes, in an embittered loneliness, soured by the judgements of the critics and his peers. On our arrival, we were shown to a flagstone patio adjoining the great house. When our tangle of cables, lights and cameras was ready, Maugham joined us. He was eighty-four then, with dessicated skin, sparse straight hair, hooded eyes and a wide downturned slash of bloodless lips, but was undiminished in intellectual vigour. He greeted us with warm cordiality.

A frequent problem in a filmed interview is the subject's nervousness. Often, a guest is at his or her best while the lights are being adjusted, sound levels checked and technical problems resolved. Knowing that the cameras aren't yet rolling, he or she is relaxed, ready with quips and observations and full of sprightly small talk. But once the interview begins, that ease may disappear and the public persona will take over – guarded, controlled and dull.

We had heard that Maugham tended to tighten up during an interview and planned to begin filming without his knowledge. I began with casual conversation and Maugham made his first response. As he did, he paused in mid sentence, his jaw set and there was a pause. The pause was broken only when he whacked the palm of his hand on the arm of the chair. For a moment, I was dumbstruck: the man obviously suffered from a severe stammer. As we continued, I glanced at the director, who rolled his eyes skyward, shoved his fists deep in his pockets and turned away. There was nothing to do but to go ahead and, between pauses and whacks, try to get the story.

Television interviews are not as they seem. Most are heavily edited. The interview may take as much as an hour, but after an editor has pieced together the newsworthy and interesting statements, it may be reduced to as little as five to twenty minutes. If the editing is skilfully done, viewers are not aware that what they are seeing is no more than snippets and patches of what was originally recorded.

As the conversation with Maugham continued, it became obvious that the stammer and the banging on the arm of the chair would make the interview virtually impossible to edit. In a counsel of despair while a film magazine was being changed, we decided that we would not use close-ups, and that Maugham should be seen in the setting in which he lived. He and I would be filmed at a distance as we walked through his estate. Later, the sound portions of the interview would be overlaid and it would seem that the conversation was taking place as we went.

Three hours later, the shoot was completed, delayed by the inevitable technical problems that are a part of working with film. We were full of apologies as we packed our gear. We said our good-byes and there was a general round of handshaking, but Maugham didn't leave. He stood to one side, frowning, apparently puzzled.

I went to him and said, "Thank you again, Mr. Maugham. You've been marvellously patient and we appreciate it."

He looked at me and said, almost pathetically, "Don't you even want to see where I write?"

In our preoccupation, we'd forgotten to ask.

The following day we were scheduled to interview Minou Drouet, a most extraordinary child who, at the age of eight, was being hailed by the leading literary figures in France as a prodigy. Hers was an astounding story.

Minou Drouet's mother was a prostitute and her father a field hand. As an infant she was taken into the home of a middle-aged woman, whose ambition to write well exceeded her talent. She adopted the child and raised her with love, surrounding her with music in a home dedicated to literature. It appeared that Minou was retarded. At six she hadn't spoken a word. The judgement of four doctors was that she would never be normal.

One day, her mother played a recording of a Brahms symphony for her. Minou swooned. When she was revived, she spoke perfect French in complex sentences. Shortly thereafter she began to write poetry. Some of the poems were published and immediately provoked debate. It was said that no child of six could possibly have such thoughts, much less express them so profoundly. It was argued that, unlike music, poetry demands an experience of life, experience that no child so young could have had. It was charged that her adoptive mother – a poet herself who aspired to recognition but had been judged second-rate – was the author of the verses.

The controversy became a *cause célèbre*. The French Academy of Arts and Sciences decided on an experiment to validate or to dismiss the claims made for the child. Minou was placed in a room behind one-way glass. She was provided with paper and pencil, and after she was alone and incommunicado, given three subjects to write about. She did as she was instructed and the results were scrutinized. There could be no question; the poems were the product of a prodigious talent. Jean Cocteau, the eminent writer and film-maker, commented: "She's not an eight-year-old child, she's an eighty-year-old dwarf."

For my interview with Minou Drouet, a picnic hamper had been purchased and a colourful blanket found. Minou and I were filmed under the Riviera summer sun at an idyllic location overlooking the Mediterranean. She was an extraordinary child: beautiful, outgoing, animated, aware, coquettish, serious. There was one problem: no one on our team had troubled to find out if she spoke English. She didn't, and I retained only the residue of two years of high-school French.

The camera followed us to the spot selected. I spread the blanket and together we laid out the food. Minou thought it great fun and was especially delighted when she discovered that some "*Co*-ca Co-*la*" had been included. She chattered on animatedly and I responded gauchely, straining for the appropriate words, often to her outbursts of laughter. Fortunately, there was enough communication to get us by, and my lack was more than compensated for by her unspoiled charm and vivacity.

When it was time to end the shoot, I took her hand and said a halting good-bye. She kissed me and said, "*Bon jour, mon ami du soleil*," and went off with her mother, leaving me enchanted for days.

There were other interviews abroad:

I spent an afternoon with writer and critic Rebecca West, who talked with me on the terrace of her country home on the outskirts of London. Pointing off toward the city, only just visible on the far horizon, she described watching bombs erupt soundlessly on London as the Battle of Britain was fought in eerie silence above the barrage balloons. To this day, I see it happening as though I had been there.

Of another stripe was a session with Lady Iris Docher, a wealthy and wildly eccentric Englishwoman, whose strawberry pink eyelashes and uninhibited escapades were scandalizing the nobility and delighting the feature writers on the Fleet Street tabloids. We interviewed her on the deck of her yacht where, to the delight of our film crew, she refused to proceed unless I personally pinned the hidden microphone on the inside of her well-filled sweater. I demurred, and finally Vi Crone did the honours.

Bernie Braden welcomed us to his handsome home; surrounded by the evidence of his enormous success in English television. He talked nostalgically of Canada and the CBC, hinting that he might give it all up to return home. But, in the meantime, there was a party for Lauren Bacall at the Milroy night club in Hamilton Place, hosted by Sir Laurence Olivier and Lady Vivien Leigh, with 150 of London's show-business nobility in attendance; a new sports car to be picked up and a successful new television season underway. Braden was a talented and charming guest.

Not so charming was Lucky Luciano's number-one lieutenant, whose name I can't recall. He had been deported to his native Italy with Luciano and was managing to make out with a few little "deals" he had going. I spent most of two days with him in Rome, much of it hanging about in a sidewalk espresso-bar open to the street. In all that time, I don't think he ever looked directly at me. His eyes searched the passing traffic, and every once in a while he would interrupt our conversation to go into the street, and with a sleight of handshake, pass narcotics to his customers.

I spent much of a day and an evening with Madame Antonina Olivetti, an international beauty and the estranged wife of a member of the wealthy Olivetti typewriter family. In Roman Catholic Italy in the 1950s, she was valiantly and almost single-handedly fighting for birth control and abortion. On the evening of the interview she showed me the Rome tourists don't see: some of the great homes and estates of her friends; unexpected enclaves of crumbling beauty, redolent with history; smoky, hole-in-the-wall night clubs where American jazz was played. Two days later, as we waited for the plane that would return us to London, her chauffeur presented me with an Olivetti portable typewriter.

While in Rome, an invitation came from the Canadian ambassador to the Vatican: "Would I like a private audience with the Holy Father, Pius XII? If so, it was possible." I leaped at the chance. Vi Crone pleaded to be included, and the arrangement was made.

We went at the appointed hour to a massive wrought-iron gate beneath Bernini's colonnade. One of the Swiss Guards ushered us through marble halls to a magnificent upstairs room. It was Renaissance in style: square, with a lofty ornamented ceiling, crystal chandeliers and pilasters of pale green marble. The walls were hung with enormous, intricately wrought tapestries.

I was surprised to see others there. In my ignorance I hadn't known that "a private audience" isn't necessarily private – we were two of a group of fourteen. Vi and I stood to one side, talking in nervous whispers. The others were doing the same, looking about, ill at ease. They seemed to be mostly Europeans. A priest came and arranged us in a line that turned at a ninety-degree angle, placing me near the end, and telling us that the Holy Father would soon arrive.

I found myself in a ridiculous dilemma: how should I greet the Pope when I was introduced to him? My parents were Protestant-Irish and, while not anti-Catholic or bigoted, were not kindly disposed toward the church. In my childhood, my father had regaled me with stories of his childhood in Ireland. He was the son of a Methodist clergyman who, as was the custom of the Methodists, was moved to a different parish every three years. Dad described in detail the pitched battles on "The Glorious Twelfth," when men and boys fought in the street with paving-stones, pickets ripped from fences, any weapon that came to hand. When I was a boy in Regina we called some of our schoolmates Catlickers and Dogans and Arsies, and sometimes threw stones through the windows of the parish hall at Holy Rosary cathedral. We didn't know why; it was simply something we did. Moreover, my father (and later, the New Testament) had drummed into my head that you "Bow the knee to no man." And now I was about to meet the Pope.

There was a sudden ringing of bells and, preceded by a half dozen cardinals and others in full regalia, the Holy Father swept into the room and began to move along the line. I had ample opportunity to observe him for he took two or three minutes with each person. The women dropped to a deep genuflection and kissed his ring; the men went to one knee and did the same. I was torn by a mounting anxiety: how should I react when the Holy Father reached me? I felt respect for the man, for what he symbolized, and for his personal accomplishments (among other things, he spoke a dozen languages), but all my upbringing was warring with my reason. Surely, on the ground of simple civility, I should follow the example of the other men and go to one knee. But I knew I couldn't do it, and the Pope was drawing near.

Now he had reached the woman to my left. I was surprised at how small he was, almost diminutive. He looked wan and tired and liver spots speckled his skin, but his face was full of animation. He was speaking fluent French, looking directly into the woman's face.

Now he came to me. Involuntarily, I put out my hand. Without a moment's hesitation he shook it, holding it for just a moment, and I knew that I had been a fool for debating the matter; obviously it had happened hundreds of times before.

Without reference to a note and without being prompted by the cardinal who hovered at his elbow, he called me by name, as he had those who preceded me. But he had been mistakenly briefed and took me to be a teacher. I didn't correct him. In slightly accented English, he spoke about the importance of teachers, about the trust imposed in them and about the fact that they write tomorrow's attitudes on the minds of their charges. He urged me to take the calling with great seriousness, made the sign of the cross and passed on. Afterwards, we were each given a medal to commemorate the audience.

Some months later, in Windsor, Ontario, I was a guest at a small, private party in the home of a couple who were devout Catholics. I slipped out of the party, went to my hotel room and got the medal. As I was leaving I called the couple aside and gave them the souvenir, explaining the circumstances under which I was given it. The husband took it in his hands and examined it, his eyes shining. His wife looked at it closely, sat down abruptly and put her hands to her face to cover her tears.

Back in Canada there was good news: the prime minister's office had approved a CBC request to be permitted to do an extended interview with the prime minister at home at 24 Sussex Drive. Mr. Diefenbaker had agreed that I do the interview with him and that Joyce Davidson talk to Olive, his wife. The broadcast would be done live on New Year's Eve.

Television cameras had never been allowed to originate a broadcast from the official residence, and so far as I'm aware, have never been since. The arrangement was that Mrs. Diefenbaker would show Joyce about the house, pointing out things of particular interest; after twenty minutes she would hand off to me for the remainder of the hour. There was one specification: the prime minister insisted on knowing in advance what my questions would be. Normally, this was an unacceptable condition, but because of the unprecedented nature of the opportunity it was agreed to.

I went with Ross McLean, Joyce and a lighting-technician to 24 Sussex Drive to meet with Mr. Diefenbaker. We conferred in a pleasant sitting room on the lower level. Olive was there, as was Diefenbaker's political mentor, now a senator, Allister Grosart. One by one I read the questions I intended to ask, twenty-four in all. One by one Diefenbaker objected to them: "No, I've told that anecdote too often." "I don't think we ought to get into that." "No, no, that's too long a story; we won't have the time." "I think not; the facts don't reflect well on the people involved." By the end, he had vetoed all but three of my questions.

I was about to remonstrate when Olive – who hadn't said a word but had been perched on the back of a small sofa – interjected. "Now, John," she said, "just *stop* that!" Her voice was sharp but the tone wasn't. It had been obvious in our conversation that there was a loving relationship between the two of them. Diefenbaker immediately accepted the reproof. "Read the questions again," he said.

He restored all but three and the telecast went without a hitch.

After a few weeks back in Toronto doing less exotic interviews, I was dispatched with a crew to Los Angeles. The prospect was exciting. Among those scheduled were Oscar Levant, Zsa Zsa Gabor, James and Pamela Mason, Hermione Gingold, Aldous Huxley, Art Linkletter and, possibly, Bugsy Seigal, the Hollywood and Las Vegas hood. And there were plans to beam to Canada a live telecast that Ross McLean ironically titled "Maturity in Hollywood." I bought a new sports jacket and slacks and packed my bag.

Ross McLean had decided to lead us on this junket, and the

time for the interview with Levant approached. Having talked to him on the telephone a number of times, Ross convinced himself that he was the person to do it, a judgement not entirely vindicated when he and Levant sat down to talk.

The interview was done in the living room of Levant's home, a sprawling, ranch-style house, designed – as so many are in southern California – in a kind of bastard Spanish. While the crew was setting up, Levant and I fell into conversation. He was a major celebrity at the time. A prominent concert pianist, he had become a film star of sorts – as he put it, the guy who always *loses* the girl – through his work in such pictures as *An American in Paris* and *Rhapsody in Blue*. He was best known to the general public as the *enfant terrible* on the popular radio and television show, *Information Please*, where his encyclopaedic knowledge and caustic wit had made him popular.

An autographed photograph of Harry Truman sat alone on top of his grand piano, and when I ventured the view that Truman was demonstrably one of the three greatest American presidents, he immediately agreed and we got into an extended conversation.

Afterwards, back at the hotel, there was a message from Levant to telephone him. Did I know any women? "No," I said, "I'm a stranger here. This is *your* territory." He sighed and said, "Ah well. Come out to the house and we'll talk. Next to women, conversation is best."

We talked for about two hours, when he suddenly seemed to tire. During the afternoon filming session he'd shown the same sudden fatigue and, during a break to reload a camera, he had excused himself "to get a glass of milk for my ulcer." He returned a few minutes later, bright-eyed and visibly revived. I learned later that he was heavily on drugs. Now he returned to suggest that he call Zsa Zsa and that we drop over to see her. (She was his next-door neighbour.) But Zsa Zsa had a date for the evening. Another phone call and he announced that we were going to James Mason's. It proved to be a most eventful evening.

James Mason was married at the time to Pamela Kellino, no mean actress herself and, like her husband, a lover of cats; they were frequently pictured in the press surrounded by half a dozen or more Siamese. (Which commended them to me. I've had Siamese and Himalayan cats continuously for thirty-seven years.) I was disappointed when I discovered that, in all of their sprawling, luxurious home, there wasn't a cat in sight.

Pamela and Oscar fell immediately into an animated conversation that ranged from small talk to contentious banter to the trading of amiable insults to the latest Hollywood gossip. I was drawn into the conversation from time to time but mostly listened. What I heard was an astounding recital of recent love affairs among the famous, of assignations, of marriages in trouble and of studio machinations.

While all this was going on, James Mason was seated to my left, cross-legged on a couch, looking handsome, listening impassively and saying absolutely nothing. He spoke no more than a few dozen words through the evening. Every once in a while he would stir himself to enquire in that extraordinary voice if my drink needed freshening. He would then provide the same service for Pamela and Oscar and resume his seat and his silence.

For some time, I'd been aware of a noisy banging from downstairs at the rear of the house. Now there was also the sound of a man's voice, angry, shouting. Pamela said off-handedly that it was a lover of hers she had just cast aside. I recognized the name. He was a six-foot-three, red-haired Irishman, who had been a prominent sportscaster in Chicago during the early 1950s. He was a volatile, controversial broadcaster, a reckless commentator who had drawn the ire of Frank Norris, then-owner of the Chicago Stadium, the Black Hawks and a stable of prizefighters. It was commonly rumoured that some of Norris's friends were in the Mafia; and the story went around Chicago that Norris had had the sportscaster run out of town. For whatever reasons, he'd departed for Los Angeles, where he soon found another job on television and became enamoured of Pamela.

She told a detailed story of the affair, while James sat sphynx-like, listening. All the while, the man downstairs was trying to kick in a door. But no one seemed perturbed, no one called the police, and no one went down to send him away. After perhaps ten minutes the din ceased.

In bed I found myself wondering: could the entire evening have been a kind of charade? Was it possible that the conversation – with all its salty details, startling candour and outrageous gossip – was simply a show put on to shock the hinterlander, a gleeful acting out of the "wild and wicked Hollywood" legend? I'm certain that it wasn't.

In the morning Oscar was on the phone. It was planned to beam the live telecast to Toronto that evening. It would feature Zsa Zsa,

Hermione Gingold, Pamela and James Mason. Oscar wanted to be part of it and pressed me to urge Ross to include him: "Mason's hopelessly dull. I'll liven things up." He might have been in need of money and he was insistent. I spoke to Ross, who was at first reluctant (perhaps because of his budget), but then changed his mind. I went to the studio that afternoon anticipating a lively time.

Zsa Zsa was first to arrive. She was at the time a Grade-A celebrity and known to be difficult. I had watched the director lighting the chair in which she would sit. There were endless adjustments, a sit-in and live cameras to assure him that all was ideal. Zsa Zsa entered, looked at the set and crossed to sit down. "Not there, Miss Gabor, but here," the floor manager said, sychophancy oozing. "I'll sit here," Zsa Zsa said and sat.

The director came from the booth and introduced himself to Gabor, who seemed not to notice him. He explained how the lighting had been carefully prepared and how he was certain she would be happier with the result if she sat in the chair prepared for her. "I'll sit *here*," she said, examining herself in a large hand mirror passed to her by the make-up girl-in-waiting. There were sideways looks of dismay and shrugs of despair. Not five minutes later, as a lighting-man was at work rearranging things at the top of a ladder, Gabor got up and, without a word, moved to the chair first prepared for her.

I took the moment to study Zsa Zsa who, preoccupied with her preening, was indifferent to everything else. Conceding that she looked like a glossy and expensive confection, I must say also that she was the most beautiful woman I had ever seen. I was told that she took three hours to prepare herself to go out in public; however long, it was worth it. Under the lights, her skin was flawless and seemed almost transparent. Her hair was carefully fashioned, soft and shining. Her eyes were a startling blue. She continued to work with the mirror – touching her hair, stroking her eyebrows, cheeks and jawline, turning her head this way and that. She spent at least five minutes flouncing her skirt so that it fell pleasingly and, in doing so, leaned forward to reveal a more than generous décolletage. At one point Ross passed behind my chair to say *sotto voce*, "Charles, we're all worried about you, so recently out of the ministry."

The other participants joined us, and as the floor manager shouted, "Thirty seconds!" the tension – as was common in live television – grew almost palpable. I took my opening cue, introduced the guests, put my first question and became almost immediately redundant. Sparks began to fly, with Levant striking the flint. When Zsa Zsa spoke grandly of the growing maturity in Hollywood, Oscar interrupted to suggest that she was indeed an authority on the subject: "More than anyone in Hollywood, Zsa Zsa, darling, you've discovered the secret of perpetual middle-age." This kindled a continuing argument between the two of them. Hermione Gingold, an English comedienne famous for her abrasive wit and comically flexible voice, tried a number of times to enter the discussion. Finally Oscar turned to her and said, "Yes, *Herman*" – emphasizing the male name – "we've all admired your *boyishness* across the many years." Fireworks. Shouting. I tried to guide the discussion from time to time but little attention was paid.

Then, suddenly, the time had expired and the floor manager was counting me down to a wrap-up. I turned to camera, muttered something about our having witnessed a sample of the level of maturity in the film capital, and spoke my outcue. Even as I was doing so, the battle was being rejoined behind me. Off the air, Hermione proclaimed her umbrage and then took a strip off me for allowing it. Oscar and Zsa Zsa adjourned to the corridor outside where they exchanged insults for another ten minutes. It was not television's finest hour but it *was* a good show.

Aldous Huxley lived on top of a Hollywood mountain, and I approached our appointment with him beset by something approaching awe. Grandson of the celebrated scientist and educator, Sir Thomas Henry Huxley, brother of the brilliant biologist and writer, Julian, half-brother to the research scientist and Nobel winner, Andrew, Aldous Huxley had himself achieved international renown through his novels and social criticism. His best known book, *Brave New World*, made Shakespeare's phrase part of every-day language. From the time he was eighteen he had engaged in a fight against blindness. In his later years he had grown cynical and disillusioned about western society. Gearing our cars up the road that led to the peak of the mountain, we were all worried about how the interview might go. It didn't go at all.

It was not Huxley's fault; he greeted us cordially and offered the crew every possible help. He was a tall, gaunt man with a shock of wiry grey hair and thick-lensed glasses that greatly magnified his eyes. For all his sixty-four years, there was about him an intense, brittle vitality and an almost childlike interest in the cameras and sound equipment.

When all was ready, he and I took our places. He had only begun to answer my first question when the sound-man interrupted: "Sorry, sir, there's a buzzing on the line. Shouldn't take more than a minute to clear it." It took, as I recall it, better than an hour and a half.

There developed a mystery. Each piece of equipment was carefully checked, but there remained a constant, overriding buzz. The master switch controlling the house's lighting was thrown; it made no difference. The sound-man put earphones on Huxley, explaining that unless the source of the interference was found and eliminated it would be on the sound track and would make the interview inaudible. But the reason for the buzzing couldn't be found. There was a KXLA transmitter tower not three hundred yards from the house; that must be the problem. But it wasn't. When a technician pointed a live microphone at the tower and passed it through an open window, the buzzing stopped. When he drew it back into the house it began again. The problem was inside the house.

Huxley had been watching with growing interest and evident excitement. Finally, he pulled me aside, and whispered, "You've got a poltergeist." (Those who investigate the occult hold that a poltergeist, literally, a "rapping ghost," is a mischievous spirit, which manifests itself by various knockings, tossing crockery about and moving furniture. It is commonly believed that a poltergeist is active only when children or teen-agers are present.) In his later years, Huxley had become much interested in the occult, and now seized upon it as the reason for our difficulties. He drew my attention to a young lad who had been hired to help carry the equipment. "*There's* the problem," he said flatly.

In the end, having tried every solution short of banishing the boy, we had to abandon the interview. Huxley was gracious, promising an appointment in New York City three weeks later. His last word to me as we went out the door was a whispered, "Poltergeist."

It was some time later that we learned what the actual cause of our problems was. Huxley's house, though refurbished, was an old one, and unused wire, circling the living room behind the baseboards, formed an inductive coil and produced the interference our sound equipment had picked up. I was disappointed that the solution was so prosaic.

In New York City some weeks later, I interviewed William ("Call me Bill") Zeckendorf, the man who built the spectacular Place Ville Marie in Montreal. Zeckendorf was the entrepreneur's entrepreneur, an energetic, ebullient, tough-minded pragmatist with a talent for showmanship. His very going to work each day was a production. His offices were the penthouse of the Chrysler Building, which he had recently purchased. Each day, he drove from his home in the country to Manhattan in a chauffeured limousine, licence ZECK-1. As he went, he kept his office alerted as to his exact whereabouts in traffic, lined up his schedule for the day and dictated to his secretary. The doorman was poised for his arrival. A private elevator was standing by to convey him non-stop to the top where his staff stood in readiness.

It had been arranged that we would do part of the interview during a lunch in his office. A table was elegantly laid, gleaming with linen and silver and imported china. From the rooftop patio that surrounded his office, Zeckendorf pointed out the sights of the city and their height relative to the Chrysler Building. He took me into his office to show off a lighting system he'd installed in a cupola above his massive desk.

"Watch this," he said, putting his fingers on a small console. "When somebody comes to see me and he's trying to sell me something, I change the lighting so that the office is predominantly blue or green – some cold colour." He pushed a few buttons. The feeling of the room changed. "Now, if somebody's coming in who *I* want to sell, I go to the yellows and the oranges. It sets the mood." He gave a pleased, boyish laugh. "Why not?"

The interview went well. Even more interesting was a story he told me off camera before he left. He had wanted to buy the entire block between Macy's and Gimbel's, New York City's two best known department stores. His plan was to refurbish the street floor and lease it to Woolworth's, so that when shoppers went from Macy's to Gimbel's, they would pass through Woolworth's, and this would surely be good for business. Using proxies to hide his intention, he bought the space needed. Only one obstacle remained: an old and decrepit fire hall in the middle of the block, which the city refused to sell. It seemed the entire project was going to founder on this one roadblock.

Undeterred, he bought a piece of property one block away and build a modern fire hall, complete with sleeping quarters, a recreation room and showers for the firemen. He then offered it to the city for one dollar. They took it, of course, and Zeckendorf completed the deal for, as he put it, "the biggest damn Woolworth store in the world."

My first two years back in Canada had been pleasant, filled with hard work made enjoyable by its variety. In addition to doing *Close-up*, from 1957 to 1959, I filled in frequently on *Tabloid* and on a long-lived CBC radio program, *Court of Opinions*, a quiz show moderated by Neill Leroy and featuring panelists Lister Sinclair, Pierre Berton and Dofy Skaith. Four of my television plays were produced. I had written and narrated a documentary on sports cars for Meridian Films, made a film for the government introducing OHIP to Ontario, and come summer, would go overseas with a *Close-up* crew to make a one-hour documentary, *Sweden's Morality*, an expensive project that would never be shown to the Canadian public because of a prohibition in the Broadcast Act — a concession to the Roman Catholic church by the Liberal party — forbidding the discussion of abortion and birth control. In the first year, I won the Maurice Rosenfeld Award for Best Newcomer to Canadian Television. The following year, belatedly, I won the Liberty Award for Best Newcomer to Canadian Television. I sent it back.

During the trip to Sweden I had received a telegram from Connie telling me that our divorce would be granted later that day. We had been married eighteen years. It was like receiving the news that a very dear friend had died. I cancelled the filming, unable to work, and went for a long, aimless walk through the streets of Stockholm. It was a chill, dark day with grey layered clouds cutting off the tops of the buildings and seeming almost within reach. I walked for an hour or more, drenched but uncaring, my mind seven thousand miles away in a tiny courtroom in Juarez, Mexico.

I had hankered to try my hand at acting, not with any intention of pursuing it as a career but simply "to have a go." Consequently, I was intrigued to receive a telephone call from Paul Almond, already recognized as one of Canada's premier film directors, asking me to read for the lead in a one-hour television play he was directing for the CBC's *G.M. Presents*. I read for him and he hired me, informing me that the female lead would be played by the featured singer on the *Jack Kane's Musicmakers* show, Sylvia Murphy.

I learned later why he had cast the two of us – I who had never acted and Sylvia who had no experience beyond high school. The play was *A Face to Remember* – as Almond described it later, "a dog he'd been handed by the drama department." Even a superb production would not hide the fact that it was a mediocre property, so Almond had decided to cast it with performers whose work in real life was similar to the protagonists' work in the play: I played a television newscaster; Sylvia, a girl singer.

The cast first met in a barren rehearsal hall on Sumach Street in downtown Toronto. There were no sets, no lights, no cameras; just masking tape on the floor to indicate the general layout. After introductions and a walk around the "set," Almond called me and another member of the cast onto the floor, scripts in hand, and said, "Act One, Scene Three. Give it a try and see what happens."

I looked at him. "No instructions? No direction?"

He shook his head. "Just start in. See how it feels."

"You're not going to tell us what to do?"

He grinned and said, "Maybe later. Just read your lines and we'll see what develops."

It was a difficult play, even for a professional. The performance would be live (videotape was still in the future) and I was in every scene save one. At the close of each scene I was required to leave one set and race to the next, sometimes removing a jacket and tie or putting on a topcoat en route. After a day or two, Almond began to guide the performances, and when we moved onto the actual set for final rehearsals, there was a growing confidence.

In one scene, Sylvia was seated in a Corvette convertible. I was to kiss her, getting lipstick on a handkerchief, which would later betray me. (Yes, the plot was that bad.) There were problems with the lighting, and it was necessary to run through the scene a number of times. Almond was aware that Sylvia and I had been having dinner together after rehearsals, and each time I bent to kiss her, he yelled, "Cut!" I obeyed, of course, but after he'd done it a half dozen times, I said, "The hell with you, Paul," and kissed

Sylvia for the first time. Within six months we were married.

On the day of the performance, I awoke with a head cold. It wasn't enough to incapacitate me, but it posed a problem. Either I had to blow my nose frequently, which removed the make-up from the area, or I had to sniff a lot. It didn't improve my sanguinity or my acting.

The performance went smoothly. The nightmare that I would freeze or forget my lines didn't come true, but when the credits had rolled and the screen went to black and I knew the ordeal was over, I was surprised by a rush of tears. Everybody kissed and hugged everybody else and called each other by endearing names — common practice among actors — and we all piled into cars and went to a cast party.

The reviews were favourable but restrained. Bob Blackburn wrote in the Ottawa *Journal*: "Charles Templeton's performance in the lead will have somewhat less impact on the theatrical world than, say, Barrymore's Hamlet." In the Toronto *Star*, after some faint praise, Gordon Sinclair wrote, "If Charles intends to do more of this kind of thing, he's going to have to learn to act below the eyebrows." I wasn't sure what he meant but knew it wasn't a rave.

There was an amusing footnote. When we met, Sylvia was engaged to a Montreal man but had decided to break it off. However, she hadn't yet removed the ring when she was interviewed on *Close-up* by Joyce Davidson. Joyce saw the diamond and asked about it. Sylvia hadn't notified her fiancé and had no option but to say, yes, she was engaged, and when Joyce pressed her for the details, had to chatter on coast to coast about the man whose ring she was about to return. He was watching the show, and it made her task no easier when, later that night, she called to tell him that the wedding was off.

II

Permit me to leap forward seven years. In the fall of 1966, Murray Chercover, then vice-president and general manager of the Canadian Television Network (CTV) asked if I would be interested in joining the network as Director of News and Public Affairs.

Following my early years on the CBC, I had been managing editor of the Toronto *Star*, had resigned to run for the leadership of the Liberal Party in Ontario, and had subsequently worked for two years as president of a company called Technamation Canada – of all this, more later. I told Chercover I would be interested but wanted to mull it over.

With good reason. There had been a recent front-page brouhaha at CTV. Peter Reilly, the Director of News and Public Affairs, had resigned at a press conference, charging that he had been subjected to intolerable interference by the chairman of the board, John Bassett. Bassett was also publisher of the Toronto *Telegram* and the owner of CFTO-TV, the key station in the new network.

I had come to know him during my tenure at the *Star*; in my bid for the Liberal leadership he had supported me editorially. I called him on the telephone:

"John," I asked, "are you aware that CTV has asked me to run News and Public Affairs?"

"Of course I am," he said in his ebullient way. "It was decided at the last meeting of the board."

"Then I have three questions: the first is, are you in favour of my appointment?"

"I've been pushing them for weeks to get you."

"Question number two: if I take the job will you leave me alone to do it?"

"Not only that," he said with a laugh, "I'll kick anybody's ass who tries to interfere." He was chuckling audibly on the line.

"Question three: is CTV going to make it? Is it a viable network?"

It took some fifteen minutes to answer that. CTV was a new and as yet unproven venture (it had gone on the air April 15, 1966), a coalition of nine privately owned stations that has now grown to seventeen. In its fledgling months, apart from a national newscast and some sports coverage, it had done little serious programming. People in the business had dubbed it "the game-show network," and there were doubts about whether its owners were committed to serious programming. And there were questions whether it could compete with the public network and with the variety of American programming flooding across the border. Bassett convinced me that the board was prepared to commit the money and air time necessary to do a responsible job.

I moved immediately on two fronts: to strengthen the national news, which lacked organization and was often slipshod in presentation, and to build a demoralized *W 5* into the flagship of the network's public affairs coverage. Both tasks ran immediately into snags.

A problem with the national news was that it was largely a one-man operation. Harvey Kirck was both news-reader and editor, and often wrote much of his own copy. He is a first-rate news-reader and a superb extemporizer, but these skills were being minimized by his involvement in preparing the newscast and operating the department. His workload was made heavier because his right-hand man, Jeff Fry, had recently been seconded to *W 5*.

I notified Harvey that I had decided to relieve him of his responsibility as editor. He was incensed and demanded to see me. In my office he began to upbraid me at the top of his voice, and with *that* voice it was audible for blocks. Gordon Keeble, who was then president of the network and whose office was the most distant from mine, finally came to the door, reached in and pulled it closed. "Nobody," he stage whispered, smiling wryly, "can get any work done." After an estrangement of a few weeks, Harvey and I became friends and have remained so over the years.

Changes were made in personnel. Some were let go; some left. New staff was hired, including a fair-haired kid from the CTV station in Calgary, Peter Kent. Unsolicited, he had sent me a half-hour documentary on Vietnam with a note that he had prepared it entirely on his own. The shooting was amateurish and the narration a bit "gee whiz," but it was obvious that Kent was a guy with initiative and guts. I hired him immediately. A few years later he was hired away by the CBC, where he read the news on *The National* and was then transferred to *The Journal*.

Chercover had asked me not only to supervise *W 5* (Who? What? When? Where? Why?) but to produce it, and I found myself directing an organization and a program about which I knew almost nothing. I had performed on-camera hundreds of times but had never worked behind the scenes, and I was immediately confronted with some of those moral dilemmas that are part of hard-nosed television journalism.

My first week on the job, I attended the preparation of the upcoming program mostly to familiarize myself with the various procedures. In the main studio, a segment of the show was being videotaped for presentation later that night. The guest was the pilot of the lead plane in the Japanese attack on Pearl Harbor. He had since become a born-again Christian and was being junketed about North America giving his testimony of God's intervention in his life. The interviewer was Doug Johnson, a tough reporter with a blunt, straightforward style. Not long into the interview he pressured the guest to admit, now that he was a Christian, that what he had done at Pearl Harbor was reprehensible. The man spoke only rudimentary English and seemed confused. It was clear however that he didn't think he had anything to apologize for. It was equally clear that Doug wasn't going to settle for anything less than a confession of guilt. The Japanese was unable to express himself clearly and Doug was badgering him. It wasn't a fair contest. Suddenly, with cameras rolling, the guest walked off the set.

Jeff Fry, the producer, came to me, elated. "Great," he said. "Great television."

"I'm not so sure about that," I said. "Doug bullied the man, and the poor guy was at a disadvantage."

Jeff looked at me in disbelief. "Are you serious? I've been hoping that one day somebody would walk out with the cameras rolling."

We discussed it for ten minutes. Jeff saw it as a legitimate and eminently desirable example of the immediacy of television. I saw it as an unfair fight in which a confused man was publicly harassed. But I was by no means sure of my position. Moreover, I didn't want to overrule the leader of the demoralized W 5 unit before his staff, so I yielded. Later, watching the item, I wished I hadn't.

The following week, there was a second dilemma. A deranged student in Austin, Texas, had bought a rifle, climbed a tower overlooking the main quadrangle at the state university and killed and wounded a number of students. The W 5 staff had prepared a piece designed to demonstrate how loose security was in public places and how easily the Texas tragedy could be repeated in Toronto. Their cameras had followed a reporter as, without difficulty, he purchased a high-powered rifle, wrapped it in butcher paper with its shape still evident, went to Old City Hall, walked in full view past a policeman, ascended the bell tower and aimed the gun over a parapet at the street below. The camera looked down

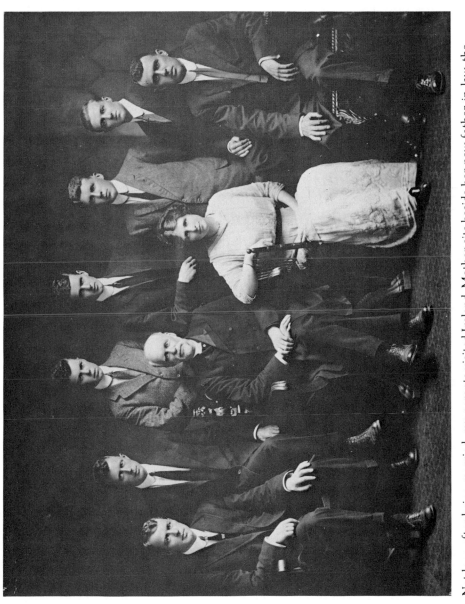

Not long after being married, my parents visited Ireland. Mother sits beside her new father-in-law, the Reverend James Bradley Templeton. My father stands in the middle of six of his eight brothers.

Standing amid the debris, the morning after the fire at Avenue Road church. That's snow falling *inside* what's left of the main auditorium.

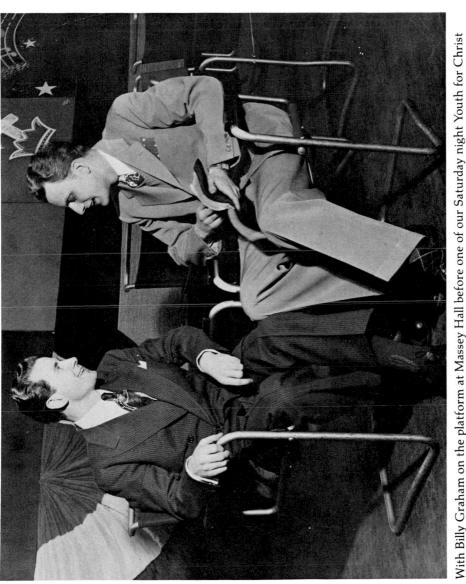

With Billy Graham on the platform at Massey Hall before one of our Saturday night Youth for Christ rallies. The year is 1946.

The audience on the closing night of the campaign in Harrisburg, Pennsylvania. It was the largest crowd in the history of the city. That night I decided to end my career as an evangelist.

Back in Toronto after the Youth for Christ International tour of Europe. Connie joined the "Welcome Home" delegation, which was out in force at the old Malton airport.

I sometimes used sports cartoons to boost attendance during my evangelistic campaigns. This is a sketch I did for the sports pages of the Edmonton *Journal*.

One of four editorial cartoons I drew (under the pseudonym, *Temp*) for the Toronto *Telegram*, while I was in the ministry. It was simply a case of needing the money.

A smile of sheer admiration for the verbal virtuosity of the late Rebecca West during an interview on the patio outside her home near London.

Novelist Evelyn Waugh signs a release form after being interviewed in London for the CBC-TV program, *Close Up.* I, not too happily, look on.

Standing with Joyce Davidson at the foot of the grand staircase at 24 Sussex Drive just before the live TV interview with John and Olive Diefenbaker.

My first – and last – starring role as an actor in a CBC television drama. I played a newscaster suspected of murder. Robert Christie was cast as a producer. The critics were less than enchanted.

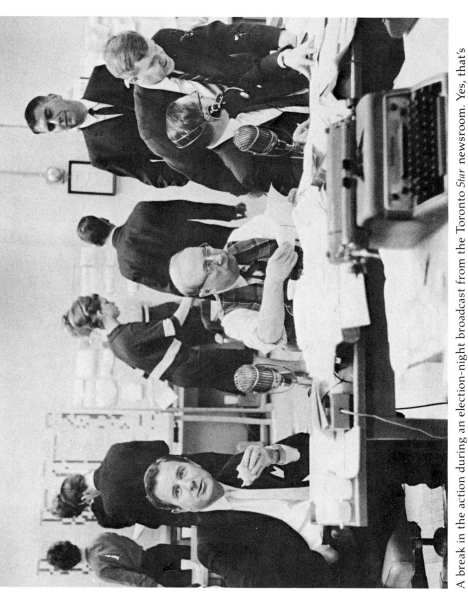

A break in the action during an election-night broadcast from the Toronto *Star* newsroom. Yes, that's CFRB's Gordon Sinclair on my left.

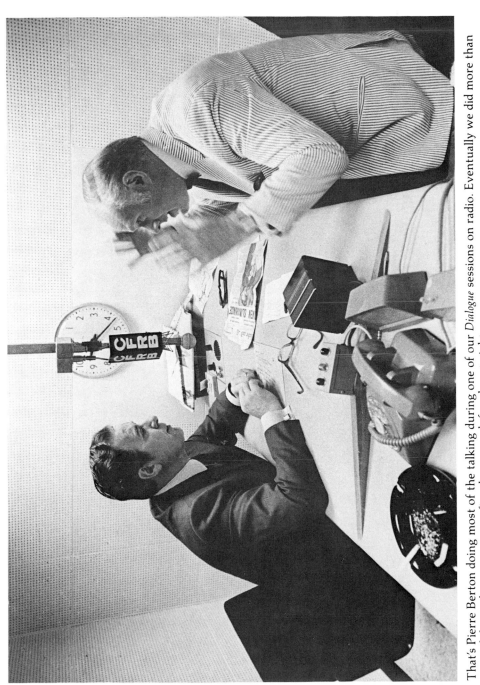

That's Pierre Berton doing most of the talking during one of our *Dialogue* sessions on radio. Eventually we did more than 4000 of them; the program ran five days a week for almost eighteen years.

Sylvia and I with our young family. That's Bradley (Brad) on my lap, then Tyrone, Deborah (now Deborah Burgess), and Michael. And, of course, the inevitable cats.

The aspiring young politician off to do some "mainstreeting" during the Riverdale by-election. Concurrently, I was running for the leadership of the Ontario Liberal party.

IF AT FIRST YOU DON'T SUCCEED...

This is how Toronto *Star* editorial cartoonist, Duncan Macpherson, saw my return to the Ontario Liberal leadership contest after the defeat in Riverdale.

the barrel and the viewer could see people on the streets fixed in the sights. It was a graphic demonstration of how easily it could be done.

The question that troubled me was: were we performing a service by dramatizing the lack of security or were we drawing a blueprint for a mentally unbalanced viewer, perhaps even stimulating him to act? Again, I yielded. In subsequent months I would act more firmly in similar situations.

There were two notable instances where questionable items went to air, not because of indecision but by inadvertence. Each was a "first" in Canadian television: the first time the word "fuck" was spoken on television, and the first time full frontal nudity was shown on the home screen.

I had developed a new program, *Crossfire*, for late-evening viewing. It had a simple format: four guests, literate, articulate men and women, would be seated on easy chairs in an informal setting. The host, Mavor Moore, now head of The Canada Council, would introduce a subject; it was hoped a sophisticated, mature discussion would ensue. As is often done, it was decided to make a "pilot" to learn what problems might be encountered and to polish the presentation. The subject discussed on the pilot was, "The Nature of Obscenity." One of the guests made a comparison between what is commonly thought of as obscene and what, in fact, is. He said, as I recall it: "If, in describing the act of human copulation I were to use the Anglo-Saxon word, fuck, that would not be obscene. But if I were to mount a defence of the use of napalm by the Americans in Vietnam, that would be." His use of the word posed no problem: the program was simply a pilot and would not be broadcast.

However, when the series had its première, a technician mistakenly racked up the videotape of the pilot rather than the program scheduled. At home, watching, I realized immediately what had happened. It was impossible to do anything so I simply hunkered down and waited. As the moment approached and the guest spoke the famous four-letter word, it seemed to my hypersensitive ears that the volume had suddenly been turned up and the sound was reverberating across Canada. It was a legitimate use of the word, of course, but unacceptable on home television in 1966. (It still is, with rare exceptions, today.) There were few letters of protest.

The "first" in frontal nudity happened on the national news. There was a member of the news department who, for his own reasons, resented my involvement and my authority. One day, in Harvey Kirck's absence, he telephoned and, by way of a briefing, informed me that one of the items being filmed that day was a special report on a class at Three Schools, an art school in down-town Toronto. In a bid for publicity and revenue, the school had started a class for businessmen with no artistic talent. As recreation, they would draw nude models. I knew the school; I'd attended life-drawing classes there. It sounded like a good off-beat feature and I okayed it, but instructed him that there was to be no frontal nudity. That night I watched the newscast. The camera slowly circled the model, going through a full 360°, and, in so doing, depicted her, pubic hair and all.

It was not in any way obscene: the model was comely, the pose was graceful and the shooting was not exploitative. But there was the problem of my directions being disregarded. I called the man and asked him why he had gone counter to my instructions without so much as a call to inform me.

"Because," he said, "there was nothing wrong with the shot."

"I agree, but you didn't trouble to tell me that."

"I was busy," he said. "More than that, I resent you telling me my job."

"I can understand that. But *my* job is to run the network's news and public affairs, and if there's a problem, the can is tied to my tail. If I give a specific order, I expect it to be followed or a legitimate reason given for doing otherwise."

He said, "Look, I've been in this business longer than you have and I won't put up with you telling me my job."

I said, "In that case, you won't have to. You're fired."

Oddly, the nudity drew a sizeable protest from viewers.

The shakedown period was over at CTV, and it was time to engage the CBC in direct confrontation. The opportunity came on June 5. Israel had launched pre-emptive strikes against Egypt, Jordan and Syria and the Six Day War was on. There was widespread concern that the fighting might escalate. The United States and USSR were making belligerent noises and the United Nations Security Council had called an emergency evening session. The Middle East was a tinderbox.

Late in the afternoon, Murray Chercover called me into the

office of Arthur Weinthal, Director of Programming. The two of them were watching the U.N. proceedings on a feed from an American network. Chercover put a question to me: "Do you think we should pre-empt our programming tonight and carry the Council session until they make a decision?"

"Is the CBC going to carry it?" I asked.

"Apparently not."

Pre-empting would mean a sizeable loss of revenue from cancelled commercials. It would also mean the disruption of normal programming and a subsequent need to juggle schedules. Even more important – for CTV was in a battle for audience – it would mean a drop in the number of viewers and complaints from people upset because their favourite programs had been cancelled. But the session was important, and if the CBC was going to be delinquent, CTV should provide the service. I said so.

"Good," Chercover said, grinning. "Arthur and I had decided that that's exactly what we should do. We'll arrange for a feed from NBC."

The decision was important to me. It meant that CTV was prepared to budget enough money to enable us to go head-to-head with the CBC, and I was itching for the confrontation. The battle would be fought on three fronts: Sunday nights, to take advantage of the new interest in public affairs engendered by the enormously popular *This Hour Has Seven Days*; the coverage of the two upcoming political conventions, in which Robert Stanfield and Pierre Trudeau would take over the leadership of their parties; and the general election that would bring Trudeau to power.

There were stories about the coming confrontation of the two networks in all the print media. Barbara Frum wrote a cover story in the *Star Weekly*, "The Battle of the Sunday Night TV Shows," calling the rivalry between *W 5* and the CBC's *The Way It Is* "the most interesting fight Canada's two television networks have entered into."

> What is particularly important is that to a very large extent, the field that television people call public affairs is the core of *all* Canadian broadcasting. It is the one field in which Canadians have learned to excel; the one thing that our networks have been both willing and able to do that the American networks – until this year at least – haven't.

It would be an uphill battle. CTV had no tradition in public affairs and relatively few resources in dollars or people. CBC's *The Way It Is*, under Ross McLean, the man who nine years earlier had introduced me to Canadian television, had a weekly budget of about forty thousand dollars. Ours was eighteen thousand dollars. Ross had a staff of fifty-five to sixty-five, W 5 had fourteen, plus five part-time. In late August, Ross and I had an amiable conversation at Pierre Berton's annual pool party and agreed that, while each would give it his best shot, there would be no dirty tricks.

W 5 seized the advantage by beginning its season two weeks before *The Way It Is*. For openers, I decided to contrast two antithetical "philosophies," both of which had enormous audiences: Billy Graham's Christian fundamentalism and Hugh Hefner's "Playboy philosophy." It would be difficult to find two men more unlike. I interviewed Billy, sitting in the pews of the Avenue Road church, putting questions to him on two or three dozen pertinent public issues. I met with Hefner in Montreal – I took an immediate dislike to the man – and put the same questions to him. We then intercut the two interviews, with each man responding in turn to the same question. The differences were predictable but interesting. We were off to a good start.

The following week we did the story that created more press attention than anything we carried that year. I had long been an admirer of and more recently an acquaintance of James Pike, a bishop in the American Protestant Episcopal church. Bishop Pike was a brilliant man. Raised a Roman Catholic, he was a successful lawyer before he felt called to the ministry. He served as chaplain at George Washington University and at Vassar before being named head of the department of religion at Columbia University. He was for six years dean of the Cathedral of St. John the Divine in New York City, after St. Peter's in Rome the largest sanctuary in the world. There, he was a leading and early opponent of the infamous Senator Joe McCarthy and a pioneer fighter for civil rights.

Later, when he was Bishop of California, he came to doubt some of the central Christian doctrines and renounced the church.

Then his only son committed suicide. The boy had begun taking drugs and had been deeply disturbed after a homosexual love affair. Pike was shattered. He blamed himself: if he hadn't been so busy, so preoccupied with his work, he might have been closer to his son. With his usual zeal and intellectual vigour, Pike began a quest to reach his dead son through experiments in the occult, and was encouraged by what he believed were messages from "the other side."

Allen Spraggett, whom I hired as religion editor on the *Star* some years earlier, suggested that Pike might be willing to appear on *W 5*, perhaps even to participate in an on-camera séance. I asked Spraggett to find out if Pike would be prepared to have the séance telecast. Spraggett reported that he would.

As the medium for the séance, Spraggett suggested Arthur Ford, then the most respected of those oddball spirit communicators who purport to contact the dead. On the night before the telecast, Ford agreed to conduct a private séance at my home. Present with Sylvia and me were Spraggett and his wife, Gary and Jackie Lautens,* Pierre and Janet Berton, and two friends of theirs visiting from Vancouver. Ford went into his trance and affected to get into a conversation with his "contact," a teenage Indian boy who began to bring "messages" to members of our group. There was some advice for Lautens, who didn't seem much impressed. My mother sent word that I should not grieve any longer (she had been dead for a number of years), and a one-time Liberal politician from London, Ontario turned up to state that I would soon return to politics. (I didn't.) There were messages for the Bertons, too, although Pierre might best have been described as a hostile if interested witness.

The following night, in the brilliant light of the television studio, with Arthur Ford in his trance, a series of men and women from "the other side" passed messages through Ford to a curiously uncritical Pike. There were some remarkable moments. A professor from Columbia identified himself by referring to an incident that had occurred when only he and Pike were present and which Pike asserted no one else could possibly know about. At the end, as Pike purportedly communicated with his son, he was in tears. It was a dramatic hour. Afterwards, Pike told reporters he was satisfied that contact had been made.

It was a front-page story across Canada and in the American

---

*   Gary was then a columnist and is now Executive Managing Editor of the Toronto *Star*.

papers, including The New York *Times. Cosmopolitan* bought the transcript. An American newspaper syndicate sent excerpts around the world.

It was not until after his death that Ford was revealed as a superlative con-artist. Among his papers were discovered some of the meticulous research he did before his séances, including his preparation for the session in Toronto with Bishop Pike.

Ross McLean thought the séance was dirty pool. He complained to the press: "When an item like that is made into a major story. . . . It is a programming decision I would have spurned." If so, he would have been wrong. Pike was among the most brilliant clergymen of his time, and spiritualism was and is a widespread religion. Our broadcast was the one time for millions of people to watch first-hand and judge the phenomenon.

The following Sunday, CBC's *The Way It Is* had its première. It hadn't been planned, but that Sunday evening W 5 was pre-empted for a showing of *Mutiny on the Bounty*, programmed to launch the ad campaign for the Ford Motor Company's new models. The film broke all ratings records.

It was an eventful year and an intensely competitive one. In my view it was healthy competition and the beneficiary was the Canadian television audience. Nor was the year without its temptation to seize an unfair advantage. One Sunday afternoon, Jeff Fry came to me, a tight, sly smile on his lips. "The film lab," he said, "has just delivered to us the film for tonight's *The Way It Is*." Each week, both shows prepared a number of items on film for that week's program. Both used the same film processor. On this occasion, the delivery man made a mistake and delivered the CBC film to us. Without the film, *The Way It Is* would be unable to mount a presentable show.

Jeff looked at me. "What do we do?"

"We call Ross and tell him we're sending his film over by taxi."

Fry grinned wickedly. "We couldn't delay a couple of hours?"

"No," I said, wanting to. "And when you call, tell him that that's . . . the way it is."

In December, 1967, I originated a series of annual programs, *A Conversation With the Prime Minister.* It was an hour-long interview with the PM, videotaped to be played on New Year's Day. I did the interviews during my tenure at CTV, Bruce Phillips has done them since. Over seventeen years, the program has invariably made front-page news.

In late fall, 1967, Lester Pearson announced that he would step down the following spring, and the Liberal party was involved in a search to find his successor. There was much speculation as to which candidate Pearson would support and, in my interview, I planned to press him with questions. However, we were no sooner in the limousine that would take us to the CFTO studios in Scarborough, than Mr. Pearson informed me that the subject was off limits. Nevertheless, during the drive to the studio, he let me put to him the names of the leading contenders while he, obviously enjoying himself, made capsule comments:

- Paul Martin, then Minister of External Affairs and at the time absent on cabinet business in Europe: "You can count on it: Paul will hurry back to make the announcement that he's a candidate. If necessary, he'll walk on the water."
- Allan MacEachen, Minister of Health and Welfare: "Allan's too canny to run.* He knows he won't have a chance – and he won't."
- Paul Hellyer, Minister of Transport: "Paul's a good fellow but he's just too stuffy. It hurts him to bend."
- Robert Winters, Minister of Mines and Resources: "Too much the Baron of Bay Street [as he was called]."
- Pierre Trudeau, Minister of Justice, and at the time an undeclared dark horse: "Charles, let me ask you a question: can you see Pierre in his sandals standing in a Saskatchewan farmer's potato patch asking the man for his vote?" I responded, "With respect, Mr. Pearson, with television you no longer need to stand in a farmer's potato patch. And Mr. Trudeau's very good on television." He shook his head. "He did a good job as my parliamentary secretary, but that doesn't take much. He's done well in Justice, but he has a long way to go before he's ready."
- Jean Marchand, Minister of Manpower and Immigration: it was obvious that Pearson favoured him. He spoke of him with affection. I raised the question of his health, which was rumoured to be poor. Roméo LeBlanc, then Pearson's press secretary and later Minister of Fisheries, turned half around in the front seat and interjected, "Jean's problems are mostly in his

---

* MacEachen did run, but dropped out after the first ballot.

head. He wears himself out worrying about every decision –
before he makes it and after it's made." Pearson none the less
insisted that Marchand was the best man available. "And he's
from Quebec, remember. There's a tradition in the party that
we alternate between a French- and an English-speaking man."

We did the interview in a sealed studio with commissionaires
guarding the doors. It was understood that the text of the interview was off the record until a transcript was released for New
Year's Day. Unknown to us, a *Telegram* reporter sneaked into the
studio and eavesdropped behind one of the enormous curtains.
He wrote the story and the *Tely* published it.

I received a call from the prime minister's office; Pearson was
enraged at the leak. I too was angry – we'd been scooped on our
own story – but my apology was only grudgingly accepted. The
PMO was certain that John Bassett had known of the interloper:
was Bassett not the owner of CFTO? Was he not the publisher of
the *Telegram*, and a prominent Tory? They were wrong, of course.
I knew that Bassett wouldn't approve a breach of security in his
own building (it would be counter-productive, if nothing else),
but I knew also that he was too much the newsman to have an
exclusive story fall into his hands and not print it.

Two extraordinary French Canadians burst suddenly on the Canadian political scene: Pierre Trudeau and René Lévesque. The two
men were as different as their backgrounds and over the next
dozen or more years, they would contest *mano a mano* over issues
as fundamental as the existence of the country. I had met
Lévesque socially through my work in television, and I liked him. I
had not yet met Trudeau. It occurred to me that the radical
differences in these two men – coming as they did from different
sides of the tracks and now moving onto the national stage –
would make an illuminating documentary and, under the working
title *One Canada: Two Nations*, set out to make it.

Lévesque was born in New Carlisle, a predominantly English-
speaking village in the Gaspé. His father was a country lawyer, by
no means poor but certainly hinterlands *bourgeois*. The youthful
René intended to follow his father to the bar but dropped out of
law school and, after a stint as correspondent for the U.S. Office of
Wartime Information, joined Radio Canada where he was a popular commentator.

I met Lévesque in 1963 when I went to Montreal to participate in a special broadcast. After the show, a number of us went to a friend's home for drinks and talk. As the evening progressed, Lévesque picked up a cane-backed chair, parked it at the centre of the living room, straddled it and expatiated about the problems and the unrest in Quebec. The people in the room, most of us in broadcasting, listened transfixed to this skinny, unkempt man as he talked about the coming confrontation. At one point he said with vehemence, "And if it finally comes down to it – to where a choice must be made – I will choose Quebec over Canada."

There was a Toronto producer there, a tall, good-looking man, impeccably dressed and impressive in manner. "René," he interjected, a pained expression on his face, "don't say things like that. *We're* troubled about the problem, too – it certainly worries *me*. And it worries my friends. All you do when you talk like that is make things worse."

Lévesque got out of his chair and walked over to the Toronto producer. They made an incongruous pair. René was almost a foot shorter; he was dressed in jeans and an open-neck shirt with the cuffs rolled to the forearms. He poked a bony finger in the producer's chest and hissed: "What do you mean, you and your friends are *troubled* by the problem? Have you given it as much as five minutes serious thought? Do you ever think about it or talk about it other than as some of your bloody cocktail-party chit-chat? Care? You couldn't care less."

Shortly afterwards, the party broke up, but a few of us stayed on. Lévesque talked almost non-stop until three in the morning.

Lévesque had entered provincial politics in 1960, working as a Liberal, and had come to power with Jean Lesage. He was part of the main thrust in the Quiet Revolution that followed the death of Duplessis and did much to popularize the cry, *maître chez nous*. He made the slogan tangible by spearheading the amalgamation of a number of private power companies into Hydro Québec. But he remained restive, even after the Liberals were re-elected in 1962. He says now, "I was a separatist as early as 1963."

Pierre Trudeau's origins were almost antithetical. His father, Charles Emile, owned an automotive-service business, and in the early years of the Depression, sold it to Imperial Oil for $1.4 million. He parlayed that sum to more than $2 million by the time he died in 1935, and his three children are multi-millionaires. Pierre Elliott was only fifteen when his father died. He spent eight years at Collège Jean de Brébeuf, a strict Jesuit school, and remains a committed if unorthodox Catholic. He studied law at the Université de Montréal, articled with a Montreal firm, and for his own reasons stayed out of the war. There were four years of bumming around, mostly in Quebec, and then back to school: Harvard for a master's degree in political economy, lectures at the Sorbonne, and work under Harold Laski at the London School of Economics. Then more travel.

Back home he participated briefly in the now-famous Asbestos strike, and went on to ten years of editing and writing for *Cité Libre*. In 1965, Trudeau, Pelletier and Marchand – the so-called "Three Wise Men" – went to Ottawa where, at first, he made little impact as Lester Pearson's parliamentary secretary and then as Minister of Justice. John Diefenbaker was outraged and the press intrigued when he turned up in the Commons wearing sandals and an ascot with an open-neck shirt. There was public attention when he bested Quebec's Premier, Daniel Johnson, in a televised constitutional conference, even more prominence when he spoke brilliantly in the Commons during the debate on Bill C-187, *An Act Respecting Divorce*, and again when he brought down his *Omnibus Bill to Reform the Criminal Code*, during which he spoke the oft-repeated, if borrowed, line: "The State has no business in the bedrooms of the nation."

While preparing our parallel documentaries on the two men, we got promises of interviews from both but had trouble nailing down a time with Trudeau. A crew was almost living with Lévesque, filming him on a trip home to the Gaspé and recording his hectic daily pace. But Trudeau was elusive. We finally were given a guarantee that when he returned from a year's end vacation in Tahiti (where, incidentally, he met Margaret Sinclair), he would meet our crew for a filming session.

During his absence the documentary took on added significance. The Trudeau boom had begun. Trudeau-for-Leader committees were springing up across Canada with the overnight swiftness of mushrooms. The absent – and to this point, reluctant – candidate was attracting impressive support. On his return he kept his promise to be interviewed, and Don MacPherson, my executive producer, and I flew to Montreal to screen the footage. We were elated by our coup; we would have the first extended interview with the man the nation was talking about.

We watched the film with accumulating dismay. The director

we had assigned, an experienced and talented man, seemed to have suffered a temporary lapse of judgement. He had placed Trudeau behind a tiny desk against a flat background, poorly lit, and had filmed him with one camera for the better part of an hour. In that hour, he had asked inconsequential questions and, without changing the camera angle, had let his subject ramble on absently and indifferently. Nor had he provided cutaways – shots from a different vantage point – so that the film could be edited. Our coup had become a disaster.

MacPherson and I held a crisis meeting in a hastily rented room at the Queen Elizabeth hotel, seeking to avoid a disaster. We were, as I recall it, not a week from our air date. MacPherson worked around the clock, snatching only moments for sleep, cadging film from sources in Montreal, Ottawa and Toronto. I returned to Toronto to work on the script. Finally, only minutes before broadcast time, we were ready. The documentary was assembled live, on air, in one of the hairiest broadcasts I've been a part of. The critics and the public hailed it (it was the first parallel examination of the two men who would dominate the political stage for the next two decades) and, although I ground my teeth at the program's imperfections, I drew some satisfaction from its timeliness and its reception.

We were now on the eve of two of the most dramatic political conventions in Canadian history. The Progressive Conservatives would select as their new leader a most unlikely politician, Robert Stanfield, in a convention that would see the public humiliation of John Diefenbaker, the man who had given them their one hour of glory and had then outstayed his welcome. The Liberals would say an affectionate farewell to their leader, Mike Pearson, and put themselves in thrall to the most inscrutable and volatile man ever to lead them. At CTV the decision was made to provide full coverage of both conventions. It was a move that surprised many but created little expectation: such events had been the exclusive preserve of the CBC since its beginning.

I had put Don MacPherson in charge of the physical and technical arrangements. He is now president of First Choice Canadian, the national pay-television service, but he was then working as a producer at TVOntario. I met him through Nathan Cohen, who had telephoned me not long after I went to CTV to say he had something important to discuss with me. We met for lunch. I saw to my surprise that he had brought a friend, Mac-Pherson. Before our food was served, he filled me in on Mac-Pherson's background and concluded by saying, "He's the most knowledgeable man in Canada on the technology of television. You need him. Hire him."

I was something less than sanguine about the decision to hire him when, the day before the Conservative convention convened, I visited Maple Leaf Gardens to check on how our meticulously laid plans were progressing. The CTV broadcast booth was being hammered together. It looked like an oversize construction shed, jerry-built with rough studding and plywood, and was perched precariously two-thirds of the way up the Gardens' slope. I was made even more uneasy when I strolled over to the CBC booth. It was virtually complete, glass-enclosed, looked expensive and substantial, and was crammed with brand-new electronic equipment.

I returned to our location. MacPherson saw the questions in my eyes and grinned. "Don't worry," he said. "We'll be fine." Then he added, the frown on his brow matching mine, "That is, if the chroma-key works. At the moment it's got some bugs."

Our hope for superior visual coverage rested in large part on this new development in television. Chroma-key is a system that makes it possible selectively to superimpose one picture on another with each picture dominant in predetermined areas. Using the system, it was possible for me to sit at the anchor-desk with an unobstructed view of the convention floor while behind me, a picture could be seen of what was happening on the floor. Without chroma-key, the CBC commentators were at a disadvantage. In order that they and the convention might be seen on the screen, they were forced to sit with their backs to the action; they could only know what was happening on the floor by watching monitors. CTV's coverage of the Conservative convention was the first such use of the chroma-key technique by any network. The system, much improved, is now commonplace at major events in Canada and the United States.

We had another advantage in the contest: the CBC had grown fat in its virtual monopoly; our people were hungry. On the eve of the convention, I gathered the commentators, floor reporters and cameramen for a briefing, and ended with a pep talk. It wasn't quite, "Get in there and win this one for the Gipper"; it was more in the order of, "Let's do a replay of the David and Goliath scenario." Hardly standard procedure in the sophisticated business of modern broadcasting, but it worked.

We'd selected our staff of floor reporters and commentators with care. I'd hired Pierre Berton, Scott Young – who was writing a featured column at the *Globe and Mail* – Doug Fisher, a former member of parliament turned journalist, and Peter Riegenstrief, the pollster. Harvey Kirck, Max Keeping and Jim Fleming (now the federal Minister of Multiculturalism), all staffers, held up their end. I manned the anchor desk from the opening gavel to the end of the convention.

We had one consuming goal: get the story and get it first. If a delegation was split or wavering in its allegiance, if a candidate was about to withdraw and throw his support to another, if the party wheels were closeted in one of the dressing rooms below or plotting amid the cigar smoke down the street at the Westbury hotel, we must get it to air first. Most of the time we did.

Pierre Berton was relishing his return to the role of reporter and was dashing about the Gardens like a cub. He took advantage of the fact that he was as much a celebrity as most of the candidates to entreat or browbeat information from Conservative officials. Twice in the early balloting he made his way to where the votes were being counted and, at the crucial moment, leaned his six-foot, three-inch frame over one of the scrutineers and said, "Here, let me see that," copied the figures and sprinted to the nearest CTV camera to report the totals long before they were announced by the chairman.

On the final ballot, after an engrossing struggle between Robert Stanfield of Nova Scotia and Duff Roblin of Manitoba, Tory officials tightened security. The area where the votes were counted was isolated by a hastily rigged rope barrier. But they had not reckoned with Berton. On the floor, he encountered Robert Macaulay, a Toronto lawyer and the so-called "Minister of Everything" in the Ontario government. "Bob," Pierre said, "do me a favour. Get me the figures on the final ballot."

I was extemporizing at the anchor desk when I saw Berton on the monitor struggling to don a pair of earphones and reaching for a hand microphone. Simultaneously, Don MacPherson's voice jangled in my earpiece. "Go to Berton! Go to Berton!" We broke the news of Stanfield's victory ten minutes before it was announced by the chairman. The CBC was forced to quote our figures – without, of course, admitting where they got them:

"While they're not official, they are from a reliable source."

Our coverage was praised by the newspapers and there was much chiding of the public network. I knew, however, that having taken the CBC by surprise the first time, it would not be so easy the second.

The contest to succeed Lester Pearson had fascinated the nation; not simply because the Liberals were in power and the new leader would become prime minister, but because of the presence of Pierre Elliott Trudeau. The excitement he engendered exceeded even that which surrounded John F. Kennedy when he made his bid for the American presidency.

Trudeau was a media dream. He was photogenic, sophisticated, contemporary, unpredictable and utterly unlike the common perception of a politician. And he embodied the new sense of itself that Canada had discovered in the extraordinary triumph of Expo '67. From the moment he disembarked from the special train that brought him to Ottawa on the eve of the convention (flanked by Edgar Benson, the Minister of Housing, and Mitchell Sharp, the Minister of Finance), and like a political pied piper strode up the ramp to the station trailing a cheering, chanting crowd, it was obvious to all but the blind or obdurate that the convention was as good as over.

Nevertheless, an engrossing and occasionally bitter struggle lay ahead. Among those grasping for the succession were: Paul Martin, Robert Winters, Mitchell Sharp (who, on the eve of the convention, dumped his supporters with unseemly haste and scrambled to board the bandwagon), John Turner, Paul Hellyer, Allan MacEachen, Joe Greene and Eric Kierans. Absent was the early front runner, Pearson's personal choice, Jean Marchand. When, for reasons of health and/or temperament Marchand stepped aside, it was the final factor in bringing Trudeau in. It was imperative that there be a French Canadian in the race – not least, because of the Liberal tradition that the leadership of the party alternate between a Québécois and an anglophone.

At CTV we had been planning for the convention for weeks. I arrived in Ottawa the day before the opening gavel, lugging two briefcases stuffed with research material, to find a Trudeau cocktail party in progress at my hotel. The entrance, the lobby, the mezzanine and the lower levels were jammed with a moiling, beribboned, hyperactive mob. It was almost impossible to move about. The frenetic adulation that surrounded the candidate was almost beyond belief. Women of every age were, quite literally, left faint when he passed by. There were squeals of excitement reminiscent of the madness I'd witnessed in the Paramount theatre in New York City thirty years earlier when a stick-thin young Frank Sinatra first burst on the scene. It has been called Trudeaumania – it was exactly that.

On the way from the airport, I'd gone to the site of the convention, to check that all was in readiness. Again, I felt a tremor of fear and insecurity. Our cameras, borrowed from CJOH-TV, were just being put in place; relatively small Phillips units, boxlike, battered and unimpressive. The CBC had purchased new RCA cameras and had eight of them positioned on the floor. They stood, hooded in slick plastic covers like sleek thoroughbreds waiting to go to the post. More alarming was the fact that the opposition had not one but two studios: a glass-enclosed announcers' booth at the ideal vantage point above the convention floor, and a second all-glass facility at floor level beneath the stands, to be used for round-table discussions and interviews. Our facility was a duplicate of the rickety booth we had used in Toronto, and in spite of the new CTV banner hanging from it, it looked low-rent and tacky.

But the CBC had learned little from the Conservative convention. Their anchorman and his associates still sat with their backs to the action. We had stolen Tom Gould, their best commentator at the Tory convention, and had brought in Berton again. We had two other advantages: their new cameras, although impressive in appearance, could not match ours under poor lighting conditions and could not produce a comparably bright picture when turned on the crowd or on the candidates' boxes at the perimeter of the floor. Moreover, I had noted during the Conservative convention that, at the climax, a horde of newsmen and photographers had swarmed about the finalists' boxes, and neither our nor the CBC's floor cameras had been able to see over them. Both we and the CBC had prepared what were called "creepie-peepies" – shoulder-borne light cameras – but I was certain they too would be useless in the crush. Consequently, I had ordered a ten-foot scaffold secretly built and stored out of the way backstage. At the crucial moment, although forbidden to do so by the arena management, we wheeled it onto the convention floor, a cameraman balanced precariously on top, and got an unobstructed view of Trudeau in his moment of victory.

Don MacPherson's voice rasped in my ear: "Charles! Charles! Martin Luther King has just been shot!"

We had just come on the air for the opening session of the Liberal party leadership convention. I was at the anchor desk in the CTV booth; MacPherson was outside the stadium in the remote unit – an oversized van crammed with electronic equipment, which housed the control room, nerve centre of the broadcast operation. The news of King's assassination was soon followed by fragmentary reports of burning and looting in a number of American cities. All our plans to set the scene at the convention, to run film clips of the candidates and to present rundowns by our regional reporters went down the chute.

The information was sketchy at best and changing every few minutes. I extemporized as best I could. A dozen times, we cut away to take feeds from the American networks and from our own newsroom in Toronto. The news of the rioting grew more ominous as the hours passed. We had no option: the opening session of the convention was put on the back burner and we "winged it" until 11 p.m. when we could hand off to the national news.

The following day, the convention returned to normal – if "normal" can describe that convention at any point. Overarching everything that happened was one obsessive question: can the Trudeau juggernaut be stopped?

An early indication of the trend came with the arrival of the Newfoundland delegation headed by Premier Joey Smallwood. Newfoundland had been thought to be securely in Bob Winters' camp; Winters was himself a Maritimer and a long-time friend of both Newfoundland and Smallwood. But a few days before the convention, Trudeau made a flying trip to St. John's and the word went out that Joey, ever the political opportunist, had defected. But there were reports of dissention in the delegation over the switch, and this led to what could have been the most hilarious gaffe in Canadian broadcasting history.

I was in the midst of presenting a round-up of reports from the floor. Each reporter was at standby with the representative of some region by his side. One of them, Henry Champ (who has since gone to NBC television news), was with a burly, beery Newfoundland delegate. Mistakenly thinking he had been given a cue and not realizing he wasn't on the air, Champ began his interview:

"There are rumours of a major split in the Newfoundland delegation," he said. "As I understand it: Joey Smallwood wants the entire delegation to declare for Trudeau but some of you aren't prepared to go along. Are you one of those? Tell me what's happening."

The delegate paused a moment to gather his thoughts, his mind unfocussed after a long night of partying and politicking. "Well," he said, "here's the way it is. I'm a Bob Winters man myself and they're tryin' to get me to switch. I'm not sure exactly what's happenin', but I'll tell you this: Joey can point my cock but he can't tell me when to piss."

I, too, was a supporter of Bob Winters and had written speeches for him during his successful run for election in Toronto York West. In my position, I couldn't show preference, but I had helped Clem Neiman, Winters' campaign manager, plan the demonstration scheduled to follow the candidate's speech. His slogan was, "It's Winters' Time," so I had proposed that, as the demonstration began, white confetti be poured into the air conditioning system, which led to great ducts high above the convention floor. At the same moment, Winters' supporters would toss foam snowballs back and forth. Somehow, the engineer was talked into permitting the confetti, hundreds of snowballs were passed out and hundreds of "It's Winters' Time" signs were brought in. As Bob finished a lacklustre speech, suddenly it *was* winter time. The air was full of confetti snow and hundreds of snowballs flew through the air. It was a hokey scene, and in the broadcast booth, a bit embarrassed, I made innocuous comments.

The early balloting went as expected. MacEachen, who had talked himself into believing he had a chance, went out on the first vote and crossed the floor to join Sharp and Benson in the Trudeau box. Others would soon follow. Pearson signalled his approval of Trudeau and the bandwagon began to roll. But the opposition was hardening. Judy LaMarsh made her famous whisper to Paul Hellyer (unhappily for us, picked up by a CBC microphone), "Paul, you've *got* to go to Winters. Don't let that bastard win it, Paul – he isn't even a Liberal."

But Hellyer wouldn't yield. Nor would John Turner, who stubbornly stayed in for the last ballot, and Trudeau carried off the prize. The final totals were: Trudeau 1,203, Winters 954, Turner 195. The building erupted in an explosion of sound and celebration. It didn't end until voices were hoarse and partisans exhausted and marching bands could no longer pucker.

So began the most tumultuous era in Canadian political history.

It was going on midnight when I packed my notes and personal belongings to leave the broadcast booth where I had spent the past fourteen hours (and won the sobriquet, "Ol' Iron Kidney"). I was feeling a variety of emotions: exhaustion – I'd been broadcasting for two and a half days, elation – the polls and the comment in the media showed that our coverage had again topped the CBC's, and uneasiness – Trudeau stirred in me a vague sense of disquiet. (I remained a card-carrying Liberal for another six years, but in five general elections could not bring myself to vote to return him to office.) And I was heartsore for Bob Winters. He had put on a brave front, as had all the defeated candidates as they gathered on the platform for the traditional show of solidarity, but I could see that he was suffering. I had some understanding of what he was feeling; I had come second in a close fight for the leadership of the Ontario Liberal party just three years earlier, of which more later.

As I walked toward the exit with MacPherson and some of the crew, the floor was inches deep in spent campaign material. The lights had been lowered and the arena was almost empty; only the cleaning crew was in sight. We paused for a moment in the foyer. From the corner of an eye I caught a movement in the shadows beneath one of the great concrete stairways. It was Bob Winters, alone. I called out to him and went toward him. We put our arms about each other and stood quietly for a minute or two. His body was shaking. An hour earlier, he had been the centre of hundreds of adoring supporters, marching with a flashing smile, hands held aloft at the head of his demonstration, the focus of millions of Canadians. Now, here he was, fighting to contain his emotions, alone in the shadows beneath a concrete stairway in a deserted hockey rink.

Second doesn't count in politics.

Within weeks Trudeau called an election, naming the date as June 25. The moment the writ was issued I moved to mount a half-hour special out of our affiliate station, CJOH, in Ottawa. Tom Gould would host the show and, after an examination of the issues, would conclude by interviewing Pauline Jewett. I was aware of the risk. It was imperative that the broadcast be non-partisan. Jewett was an academic and an incisive political commentator, but she had been active in the Liberal party.* To avoid partisanship, I drafted a list of questions and sent them by telex to Ottawa, instructing Gould not to depart from them.

The show went well and Jewett was even more than usually succinct. As the program continued, I realized with a touch of trepidation that the questions I had drafted would be exhausted before the time ran out. With a minute left, Gould unwisely asked Jewett to hazard a guess as to what the result of the election would be. She predicted a Liberal sweep, with a mere seventy-four seats for the Tories. (In fact, they won seventy-two.) I flinched.

Not long afterwards, the telephone rang. "John Bassett," the voice said – Bassett's usual opener for a phone call. "I've been sitting here watching television with some of my friends, [Eddie Goodman, Finlay MacDonald and George Hees, as I recall it, all prominent Conservatives] and I've just seen my station used for a partisan political broadcast." He then launched into a tirade, charging me with using my position at CTV to help the Liberal party. He continued, in full voice and without a pause, stating that, in future, he would vet any programs produced by me before putting them on the air and would not allow me to host another show on his station. I said nothing, waiting until he finished. From the day I joined CTV, I had known that the time would come when Bassett and I would clash. I knew he was a fighter who granted no quarter and I had planned what I would do if we ever bumped heads – I would counter-attack with equal vigour.

When he paused to draw breath, I said, "John, you're dead wrong. You haven't heard one partisan word from me from the day I joined the network. If anything, I've leaned over backwards.

---

* She subsequently crossed the floor to the NDP.

You're accusing me of slanting our programming; you *know* that's absolute crap. When our coverage of the conventions was being praised from every side, you were happy to get the benefit; now you say you'll vet any program I do before it goes on the air. I say: if you change one of them or refuse to carry any of them, I'll resign."

We fumed at each other for the next few minutes, until he banged down the phone. I called Chercover at home. "Murray," I said, "we've got a problem." I told him the story. He said, "Look, don't do a thing. Go to bed. We'll see what happens tomorrow."

The following morning my telephone rang.

"John Bassett," he said.

"Charles Templeton," I said.

"My wife gave me hell last night for shouting at you."

"Mine was in the bedroom above my study, and when I went upstairs she asked me what the ruckus was all about."

"I'll tell you what; I'm prepared to forget it if you are."

"I certainly am."

"Good," John said. "Now I want to talk to you about hosting a new show for me on CFTO."

We both laughed.

Not long after the shouting incident, I found myself facing the possibility of another clash with Bassett. Chercover said to me one day, "You're looking for a new research assistant. I may have just the right person for you. But there's a catch."

I was indeed looking for a research assistant. I was planning a summer replacement series and hadn't been able to find the person to do the preliminary digging and the research needed for each show. Chercover's nominee was Isabel Gordon, whom I knew only as a former women's editor of the *Telegram*.

"The catch is," Chercover said, "she's John Bassett's lady friend, the woman he's going to marry." "Oh," I said, considering the land mines that might lie ahead. "I'll hire her," I said, "on one condition: that if she doesn't work out, I can fire her."

She came to see me the following day. I explained the job, told her what would be required of her and named the salary. All was agreed to and I hired her.

For the next two weeks I hardly saw her. She would come in

mornings, more or less on time, spend less than an hour in the tiny office I'd assigned to her, mostly on the phone, and then leave. I might not see her again all day. I was beginning to think I would have to dismiss her. One morning she knocked on my door and asked if she could speak to me. She then showed me the results of the research she'd been doing. It was innovative and went far beyond what I'd asked for. I said, "Isabel, this is absolutely first rate. Unfortunately, I can't use more than half of your suggestions. It's a summer replacement show. I simply don't have the budget. Nevertheless, great work."

The following morning my telephone rang. "John Bassett," the voice said. "I hear you don't have enough money in your budget to do that summer replacement show." I said, "I'm afraid not." He chuckled. "You do *now!*"

A week or so after the election was called, I had a phone call from Finlay MacDonald. I knew him as the owner of the CTV affiliate in Halifax and as a prominent Conservative. He came to see me and brought with him Eddie Goodman, a distinguished Toronto lawyer. Eddie (known to his friends and the press as "Fast Eddie") had been chairman of the recent Conservative leadership convention and was one of the major figures in the party. Both men were convinced that Robert Stanfield was a better man than Trudeau and felt certain that, if Canadians could see the two of them in personal confrontation, they would recognize Stanfield's worth. They hoped to accomplish this through a nationally televised debate, but wanted to restrict it to Stanfield and Trudeau. They knew that if the CBC mounted the debate, it would, as the public network, insist on including Tommy Douglas, the leader of the NDP, and Réal Caouette of the Créditistes. Their proposal was this: Stanfield is prepared to commit himself to a televised debate on CTV, if you can get Trudeau.

I grasped the opportunity. As a private network, CTV would not be bound to include Douglas and Caouette. It was my view that a face-to-face debate between Trudeau and Stanfield would not only be great television, it would provide an invaluable public service, enabling the Canadian people to take stock of the two men, both of whom were new to the national political scene. I called Keith Davey, who had been Pearson's campaign manager and was performing the same function for Trudeau. He liked the idea, said he would take some soundings among his associates and get back to me. To my surprise, there was immediate agreement. But by the time Goodman and MacDonald met with their Liberal counterparts to discuss the format and the rules, it was evident that the initial enthusiasm was cooling. Within days, it became obvious that, for all the positive noises being made, the Liberals had no intention of proceeding.

Their first objection, that there would be widespread resentment at the exclusion of Douglas and Caouette, was raised despite the fact that the two-man confrontation had earlier been perceived as a plus. They then questioned whether CTV's coverage would encompass most Canadians, particularly in Quebec where the network had only one station, CFCF Montreal. It was a valid objection. Chercover got on the telephone and within a day arranged for the broadcast to be carried on a number of independent stations, including Quebec City, Sherbrooke and a French station in Montreal. As well, a simulcast would be transmitted nationally on radio. The nation would be covered.

But the Trudeau strategists were now firmly opposed, and for understandable reasons. Trudeau was dominating the media coverage. Why share it with Stanfield? Trudeau was well ahead in the public-opinion polls. Why risk a major gaffe before the entire country? Even though they were confident their candidate would win against Stanfield, a four-man debate would be safer. Trudeau now made a public statement that he wouldn't participate unless the minor parties were invited, and added that he favoured including the public network. There was no option but to agree.

From that point things went downhill. I met a number of times with the operational brass at the CBC and found myself involved in endless convoluted discussions about format, rules of debate, personnel, locale, equipment and so on. On the eve of the debate, in which I would act as moderator, I flew to Ottawa knowing that "The Great Debate," eviscerated by politics and bureaucratic caution, would probably end as "The Great Bore."

A rehearsal was scheduled for the early afternoon on the day of broadcast. Its purpose was to familiarize the principals with the physical arrangements and the tangle of rules that now restricted the participants. Each man arrived separately; first Douglas and then Caouette, both apparently relaxed. Stanfield, shepherded by a coterie of tense advisors, came next, appearing subdued and serious. Trudeau was late; he'd attended a funeral and was dressed in formal attire. However, his mood was anything but funereal; he was bouncy and ebullient. He gave me a smile and a wave, winked at Sylvia (caught up in Trudeaumania, she'd insisted on attending the rehearsal), went to his assigned position and swung a leg over the top of his desk. Then, affecting a sudden schoolboy primness, he sat on his high stool, the model of decorum, his hands in his lap. The producer gave him a rundown of the procedures and he listened impassively. When the red light, which would signal the expiration of his time period, flashed, he burlesqued an appalled grimace, leaned over his desk and covered the light with a hand.

For all the bravado of the rehearsal, it was evident as the telecast began that Trudeau was frightened. At the moderator's desk I was no more than a dozen feet from him and could see the working of his jaw, the frequent swallowing and the tension in his body. Little wonder — the potential for disaster was there. He had vaulted from the House of Commons to the zenith after only three years in Parliament. There were dozens of current issues on which he hadn't had time to brief himself. Caouette (who was not permitted to join the debate until the halfway point, as the Créditistes were not a national party) was no threat but Tommy Douglas was; he was an experienced and incisive debater and had been in the Commons for years. Moreover, it was known that Stanfield had prepared himself with long and careful briefings. The possibility existed that, in full view of the nation, the Trudeau skyrocket might descend a charred stick.

As in most televised political debates, there was no clear winner. The followers of each man could extract some satisfaction from his performance. Douglas and Caouette, who had less at stake than the others and had been around for years, did acceptably. Stanfield did better than many expected, but that is faint praise. Trudeau was restrained and flat and monotonous of voice, but he made no mistake of consequence and was generally credited with handling himself well. But the debate itself never caught fire.

The election campaign was a royal tour; the election a coronation. The Liberals won 155 seats — 27 in the western provinces — to the Conservatives' 72. Stanfield fumbled a football and the election. Tommy Douglas lost his seat. The universe was unfolding . . .

The morning of election day I drove into CTV's underground parking area. As I got out of the car, the accumulated fatigue of the past nineteen months suddenly settled on me and I hadn't the strength to walk across the floor to the elevator. I rested on the fender of the car for ten minutes until I gathered the strength to make my way to my office. The previous three days had been spent incommunicado in a hotel room, fixing in my mind the myriad details necessary for making pertinent comment and swift analyses during an election broadcast. It was the first general election in which computers would be used and we were fearful of a breakdown. That possibility added to the pressure. Our weeks of meticulous preparation had focussed on this day; but now that it was here, I found myself doubting that I would be able to do my job.

It was late June. The hot studio was hotter because of the lights and the large number of people working on the floor. To counter the heat, I wore walker's shorts instead of trousers – when I was seated behind the anchor desk, who would know? The desk where I would spend the next four hours was raised above the floor and it was necessary to mount a riser to climb into my chair. On the desk before me were a red telephone connected to Don MacPherson in the control booth and a television monitor sunk flush with the desk top. Tom Gould sat to my left, sifting through the first computer print-outs, the trickle that would soon become a flood. Seated at a table behind and below me – at floor level and hidden from the cameras – was Susan Dexter, a *W 5* staffer seconded for the evening. I had her tie a string to my ankle. As new print-outs were delivered to her, she would cull from them those I needed, and when they were in order, tug on the string. I would then put my hand below the desk and take them. Computers and string . . . !

During rehearsal, I felt a pervasive trembling in my body and a wooliness in my brain. I seemed oddly removed from what was happening. We were scheduled to go to air at 7:30 to get a jump on the CBC, which would begin its broadcast at 8:00. At one minute to air time – to warm up my brain, as an athlete might his body before a contest – I commanded my mind to run through the names of the ridings in Prince Edward Island and Newfoundland. I couldn't recall even the four ridings in PEI. Panic. I was suddenly drenched in sweat and overcome by dizziness.

The floor manager was giving me the countdown. "Five-four-three-two . . . " a pause and then the stab of the forefinger. I began to talk, almost automatically, the sentences forming themselves in the murk of my brain, setting the scene for the election and giving a rundown on the features we would be providing. Then, mercifully, the floor manager gave me the cue for a commercial break.

The light on the telephone flashed. It was MacPherson. "Are you all right?" he asked. "You don't look good."

"I don't know what's the matter. My head's full of wet Kleenex. I'm dizzy and faint. I'm not sure I'm going to make it."

"What do you want to do?"

"Keep an eye on my right hand," I said. "If I'm in trouble, I'll tap with my forefinger on the desk. If you see that, cut to Gould."

"Will do," he said. "Ready to come out of commercial."

The next four hours were nightmarish. I had lapses of memory and moments when I thought I was going to faint. But as the evening progressed the tension eased. I leaned on Gould more than had been planned and his solid professionalism took up the slack. But we didn't do as well as we had hoped and not as well as the CBC.

The following morning I went to my office at CTV headquarters and stopped by Murray Chercover's office. He looked up at me. "What are you doing here?" he said. "Go on home."

I told him I had a few things that must be done and then said, "Murray, I love my work and I love CTV, but I'm not ready to die for it."

He looked at me and grinned. "Go to bed for a week."

Chercover is one of the most important men in Canadian broadcasting but is unknown to the public. His knowledge of the complex details of broadcasting is astonishing. He knew the operation and the budgetary details of my department – and every other department – better than I did. But in all the time I worked with him, he never interfered. He counselled, he advised, he proposed, but having trusted you with the job he left you free to do it.

His managerial capacity can best be seen in CTV's coverage of the historical Apollo 11 lunar landing. The United States' manned flight to the moon and back spanned nine days, included a landing on the moon, an exploration of its surface and a safe return. NASA announced that, during the nine days, it would transmit seventeen hours of television pictures, from blast-off to splash-down and recovery. The CBC announced that it would carry seven hours.

Chercover asked for my recommendation as to what CTV should do. I thought about it overnight and went to his office the following morning.

"We should carry all seventeen hours," I said. "Every available minute."

He looked at me. "I agree with you," he said. "That would be ideal. But do you have any idea what it would cost?"

"Murray, this is Columbus and Magellan. It's as though there were cameras along when they set sail."

"Okay, so you're fascinated and I'm fascinated, but will the viewer watch seventeen hours of it?"

"They'll watch."

"You sound sure of it."

"I am."

He looked down at his desk, frowning. Then he lifted his head and said, "Okay, we do it."

If he had been wrong, it could have cost the network more than a hundred thousand dollars. It could have cost him his job. In fact, every commercial slot was sold. The CBC, which began with partial coverage, quickly expanded its service to match ours. It was the greatest event in television history and was watched around the world by the largest audience of all time.

III

The period during which I was at CTV happened to be among the most exciting in Canadian journalistic history, made more exciting to us because we were finding our way, taking chances, experimenting. I was teamed with committed and imaginative people, most of whom worked far too hard.

There were encounters with extraordinary people, of course: the justly famous and the merely notorious, the pompous, the sleazy, the ambitious, the godly, the kooks and the rogues – a cross-section of the men and women who "make news." Television is a magnet; it draws to it people of every imaginable diversity to present themselves before its lenses, and draws others to watch transfixed. The television camera is a kinky voyeur: it lusts with equal passion for mangled bodies and widows' tears and slaughtered seals. It mingles with angry mobs, dogs the steps of preening politicians and crowds close to catastrophe. It makes nonentities celebrities and licenced brawlers rich. If Andy Warhol is right and the day comes when everyone will be famous for fifteen minutes, it will be because of television.

For me, television was work, opportunity and a stepping-stone. In 1959, an interview I did on the CBC led to the offer of a job at the Toronto *Star*. In 1969, when I returned to television, programs produced at CTV led to becoming editor of *Maclean's* magazine. In each case, my work in the electronic medium led to print journalism, which runs counter to the flow – television usually recruits from the press. There was no deliberate going against the grain; it merely happened that way.

I was never fully committed to television. To individual programs and to special challenges, yes, but never to the medium itself. It is possible to do some things superlatively well on television, but they are the exceptions. Commercial television, by its very nature, breeds mediocrity. It is an insatiable dragon, whose keepers must feed it every hour of every day of the year. A result is that those who work in television find themselves, for all their high resolves, living with compromise. There is little time for contemplation, there are few opportunities to step back and scrutinize what you are doing. A valid and shining idea is inevitably diminished as it becomes subject to the limitation of budgets, the caution of bureaucrats, the exigencies of time, the complexity of the mechanism, the shortage of first-rate technicians, the low level of public expectation and the hundred other woes that bedevil the production process. As has been said, "Television is a one-ton pencil." It is a powerful means of communication; it is also unwieldy and expensive.

None of this justifies or excuses the banality of 90 per cent of television programming, but it does explain it. And it reveals why most television programs are tired imitations of earlier successes. They may amuse but they seldom stimulate robust laughter. (Most television laughs come from studio audiences responding on cue, supplemented by ancient guffaws recycled on tape.) The best programs available on a given night are usually something unscripted, such as sport, or something borrowed from another medium, the cinema.

Television does some things well: political conventions, public affairs, sports, examinations of nature. It does some things poorly: news (with a few exceptions), political campaigns, live theatre, classical music. It has gone to seed (as has public affairs radio) on "causes," among them homosexuality, environmental pollution, abortion, racial prejudice, rape and, lately, incest. Each is important and needs the focus of attention, but one tires of the onslaught, and the end result is informed indifference. Television builds callouses on our compassion.

In the beginning, television news was presented in a straight-forward manner. The news-readers were staff announcers who presented little more than radio with pictures. The shooting and preparation of film excerpts was a slow, laborious process, and the film portions of the "telecasts," as they were then called, were usually a day or more behind the events.

But as techniques improved, portable videotape cameras appeared and satellites began to transmit pictures worldwide, viewers discovered television news to be an undemanding and entertaining way to keep abreast of what was happening in a world that had become, in Marshall McLuhan's phrase, "a global village." There was an immediacy, an apparent authenticity to television reporting. You could sit in your living room and be an eyewitness as politicians made pronouncements or bombs shattered villages or billy-clubs crushed skulls or firefighters poured their torrents into infernos. And audiences increased.

Businessmen saw this gathering crowd and sought the opportunity to proclaim the virtues of their wares before it. As the number of viewers increased, the income from commercials sky-rocketed and "the news" no longer showed as a debit on the balance sheet. Inevitably, the quest for the advertiser's dollar led to a competition for viewers. Networks and local stations strove to provide more news, more immediate news, more interesting news. The news-reader gave way to the anchorman (more accurately, anchorperson, for there are an increasing number of women in the business) and, especially in the United States, he or she became as much a media star as the singers, dancers and comedians in the entertainment part of the industry. Walter Cronkite, a former CBS anchorman, was selected in a national pool as "the most trusted man in America." Surely the CBC's Barbara Frum is the best known television "personality" in Canada.

The growth and popularity of television news has produced problems. The time allotted must be filled. If there isn't enough news it must be manufactured. If there is a shortage of hard news, gussy up an inconsequential item. Seek the human-interest story. Create a media event, transforming a non-story into an apparently important happening. Develop stories about "problems" in the society. And even more important, seek news that makes for interesting pictures. A line-up editor will be disposed to allocate more time to a riot at a rock concert than to a Nobel presentation. A protest provides better footage than a press conference. Responsible broadcasters will strive for a balance between legitimate news and trivia; others will major in ambulance-chasing, fires and police work.

Television is subject to the need for pictures. Its reason for being is to transmit visual images. This is its strength and its weakness. No reporter's words could communicate so graphically the defeat of the American withdrawal from Saigon as did the pictures of the Vietnamese clinging to and falling from the helicopter skids. And nothing was more boring than those dated "file tape" shots of the British navy in the Falklands. Therein lies the problem: television must put up pictures, even when there are no pictures worth putting up; the "talking head" is no more than picture-postcard radio.

Television will undoubtedly get both better and worse, in large part because of the proliferation of channels brought about by cable and satellites. There is little reason to believe that the increase in the number of programs will lead to higher quality programs. There will be one improvement; as has happened with radio and print, the proliferation of channels will generate a full spectrum of highly specialized offerings. Already, there are channels that offer nothing but news or sports or religion or motion pictures. Their number and their diversity will increase exponentially, as will the viewer's ability to determine programming through videocassettes and other systems of storage and retrieval.

I was present at the beginnings of television. I expect to be part of its continuous evolution. It wasn't, for all the nostalgia, better in the old days, although it *was* more exciting because it was new and live and had to be innovative. But for all the proliferation and scope, the task remains the same — to communicate with that one individual in his or her living room. It is an exceedingly difficult thing to do well.

Inside the Toronto *Star*

INSIDE THE TORONTO *STAR*

I

On February 22, 1959, on the program *Close-up*, I did simultaneous interviews with three subjects in three locations in Canada and the United States. That the interviews were not memorable is attested by the fact that I can't remember who they were with or what we discussed. But the following morning I received a telephone call from Herb Manning, managing editor of the Toronto *Star*, asking me to come and see him.

The previous Friday ("Black Friday" as it was being called in the press), Prime Minister Diefenbaker had announced the scrapping of the Avro Arrow because of high development costs and the inability to find another country to share the expense. The five completed planes, each worth $3.75 million, were cut to pieces with a welder's torch and sold as junk. Hundreds of workers, many highly skilled, were laid off.

The prime minister's decision kindled a national controversy. The Arrow, a jet fighter of advanced design, was believed by many to be the best aircraft of its type in the world. It was a time of rising nationalism and the decision to junk the Arrow was seen, among other things, as delivering Canada into the hands of the Americans, threatening our sovereignty and making the defence of Canada entirely dependent on the U.S.

Beland Honderich, then editorial director of the *Star* and now its president and publisher, had seen my multiple interview on *Close-up* and had suggested to Manning that he get me to adapt the technique to print. Manning linked four experts in a conference telephone call: Maj.-Gen. W.H.S. Macklin, former deputy chief of staff, Canadian army; Lt.-Gen. Guy Simonds, former army chief of staff; Professor A.R.M. Lower, Queen's University historian, and Walter Gordon, Chairman of the Royal Commission on Canada's Economic Prospects. I plied them with questions. The discussion was recorded and three stenographers set to work preparing a typescript.

As I was preparing to leave, Manning drew me into his office. "Would you be interested in doing an edit of the interview?" he asked. "We're going to carry a full page on the story but it needs to be cut by about half." I'd never edited copy and said so. Nevertheless, he found me a cubicle off the newsroom and left me alone. I sweated my way through it. From time to time a young woman brought additional pages and fresh coffee.

Three days later, Manning called me in again. He explained that the *Star* had recently begun a new feature. The page opposite the editorial page (known in the business as the op-ed or egghead page but at the *Star* called Page Seven) had been set aside to provide background to the news. Would I be interested in the job? I expressed doubts as to whether I could handle it and asked for the weekend to consider it.

The following Monday I was standing on the sidewalk outside CBC headquarters on Jarvis Street talking with Pierre Berton. We had just taped a radio show, *Court of Opinions,* on which he was a panellist and I was a frequent guest. Berton and I had met on the *Close-up* set but were no more than working acquaintances. He was at the time a featured columnist on the *Star.*

"Pierre," I said, "I need some advice. I've been offered the job as editor of Page Seven on the *Star.* What do you think?"

He looked at me, incredulous. He had written a column about me and knew something of my background in the ministry, not the usual apprenticeship for a newspaper editor. He was confused further by the fact that he had recommended Ross McLean for the job and had the impression that it would be tendered to him.

"Is it a hard offer?" he asked.

"Yes."

He looked at me again, not yet at home with the idea. "Have you ever worked on a paper?"

"Only as a sports cartoonist."

"Have you ever handled copy, made up a page, written heads?"

"No."

"I don't know, Chuck," he said, shaking his head. "It's not an easy job. I really don't know how to advise you. If I were you, I'd think about it. Hard."

I did, and the prospect intimidated me. But I was planning to get married and needed the money. I called Herb Manning and asked him when he wanted me to start. "Tomorrow," he said.

My first day on the *Star* was a terrifying experience. Manning introduced me to Norman Phillips who had been handling the page until an editor was appointed. Phillips was a thirty-year veteran newsman who had done every job in journalism from junior reporter to foreign correspondent. He was a tall, quiet man, withdrawn, not at ease with strangers, and had been less than overjoyed when told that he was to be replaced by an amateur and an outsider. At the moment he was under pressure of his deadline.

He handed me a galley proof of one of the stories scheduled for that day's page. "Here," he said, "read this and give me a K-5-36."

I retreated to a nearby desk in an agony of indecision. Dare I confess to this old pro in my first five minutes on the job that I had no idea what a K-5-36 was? The offhand way in which he had asked for it suggested that it was something elementary.

"Mr. Phillips . . ."

"Norm," he said without looking up.

"I'm sorry, Norm, but I don't know what a K-5-36 is."

He looked up, sighed heavily, turned up the newspaper on his desk and stabbed a finger at the page. "You do know what a head is?"

"A headline," I murmured.

"Right." He pointed at the page. "This," he said, "is a K-5-36. The K stands for kicker – the small head above the big one. Eighteen-point Bodoni bold is the typeface we use for kickers. The five means five columns. The thirty-six stands for the main head, which is thirty-six-point Century bold italic. Read the galley and write a head. You can figure the character count from this head here. Allow one and a half spaces for Ms and Ws and a half space for Is and lower-case Ls." He returned to his work.

Head spinning, I went to my desk and wrote half a dozen heads. He glanced at them, pursed his lips and put them aside. "Better come with me," he said, grabbing a fistful of galley proofs and heading in long strides toward the composing room. "We're running late."

The production of a big-city newspaper has greatly changed

with computer technology but it was and is a small daily miracle. In 1959, it was a much more labour-intensive task. News stories came to the editorial department from the paper's reporters and feature writers and from hundreds of sources around the world: wire services, legislatures, free-lancers and special correspondents; from war zones, sports arenas and entertainment centres; from stock markets, picket lines, corporations, public-relations agencies, political parties, hospitals and police forces. Many of the stories were rewritten. All were edited. Each was changed to conform to the newspaper's style. Then, having been assigned a specific place in the newspaper, the story was slugged (given an identifying one-word title), a head was written and the entire, scruffy, scrawled-on bundle was dispatched to the composing room.

There, it was set by a man at a great, clacking linotype machine, which cast type in lead slugs a line at a time. The story, now in a column width, was placed in a galley, a long metal tray, and after proofs had been pulled, was dispatched to the designated page form. In the meantime, the head had gone to another typesetter who set it by hand, cast it in lead and forwarded it to the appropriate page.

The *Star*'s composing room was a great, low-ceilinged room, ablaze with fluorescent light and stinking of printers' ink and hot lead. Dozens of harried men toiled in an apparently uncoordinated chaos. I stood with Norm Phillips at one end of a metal form enclosing Page Seven. A compositor was bent over at the other end, working from a layout indicating where each story should go, fitting together the jigsaw puzzle. From my vantage point the page was wrong-end-to, reversed, and a three-dimensional negative. Norm and the compositor easily read the tiny slugs of type; I could barely decipher the headlines.

It is not, on a newspaper, "All the news that's fit to print," but all the news that *fits*. Lead is not compressible. A head is too long and has to be rewritten on the spot. A paragraph is removed here, a line deleted there, and a too short story leaded-out. Norm was bent over his proofs looking for matter he could delete without doing injury to the story. He passed me a proof and said, "See if you can cut this by six lines." Minutes later, as I wavered in indecision, he snatched it from me and did it himself.

I stood at the head of the form dizzied by the frenetic activity and banshee noise of the composing room. The page was running late, and the foreman, a large-bellied, ruddy-faced man, came by to badger us with shouts of, "Let's go! Let's go! Lock 'er up!" Newspapers speed to their destinations on planes, trains, buses and trucks and must meet schedules. As the pressures mounted and the din increased, I was in despair. In one week I had to be ready to go it alone.

But as I would soon learn, "making up" the page was the simplest part of the job. Page Seven had been established in part to counter the competition of public-affairs television. Its purpose was to "background" the news, to present expert opinion, to offer insights and information on the complicated issues of the day. The job was really the production of a small magazine six days a week. Ideas had to be developed and assigned, fees negotiated, photographs or illustrations found. A balance had to be maintained among local, national and world stories, with the occasional spice of lighter stuff.

A week later, Norm Phillips gave me a laconic, "Good luck," and left me on my own. I could barely work for the trembling of my hands. I soon learned, however, that the problem didn't lie in getting the job done; but in doing it well.

I was entirely unprepared for the resentment that followed my appointment. I wasn't expecting flags and banners but would have been heartened by a "Welcome aboard," especially from the senior people. At the daily staff meetings, where the following day's paper was planned, the atmosphere was chill. As we were expected to do, I made suggestions. In my zeal I made many. The city editor, especially, dismissed them as impractical or "old stuff." Harry Hindmarsh ("Young Harry") the managing editor, chaired the meetings. He listened to the comments and then said something like, "Wait a minute. I think Charlie [as he called me] has a couple of good ideas here. Let's get on them."

I now understand the resentment. I had been handed one of the most desirable jobs in the newsroom and I wasn't even a newspaperman. I'd never filed a story. I hadn't come up through the ranks. I was "a former evangelist, for Chrissake!" And "a goddam television personality!" Was there a background less likely to commend?

Things were not improved when, eight months later, I was

named features editor and assigned a staff of three. Or when eight months after that I was appointed executive managing editor, with responsibility for the editorial content of the paper, excepting the editorial page. Or when, a few days later, I was moved into the corner office at the southeast end of the editorial floor, succeeding Hindmarsh, who had been transferred upstairs to deal with the ailing *Star Weekly.*

Writing about it in *Maclean's* some years later, Alan Edmonds quoted Pierre Berton as saying,

> It was a shock for newspapermen to discover the awful truth that any man of reasonable intelligence can learn the basics of newspapering in a few months and then take over. A lot of people who had been there for years found it an affront to their egos.

Not long after I was named managing editor, I went to Pierre and Jan Berton's annual pool party. Berton serves a punch at these affairs that is about 99 per cent Pimm's Extra and 1 per cent fruit juice. It *does* get the party moving.

Late in the afternoon I approached the punch bowl for a refill and encountered McKenzie Porter, a *Telegram* columnist, there on the same mission and not for the first time. Porter is a professional Englishman and is known among journalists as "the belted Earl." He is much attached to tradition and is often sticky about what he regards as the proprieties. He greeted me with, "Well, Templeton, how are things with God these days?"

"I'm not quite sure," I said lightly. "Haven't checked lately."

He emptied the ladle into his glass with careful deliberation and then said, "What in hell does a goddamn evangelist know about the newspaper business?"

"Not much," I said. "That's why Honderich gave me the job."

He was working hard at fixing me with his gaze. "I mean, what the fuck does an *evangelist* know about getting out a newspaper?"

I didn't quite know what to do. It would have been simple to give the Earl another belt, but I'm not given to violence as a solution to problems and am, in general, opposed to hitting old men or drunks. Without another word, I filled my glass and turned to leave. He followed, his voice rising, the insults becoming obscene.

It was one of those times when you think of the right riposte at the moment, rather than later that night in bed. I turned and said to him, "Look, you have the advantage. You obviously know a lot about me. I don't even know your name."

Some months before, when I was first appointed features editor, I had a phone call from Val Sears, now Ottawa bureau chief for the *Star*, then the paper's Washington correspondent. He said, "I've been wondering whether you'd like a story on Senator John Kennedy?" Kennedy had been returned to the Senate in 1958 with an overwhelming majority and was beginning to be touted as a leading presidential possibility.

"What story on Kennedy?" I asked.

Sears told me that Kennedy and his wife of six years, Jacqueline Bouvier, weren't getting along and that Kennedy, whose womanizing tendencies were only becoming known, had a mistress whose name was, appropriately, Smith. He wanted to know if he should file a story on the subject.

"Val," I said, puzzled, "why would you think I'd want to run a story like that?"

"No reason, really," he said. "Just testing."

I seldom talk with anyone about the newspaper business in Canada without the question being asked in some form: "Beland Honderich — a real son of a bitch to work for, eh?" My response has always been, "Sometimes. But I wouldn't have had it any other way."

In 1955, at the age of thirty-eight, Beland H. Honderich was appointed editor-in-chief of the Toronto *Star*, a newspaper that had been the foremost Canadian practitioner of William Randolph Hearst's yellow journalism. Almost single-handedly, he turned it around. Within five years he put together the finest staff that has worked for any Canadian newspaper at any time and made the *Star* the antithesis of what it had been.

There is among newspapermen much mythologizing of Honderich's predecessors, Joseph E. "Holy Joe" Atkinson and his son-in-law, Harry A. Hindmarsh. Little wonder: they were extraordinary men and the stuff of journalistic legend. Bizarre tales about them and their exploits still warm the hearts of veteran reporters downing a beer at the Toronto Press Club. The gloss of nostalgia and a rueful affection skip lightly over the gargantuan excesses and shudderingly irresponsible journalism they often indulged in. In the first half of the century, the *Star,* for all its merits and its crusades for the underprivileged, was a biased, dishonest and unprincipled newspaper. Its polices were often unethical, its passions were mostly purple, its treatment of the news was often outrageous. When it suited Atkinson and Hindmarsh, the *Star* was more British than the flag, more royalist than the Queen and more Liberal than Mackenzie King. Warts and all, it grew to become Canada's largest daily.

In the federal election of 1949, the *Star* established a record in the scurrilous coverage of an important story. The Liberal party under Louis St. Laurent was seeking re-election. The leader of the Conservative party was George Drew, the former premier of Ontario. Atkinson had died the year before, leaving the bulk of his estate to the Atkinson Charitable Foundation. The Ontario government – with whom the *Star* had had a bitter and long-running feud – subsequently introduced The Charitable Gifts Act, frustrating Atkinson's intentions and arguing that the bequest was an attempt to avoid paying succession duties. When the bill passed, Hindmarsh wheeled his heavy artillery into position.

In the election fight, the *Star* abandoned every vestige of responsible journalism. During the final weeks of the campaign it carried as many as eight election stories on page one, all biased. It purported to expose what it called "a secret deal" between Drew and Maurice Duplessis, then premier of Quebec. Drew, the *Star* trumpeted, had agreed to appoint the former mayor of Montreal, Camillien Houde, to the Tory cabinet as leader of the Quebec Conservatives. Shame, cried the *Star* and launched an anti-Houde campaign. They had an ideal target. During the war years, Houde, while mayor, had urged Québécois not to register for what was in effect the national draft, and was imprisoned.

To spearhead the crusade, Hindmarsh dispatched a reporter to Quebec, and with him, photographers under orders to dog Houde's steps and photograph him in the most unflattering poses possible. It was not a difficult assignment; Houde was a grossly obese man with an exceptionally ugly face and a great paunch. The photographers shot hundreds of pictures, managing to get some dandies at banquets.

The final low blow was delivered on the front page of the first edition on the Saturday before the election. It remains the most infamous headline in Canadian newspaper history. Three lines of the blackest condensed Gothic type spanned the top of the page:

KEEP CANADA BRITISH
DESTROY DREW'S HOUDE
GOD SAVE THE KING

Below was a grotesque photograph of a shirtsleeved Houde, looking positively evil. The cutlines read:

This man will become one of the leaders of Canada if voters Monday elect George Drew as head of a Conservative government. He is Camillien Houde, isolationist, ex-internee, foe of Britain.

Every story on the front page attacked Drew. It was too much for Alexander Stark, a member of the *Star*'s board of directors. He deleted the third line for the second edition, substituting, VOTE ST. LAURENT, but was only able to do so because Hindmarsh, who had written the heading, had gone for the day.

In the 1951 provincial election, the *Star* topped even this shabby performance. To defeat the incumbent Leslie Frost, it championed the Liberal leader, Walter Thomson, an uninspiring candidate. It was decided in the *Star* offices that the Liberals should base their campaign on a promise to introduce a prepaid hospital-care plan; they would attack Frost for purportedly refusing an offer from the federal government to aid Ontario hospitals. It is difficult today to credit the astounding reach of the *Star*'s vendetta. Speeches by Conservatives went unreported. CCF candidates were reported only if they had something complimentary to say about Thomson. In the last week of the campaign, according to Ross Harkness, in his excellent book, *A.E. Atkinson of the Star,* the *Star* devoted 312 columns of type and pictures to Thomson, but carried only 44 columns of international news and 83.5 of local news. On the eve of the election, the *Star* did not carry one line of international news!

The front page of the November 10 issue is a classic. The main headline read:

MAY BE YOUR MOTHER — THOMSON

Beneath it was a five-column picture (not of an actual Ontario couple, but a stock photo from a model agency) of an aging couple. The caption: *Should dear old people like these go to mental institutions?* Across the entire width of the page, in bold type, was a quotation from Thomson to the effect that the minds of ten thousand elderly folk could have been saved if Frost had accepted the hospital plan offered by the federal government.

Despite this fulminating, the Ontario Liberals suffered the worst defeat in their history, electing only eight members to the legislature and polling only one-third of the vote. Yet, while this astonishingly irresponsible campaign was underway, the *Star* had a steady and sizeable increase in circulation, and suffered a sharp drop after polling day.

Despite its excesses, the *Star* had many notable achievements in legitimate journalism. Its reporters were dispatched around the world; some filed excellent news stories and features on significant events. In pursuit of a breaking human-interest story, the *Star's* efforts were sometimes awesome: it didn't merely double-up, it sent *teams* of reporters and photographers. It once hired an entire railroad train – to transport staffers to the site of a story and to keep its rivals out of the area. Reporters for the *Star* and the *Telegram* (whose standards were not much higher) sometimes kidnapped newsworthy persons, wining and dining them in locked hotel rooms to keep them from talking to the opposition. Gangs of "kidnappers" sped across Toronto corralling Irish Sweepstakes winners, witnesses to bizarre murders or others who could offer exclusive or inside comments on stories of broad interest. Hindmarsh formed a famed Flying Squad, complete with staff cars and a portable wire-photo unit. It was on call twenty-four hours a day, seven days a week, ready to go anywhere in the province and nearby American states in pursuit of a story. The Flying Squad cars, jammed with reporters and photographers, would descend on a scene and drop off men at likely points to ferret out information and round up every available picture before the opposition arrived.

The *Star* was the first Canadian newspaper to use wire photo. In 1928, it was the first to distribute papers by plane – albeit to St. Catharines, Ontario, and mostly as a publicity stunt. A *Star* reporter made the first long-distance telephone call from Canada to Mexico in pursuit of a story, and in 1932 to South Africa to interview the governor-general who had once been an Ontario farmer. Beyond that, it founded the Star Fresh Air Fund and the Santa Claus Fund and did many other good works.

Beland Honderich clamped down on the excesses. *Time* magazine took notice of the metamorphosis. Its February 25, 1955 issue stated, "The Toronto *Star* turned grey one day last week." Banished overnight were the sensations, the sudden deaths, the nude bodies and grisly scenes once played large on the front page under blazing headlines. Crime reporters were no longer permitted to identify criminal suspects until they had been formally charged.

These were first of the many notorious "Honderich rules" as he dragged the *Star* kicking and screaming into the realm of responsible journalism. In enforcing his view of what the *Star* should be, he was often arbitrary and unreasonable. He seldom praised and was inflexible in disciplining carelessness or slovenliness. Sometimes he was crotchety about trivial matters; among them one that particularly irritated staffers, an insistence that they leave their desks tidy at the end of the day.

Shortly after I joined the *Star* I was told the story of staff resistance to one of Honderich's economy drives. Reporters were notified that, before a new pencil would be issued, the stub of the old one must be turned in. It was an invitation to journalistic inventiveness. A reporter would turn in a stub, get a new pencil, cut it into five pieces, sharpen the tips and turn them in for five new pencils.

Reporters traditionally resist management, but Honderich's zeal stimulated more than the usual amount of vilification. Wherever reporters met to talk shop you would likely hear the familiar one-liners: "Beland's not in today; he's over at the foundry getting a heart transplant." And after the *Star* moved from 80 King Street West to Yonge Street at Queen's Quay: "Honderich moved the plant to the waterfront so he could be near his U-boat."

Most of the Honderich rules were wise: let the main headline on the front page (the so-called "black line") be no larger than the lead story demands. The black line may not be used for crime stories, unless the story had other human-interest aspects. There must be balance on the front page: news of the world, news from Ottawa, news from across Canada, local news. But with the seriousness, news must be balanced by a change of pace, a lighter piece. Moreover, every story must include, within the first half-dozen paragaphs, a background paragraph, so that a reader unfamiliar with the subject matter is given a context.

One of the rules led to bad journalism. Honderich was and is an admirer of Walter Gordon. Gordon was then one of the leaders of the new nationalism that was sweeping Canada. Later he was the accident-prone finance minister in the first Pearson government. Honderich insisted that, whenever Gordon made a speech, the story be carried on page one. Sometimes such display was valid; Gordon often made news. At other times, the story was unimportant and trivialized the front page.

There were many other rules; some of which often made a *Star* story pedestrian compared to the matching story in the *Telegram*. A classic example may be seen in a comparison of the lead paragraphs in the two papers on the morning astronaut John Glenn first orbited the globe. The *Star*'s lead was long and leaden, cluttered with background information that would have been better handled further down in the story. The *Telegram*'s lead read: "This morning, in the time it took a suburban commuter to drive to work in downtown Toronto, U.S. astronaut, John Glenn, blasted off from Cape Canaveral, Florida, and circled the globe."

In the 1960s, the rivalry between the two Toronto afternoon papers was intense. The *Globe and Mail* was a competitor but the *Telegram* was the enemy. Nothing gave *Star* staffers more satisfaction than to score a beat on the *Tely*.

The two newspapers were as different as the men who controlled them: John Bassett was Honderich's antithesis in almost every way. Politically a Liberal (at the time), Honderich was conservative and introverted as a man; Bassett, a Tory's Tory, was flamboyant and unconventional. Honderich came "from the wrong side of the tracks" in Kitchener, Ontario, and had worked his way up from general reporter to editorial director and eventually publisher. Bassett was the son of the publisher of the Montreal *Gazette*, was himself owner and publisher of the Sherbrooke *Record* and had been born with a mouthful of silver spoons. Honderich seldom speaks in public and his photograph is rarely seen; Bassett is a buoyant extrovert and a celebrity. Honderich's *Star* sought to remove itself from the raucous, jaundiced journalism of its earlier days; Bassett's *Telegram* was a free-swinging, Fleet-streeting, punchy-headlined journal — even its pages were pink for a time. It is not suprising that the men who founded the tabloid Toronto *Sun* were mostly former *Tely* staffers.

I came to know John Bassett through an incident that is typical of the man's unconventional directness. One morning, my telephone rang. Bassett wasted not one sentence on preliminaries. "I'm told that Beland Honderich is out of town and can't be reached, and that you're in charge of the paper. Is that right?"

"That's right," I said.

"Then let me tell you the reason for this call. I'm informed — and I have every reason to believe it to be true — that a *Star* reporter is preparing a story on my forthcoming divorce. Are you aware of that?"

"No," I said.

"Good enough," he said. "Well now, we haven't met and you don't know me, but I'm sure you'll accept my word when I tell you what the situation is. Beland and I have an agreement: the *Telegram* won't carry anything on his divorce if the *Star* doesn't carry anything on mine." He paused to chuckle. "Not that there would be that much interest in Beland's case, but there sure as hell would be in mine. At any rate, in Beland's absence I wanted to let you know about that agreement."

"Thank you for calling."

He paused for a moment. "You accept what I've just told you?"

"Of course. If you tell me straight out that you and he have an agreement that's good enough for me."

"Good," he said, and hung up.

I called the city desk and asked if someone was preparing a story on Bassett's divorce. Yes, I was told. "Kill it," I said.

The reporter who had been working on the story came to see me, wanting to know why it was being killed. I didn't give him a reason but simply repeated that we weren't going to run it.

"I was assigned the story by the city editor," he grumbled, "and was told to double-check my facts. I've been working on it for days and I've done a lot of hard digging. I have a right to know why it's being killed." I told him that I'd made such a decision. He turned to leave, muttering half to himself, "What I'd like to know is; who's running this goddamn paper?"

"Sometimes I'm not sure," I said. "But I know one thing — *you're* not."

For a brief period the *Star* had informal monthly meetings of senior editorial people. They were held after hours in a conference room at the Lord Simcoe hotel, now razed but then only a block from the *Star* building. After drinks and a meal, all present were encouraged to talk candidly about the news operation and to put forward suggestions for improvement. Few said anything pointed or critical; the only exception I can recall being Ron Haggart, who wrote an influential column on municipal politics.

On one occasion, after the others had gone, Beland and I were sitting alone, drinks in hand, relaxing. He turned and said, "It wasn't a very productive meeting."

"I thought it went pretty well," I said.

He took a sip of his drink and was silent for a long moment. "The staff doesn't respond to me very well. What's the problem?"

Although the question was entirely out of character, I wasn't surprised. The hour was late. We were tired. We'd had more than a few drinks and the moment seemed conducive to candour. I rested an arm on his shoulder, and with all the presumptuous wisdom of a number of scotches, said, "You want to know what your problem is? I'll tell you what your problem is – you're a Mennonite and you've never learned to enjoy sin."

It was a fatuous comment; the kind of thing that only gets said with an evening far gone. Today, in retrospect, however, I think it may well be true.

The staff on the *Star,* put together by Beland Honderich during the late 1950s and early 1960s, was the best ever assembled in the history of Canadian journalism. Pierre Berton wrote a daily column. Nathan Cohen was entertainment editor and drama critic. Ron Haggart covered Metropolitan Toronto politics. Martin Goodman was in Washington and Val Sears in Ottawa. Robert Fulford wrote about books and the arts. Dennis Braithwaite (and later, Roy Shields and Bob Blackburn) covered television. Mark Gayn was a roving correspondent and editorial writer. The veteran, Roy Greenaway, was at Queen's Park. Jocko Thomas was at "police headquaarrters." Milt Dunnell was sports editor and Jack McArthur headed the financial department. Lotta Dempsey reported on women. Leonard Bertin covered science. Jack Brehl, Rae Corelli and George Bryant wrote features. In the newsroom, Richard Needham was city editor and Andy Lytle news editor, with that nonpareil of headline writers, Willis Entwistle at the heart of the "rim." Norm James was the chief photographer. On the editorial page, Duncan Macpherson raised the newspaper cartoonist's art to new heights.

In October, 1962, Berton decided to leave his enormously popular column to major in television. I considered a number of writers from across Canada but couldn't sell myself on any of them. One morning as I passed Milt Dunnell's desk, he asked, "Are you still looking for a columnist? If you are, have you considered Gary Lautens?" Lautens wrote a column on sports for the Hamilton *Spectator* but I'd never heard of him. "He's good," Milt said. "And funny as hell."

I read some of Lautens' columns and invited him to come to see me. He was entirely lacking in self-confidence. It took some persistence to convince him that he had the stuff to make it in Toronto. He wrote wonderfully zany material, but each day he would endure an agony of self-doubt, and when he encountered me in the newsroom would denigrate his last column. I made it a practice to read his stuff in advance, and when it was particularly good, to tell him so. He wrote the column for twenty years and is now executive managing editor of the paper.

I also needed a religion editor. One day while involved in a search for the right man, Allen Spraggett strolled in to ask for the job. He was pastor of a tiny church in Frankville, Ontario, a hamlet of fewer than a hundred people.

"What makes you think you can do the job?" I asked.

"I would certainly do it better than it's being done," he said.

I told him to return home and write a story about any religious event in his area. "With it," I said, "include a list of the half-dozen things you would do were you religion editor on the *Star*." A few days later I received a news story about an evangelistic campaign in a nearby town along with a list of more than a dozen projects he would launch if he had the job. I hired him.

Immediately he became a target of fun among the staff. The incredulous report went out: "The guy types with *one* finger." Most newsmen use the hunt-and-peck method, but Spraggett picked out his stories with one finger on one hand. It was viewed as a small wonder. But he did an imaginative and thorough-going job with the weekly religion page and left only after he wandered into the cloud cuckooland of the occult. He prospered there but it finished him as a credible journalist.

Nathan Cohen had been hired to do one thing: to write a daily column on the entertainment scene, specializing in drama criticism. Canadian theatre had just begun the flowering that would take place over the next twenty years. Nathan was inflexible in his determination to serve the theatre by insisting on excellence; he made few allowances for the fact that Canadian companies lacked money, had inadequate facilities and drew sparse audiences. He adamantly refused to excuse second-rate productions merely because they were Canadian and better than the norm. He was hated with passion in those early days, and I was frequently berated by actors and producers for permitting his "negativism," which, they argued, discouraged attendance and was delaying the emergence of a distinctive national theatre. They hail him now; they railed against him then.

Nathan was thought by those who didn't know him to be pompous and imperious, indifferent to others' opinions. In fact, he was shy and easily embarrassed. He was courtly around beautiful women and florid in his compliments, but he was ill at ease and more than once I saw him blush. He smoked heavily, an unfiltered American cigaret, but didn't inhale. He never learned to drive a car and was driven about by his wife. In some ways he was rather Victorian: he seldom swore and didn't enjoy off-colour jokes. After a friend gave him a cane, he was never without one. Over the years, he was presented with walking-sticks of various designs – one enclosed a rapier – and he took a boyish delight in showing off his latest acquisition.

Although he often denied it, he enjoyed public attention and relished the craning of necks when he entered a theatre. He and I once gleefully fashioned a conspiracy, in which he would attend an important opening at the Royal Alexandra theatre and, two minutes before the curtain, make a grand entrance, sweeping to his usual seat on the right aisle, a cape billowing behind. He went as far as to enquire at Malabar's about renting a cape and a top hat but never did do it.

His great gifts were a sure understanding and a love of the theatre. He harboured one dominant ambition – to be drama critic on the New York *Times*. The opportunity never came. He was invited to join the New York *Post* but refused, probably because it would make difficult a move to the *Times*. He was respected by American producers and, when their companies came to Toronto, a major concern was Cohen's reaction. In 1960, when Lerner and Loew's *Camelot* opened the O'Keefe Centre, Nathan wrote an extraordinary review in which he made specific suggestions for the improvement of the production. As I recall it, all but one of his suggestions were incorporated in the play.

Nathan made a great show of resisting the job as entertainment editor of the *Star* — it was not his metier, he would be spreading himself too thin, he wasn't sure how well he would handle staff. It was his fashion to demean his own capacities so you could take issue with him. I played the role, offering him secretarial help and an editorial assistant. Slowly but predictably he came around, shaking his massive head in mock wonder at his departure from sanity. He ran the best entertainment section in the country.

Nathan and I played a weekly charade. I would notify him each Thursday of the size of the Saturday entertainment section "news hole" — the amount of space left over after the advertisements had been blocked in. Friday mornings, I would hear the singular sounds of Nathan approaching along the hall: the heavy shuffling of feet, the muttered imprecations, the murmurings of despair.

He would throw himself heavily into a chair across from me, toss a wad of tattered page-dummies onto my desk and roll his eyes toward the ceiling. "Charles," he would mourn, "what are you doing to me? You're asking the impossible. How can I possibly produce an entertainment section if I have to jimmy the material into this pathetic, minuscule space?" He would then toss a sheet of paper onto the desk on which he had scrawled the features he had planned. He would huff and puff and fulminate, place spread fingers against his shirtfront, and with the overdone expression of a man betrayed, demand more space.

I would hear him out, enjoying the performance. When he was finished, I would say to him, "Sorry, but that's it. There ain't no more. We have to earn enough from the advertising to pay your princely salary." Groans and appeals to heaven. After a while we would tire of the game and go on to gossip about the newspaper and entertainment businesses.

He came into my office one day and dropped a photograph on the desk before me.

"Any idea who that is?" he asked, a slight smile on his lips.

I studied the picture. It was a candid photograph — what is called in the business a "grab-shot" — of a very old woman. The contours of her face sagged; the eyes looked hunted and flashed with anger. She was turning toward the camera, obviously caught off guard in what appeared to be a theatre dressing-room. There was something familiar about the face.

"No idea," I said.

"She's playing in town right now," Nathan hinted. I shook my head. "Marlene Dietrich," he said.

I looked at the photograph again, barely crediting my eyes. Marlene Dietrich had been one of the most exquisitely beautiful women in the world.

"The question is," Nathan was saying, "do we run it?"

"Of course we don't run it," I said hotly.

Nathan's smile broke widely. "I'd already made that decision," he said. "I merely wanted to remind you that time is the enemy."

Honderich was a notoriously difficult man to work for. He kept a close watch on every part of the paper and arrived at his office by seven to read all the galley proofs. His criticisms of stories and headlines were usually valid and, although sometimes you would go from a meeting grinding your teeth with rage, you would have a grudging admiration for his editor's eye.

He and I clashed seriously only once. It had been decided to devote the entire front page of the second section to a series on the virtues of Metropolitan Toronto. On five consecutive days we would present some of the reasons for pride in the city: the superb harbour, the swiftly burgeoning downtown, the diversity and excellence of services, the public transportation system, the parks and green spaces, the tree-lined streets and magnificent homes. For a week, we would unabashedly brag about our

I assigned the project to Bob Needham, the city editor. (He now goes by Richard Needham and writes for the editorial page of the *Globe and Mail.*) He did an excellent job of assigning, supervising and editing the various features. I laid out the pages, cropped the photographs and wrote the heads. When the first of the five pages was proofed, I took it to Beland.

He examined it, making approving noises. Then he said, "Charles . . . this picture: wouldn't it be better if you ran it four columns? . . . This head's too strong. . . . And this story below the fold; I'd think you'd want to give it more prominence."

The entire page had to be remade, and the result lacked balance and cohesiveness. The following day I took him a proof of the Tuesday page. He went over it and made half a dozen criticisms. Again, a major revision was required. On the third day a similar thing happened. As he finished his comments he said, "Now Charles, if you'll just have those changes made."

"I'm sorry, Bee," I said. "I can't do that."

He looked at me, puzzled. "What do you mean, you can't do it?"

"Simply that I won't do it. The page is fine as it is."

There was an extended pause. When he spoke his voice was soft. "Charles, I would like the changes made."

"I'm sorry, Bee."

"What's the problem?" he said.

I was aware of an inner trembling. I was also aware that I was suddenly inflexible. "I changed Monday's page, and Tuesday's, but I have no intention of changing this one. It's a good series and it's well presented. More important than that, it's the best I can do. Three days in a row you've indicated dissatisfaction, so obviously my best isn't good enough. Perhaps you should get someone else."

He didn't respond for a moment but looked down at the page proof before him. "Charles," he said, "I would like the changes made. If you aren't prepared to make them, will you pass the page to someone who is?"

"Yes," I said, "I'll send Phil Sykes to see you." Sykes was then assistant managing editor.

As I opened the door, he said, "Are you sure you've given this enough thought?"

"Yes," I said. "I've thought about it for three days. Longer than that, actually."

"You realize, Charles, that if it comes to an impasse between the editorial director and the managing editor – you know what the outcome will be?"

"Yes," I said. "I know that."

"Please ask Mr. Sykes to come and see me."

I did, and went to my office, closing the door. I sat numbly reviewing what had happened, deeply saddened. I loved my work on the *Star*. Apart from the long hours and the unremitting pressure, there was no part of it I didn't delight in. Yes, Honderich was a demanding superior, and sometimes exasperating, but I was in sympathy with what he was trying to do. The *Star* had become a fine newspaper. A recent study had listed it among the twelve great newspapers in the world. I liked the challenge and the scope of my work and the assurance I felt in doing it after years on the job. Had I been too precipitate in bringing on the confrontation? No. It is impossible to work creatively and well if someone is constantly second-guessing you.

There was a tap on the door and Honderich entered. He crossed the office and stood with his hands in his hip pockets looking out of the window at the excavation that would soon house the footings for the Toronto-Dominion Bank tower.

"Am I really that impossible to work for?" he asked.

"Sometimes."

"What we're trying to do, you and I, is to turn out a good newspaper. It's not easy."

"Beland," I said, "wherever I've worked, I've asked only one thing of my employer – leave me free to do my work. If I'm not good enough, fire me. But if I am good enough, leave me free to do my job. The prerogatives are yours. I don't resent direction or instruction – you're the guy who's finally responsible – but, day to day, let me do my job. It's impossible to work with the knowledge that somebody's looking over your shoulder."

He turned from the window. "You're tired," he said. "Take a week or two. Go off to Florida or somewhere and send me your expenses. We'll have a talk when you get back."

I took ten days off and sat in the sun. When I returned, neither of us said anything about the confrontation. Honderich stayed away from the newsroom and, apart from our usual morning briefing sessions, didn't interfere. After six weeks, the earlier pattern resumed.

The second time the *Star* and I almost parted company also had to do with editorial interference.

Harry A. Hindmarsh was managing editor at the time and a member of the board of directors. Although not named to the position, I was acting as assistant managing editor. Harry was fighting a health problem and frequently arrived late at the office. I was on the desk each morning, making the decisions, laying out the front page, getting the paper out. Hindmarsh would arrive, check on what was in the works, and then sit in the spare chair at the news desk to take over principal responsibility.

But there was a growing problem. He was arriving later each morning and would order changes that would delay the edition. Three mornings in a row the paper closed late. One morning, he arrived later than usual and went, as was his custom, to the photo desk to look over the available "art," as photographs are called. "Charlie," he called out, photograph in hand. "Why isn't this on the front page?"

It was an excellent picture, not a news photo but a good human-interest shot. I had considered it, but had rejected it, because it would need to be played large to be effective. Using it would have meant cutting back on an important story, and it was a heavy news day.

"It's too good a picture to miss," he said. "Run it."

The men at the photo desk were watching. "I'll have to remake the page," I said. "We're running late now. We've closed late for the past three days."

"Charlie," he said, "I told you to run it."

"I'm sorry, Harry. We're late now. I've got to get back to the desk."

"Run the goddamn picture!" he flared.

"No, goddamn it!" I said, suddenly angry. "You want it, you change it. And while you're at it, get the goddamn paper out."

I turned and went to my office. I began to empty the drawers of my desk, waiting until the paper was away, when I would be fired. An hour passed, and then two. Then Harry was at the door. He came in, closed the door behind him, and for a few minutes made inconsequential talk. Finally, he smiled his lopsided grin.

"I had a talk with Beland," he said, "and he tells me I was wrong. Especially having a row in front of the guys at the photo desk." He stuck out a hand, "Okay?"

I gripped his hand warmly. "Okay."

There was no one in the upper echelons of the *Star* less well known to the staff than the president, Joseph S. ("Young Joe") Atkinson. In the almost five years I was on the paper I met him only once and never saw him in the newsroom. Shortly after I'd been appointed executive news editor, we passed in the hall outside his office. He invited me in and we chatted for a few minutes. I can't recall what was said; my mind was preoccupied with a story going around the newsroom that embodied the light regard in which he was held, rightly or wrongly, by the editorial staff.

According to the tale, Atkinson, who had a fondness for gadgets, had a console installed on his desk: simply by depressing buttons, he could open or draw the drapes. One morning he was with an important visitor. The brilliant sun pouring through the window provided the opportunity to show off his new device. He depressed a button and the drapes moved silently closed. But rather than rest there, they immediately opened, and that cycle completed, drew once more. Back and forth they went until aid was summoned.

Conventional newsroom wisdom had it that Burnett Thall, the production manager and a vice president, was next in line to Atkinson, who was believed to be more interested in things mechanical than things editorial. Thall had impressive credentials: he held a Ph.D. from the University of Toronto as a research engineer and, before coming to the *Star*, he had worked on atomic reactors with the National Research Council and as a research physicist at the Chalk River atomic energy installation.

The newsroom gossip also had it that Honderich, although undoubtedly competent and also a member of the board, was an outsider and unlikely to move higher than his present position as editorial director. I had heard the speculation but had paid little attention. Atkinson was a young man, and the possibility never crossed my mind that a boardroom struggle to be his successor was going on.

One morning Beland called me to his office and asked me to begin a file listing every foul-up or delay in the composing room and the reasons for each one. It seemed a reasonable request. There is on-going tension between the editorial department and the composing room on any newspaper. Deadlines are important: the "product" must be rushed to market while it is fresh; connections have to be made with planes and trains and buses. A newsman, a breaking story in hand, will continue to send copy to the composing room up to the last possible minute, as the composing room foreman fumes and fulminates. The journalist wants to get out the latest news; the foreman wants to get out the paper. Consequently, each department tends to blame the other for its problems.

There was little trouble in fattening Honderich's file: almost every morning there were delays or problems to document. A few weeks later, Honderich requested the file, and shortly thereafter, asked me to meet him at ten the following morning in Thall's office.

We gathered, the three of us, around a glass-topped coffee

table. Thall, an open, gregarious man, was relaxed and cordial. Honderich was unusually tense. Thall offered coffee; Beland dismissed it. He dumped the file on the coffee table and began to read selected items chosen to demonstrate the inefficiency and ineptitude of the composing room. It was an intimidating litany.

Early in the conversation, Thall had attempted a light-hearted response, but he grew silent as it became clear that Honderich was going to make his case without interruption. Beland closed the file and slammed a fist on it. I feared for the table top as he pounded it, emphasizing his words. There would be an end to this costly ineptitude, he thundered. Unless there was a marked improvement in the next ten days, he would take the matter to Mr. Atkinson and the board. Before Thall could reply, Honderich rose, picked up the file and left. I followed, awkwardly.

There was some improvement in the composing room the following week, but the process was a labour-intensive one and subject to breakdowns. It occurred to me that, if this was the opening salvo in a showdown fight for power, Honderich would win hands down. As indeed, in the best interests of the paper, he should win. He was tougher, more ambitious and better equipped as a journalist to be the publisher than was Thall. I had left the *Star* when, in 1965, he was named assistant publisher, then president and publisher the following year when Atkinson became chairman of the board. When Atkinson died unexpectedly in 1968, Honderich stood alone at the top.

I began to have problems with Needham. I had inherited him from the *Star* editorial page when Honderich proposed that he be made city editor. From the beginning, I found it impossible to be at ease with him. He's an odd man; withdrawn, punctilious, awkward in social intercourse. When I would assign specific tasks, he would listen, head down, his attitude almost servile, saying little or nothing. At the end, he would give a quick bob of his head and be off.

He was a good city editor; imaginative and resourceful, careful about details. And he worked long hours. I would come in Saturdays to get the first edition away, and leaving, would see him in his office, often with a group of people. He would neither say hello nor introduce his friends. He was there sometimes on Sundays. I got the impression that he preferred the office to the place in which he lived.

He began a vendetta with Arnold Brunner, a reporter. Prior to Needham's coming, we had hired Brunner away from the CBC to run the world news desk. It hadn't worked out, and I had shifted him to features, where he did excellent work. Brunner was that rare breed of reporter, the "digger," the man who will pursue a slim lead with stubborn and indefatigable tenacity. He'd handled a number of stories creditably and without problems, and I was surprised when he came to me, complaining that he was being harassed by Needham.

I talked to Needham about it. He was irritated, it seemed, by Brunner's unwillingness to accept certain small routines. Brunner was expected to report mornings at eight o'clock, but would often arrive a few minutes late. It became an issue, with Brunner – who worked hours of unpaid overtime – resisting what he regarded as a martinet demand for punctuality. Needham cut him back to inconsequential assignments. Brunner began to arrive early and then dawdle so that he could walk in one or two minutes past the hour.

I had them both in and told them to act more sensibly, but things grew worse. Brunner was talking about leaving and I didn't want to lose him. And he had become convinced that Needham disliked him because he was a Jew. It was a silly quarrel.

All this came to a head one morning when I was with Honderich for a briefing session. He mentioned that he had received a memo from Needham recommending that Brunner be fired; he was surprised when I told him that I knew nothing of the recommendation. Honderich said that he would return the memorandum to Needham and tell him to discuss such matters with me. "What's the problem?" he asked. "I thought Brunner was doing good work." "He is," I said, "but he and Needham have been feuding." "Nevertheless," Honderich said, "I think you should accept the recommendation of the city editor in matters pertaining to his staff." I told him I wasn't prepared to do that in this instance. Brunner was one of the better reporters on staff and, more important, he was being badly treated. Later, I told Needham to resolve his problems with Brunner, and in future to pass such recommendations to me and not to Honderich. I told Brunner to settle down and stop playing games. They established an uneasy peace.

On December 1, 1962, the Hamilton Tiger Cats and the Winnipeg

Blue Bombers met at Exhibition Stadium in Toronto to decide the winner of the Grey Cup. The game would be remembered as the "Fog Bowl"; it was the only game in the history of the Canadian Football League to be played over two days.

The forecasters warned of dense fog, and there had been talk of postponing the game. But as the time for the kick-off approached, visibility at the CNE stadium was adequate. Four minutes into the second quarter, a cool breeze moved in, chilling the moist Lake Ontario air and forming a dense ground fog. Within minutes the game was almost invisible from the stands; as the fog thickened, even those on the sidelines were unable to follow the play. The spectators, feeling cheated, began to boo and call for a postponement of the game.

I wasn't at the game; I was in the newsroom supervising the various editions. There had been reports that the *Telegram* was organizing to print the latest results and pictures first and we had laid elaborate plans to beat them at their own game. Needham had worked out an ingenious system to provide photographs with the least possible delay. A team of motorcyclists would carry the film from CNE Stadium to the *Star*. Their ability to slip between lanes of clotted traffic and to skirt bottlenecks guaranteed that we would get pictures first. Open telephone lines, as well as radio and television sets tuned to the game, ensured instantaneous play-by-play results. In addition to front-page coverage, I had allocated four inside pages for pictures. We were geared to "beat the *Tely*."

In the newspaper business it is regarded as a matter of great importance to "scoop" the opposition. Reporters are intensely competitive and will go to almost any ends to break an exclusive story, even though beating the opposition is of little practical importance. Decades ago, when there was no radio and television, many readers bought two and three papers a day. Then "the scoop" was useful. Today, if you are beaten, you scalp — a euphemism for steal — the opposition story and immediately go to work to match or better it in the following edition. The public is seldom aware which paper broke a specific story, nor does it much care. Nor does a scoop increase sales.

It is a common myth among laymen that headlines sell newspapers, but most of a newspaper's circulation consists of home delivery; increased sales at the newsstands are usually a small proportion of overall sales. There are exceptions, but they are few. The principal benefit in beating the opposition to a story is to staff morale. When a newspaper breaks a significant story that the opposition doesn't have, there is an almost palpable sense of exultant satisfaction in the newsroom.

Back at CNE Stadium the situation was deteriorating. After an abbreviated half-time the game had resumed but now seemed likely to be postponed. The pictures arriving at the *Star* were diffuse and we were having trouble finding enough clear shots to fill the inside pages. But we knew the *Telegram* was faring no better and so consoled ourselves.

As the deadline for the All Star – our final edition – approached, the time came to choose the best available photograph for the front page. I was tempted to go with a close-up action shot but held off. A touchdown had just been scored and it had put the Blue Bombers ahead by one point; it might be the most important play of the game. I had Needham check the stadium to see if a picture of the touchdown was on the way; if so, I would consider delaying the paper. No, came the answer, it hadn't been possible to get a picture of the touchdown.

I scanned the photographs coming off the wire-photo machine. There! – Canadian Press had a picture of the crucial play. It was faded by the transmission process and would reproduce badly, but it showed what was likely to be the winning touchdown. I ordered it onto the front page.

I was in the composing room supervising the lock-up of the page when I saw Honderich and Needham on the far side of the room in a head-close conversation. As the page was wheeled away, Honderich came toward me. We went to one side, apart.

"Charles," he said, "Bob tells me he went to a great deal of trouble to organize a system of delivery to get pictures from the CNE Stadium. Is that so?"

"Yes it is," I said. "And it worked perfectly. You may have noticed that we've been ahead of the *Tely.*"

"I've seen that," he said. "But he tells me that, on the front page of the All Star, you've gone with a picture from CP."

"That's right."

"He says there's a real feeling of let-down among the staff. All that organization, all that planning wasted."

"Bee," I said, "I went with CP because they had a picture of the touchdown. We didn't. At the moment, I'm more interested in being first with the news than I am in staff morale."

He was silent for a moment. "We didn't have the touchdown?" I shook my head. "I see," he said.

I wanted to find Needham and kick his tail, but decided, the hell with it. I went to my office to wait for the edition to come off the presses. In the meantime, I was told that the final nine minutes and twenty seconds of the game had been postponed until the following day.

Not long afterwards, Needham left to join the *Globe and Mail*.

In February, 1963, John Diefenbaker's erratic government lurched toward extinction, marking the pathetic end of one of the great missed opportunities in Canadian politics. The end had come in disarray, with name-calling and some of the cabinet in revolt. It was a tawdry and untidy disintegration.

In the aftermath, the *Star's* editorial page had upbraided George Hees, who had been minister of Trade and Commerce, charging him with vacillation and inconsistency. Hees wrote Beland Honderich, arguing that his resignation and his motives were being misinterpreted and asking for an opportunity to set the record straight. Honderich gathered his editorial writers and invited me to sit in. We met with Hees in Honderich's office.

Hees presented a credible defence of his actions. As the meeting broke up, I found myself standing with Hees, Honderich and Bob Neilson, the *Star's* chief editorial writer. I liked Hees and wanted to see him in the Liberal party, and although I had no formal connection with the party, said, "George, what would you say if some senior person in the Liberal party were to ask you to join?"

He paused, looking down, fingering the chain stretched across his vest. "Well," he said cautiously, "I'm happy to talk to anyone at any time. . . ."

"Now, George," I said, "that's a politician's answer. You've been talking openly here. What would you say if someone in authority among the Grits were to try to recruit you?" As he was considering a response, I added, "There's a pretty fair precedent – Winston Churchill crossed the floor to join the Liberals."

He brightened. "Say, that's right. He did." Then he added, "I'd be happy to talk."

Afterwards, he and I repaired to my office to talk a little politics. He was greatly exercised about Diefenbaker and at one point called him "the most dangerous man in Canada."

"All the more reason for joining the Liberals," I said. "If you're seriously interested I can have someone in the prime minister's office invite you in. Perhaps Pearson himself."

He sat, frowning. "But where would I run?"

Mischievously, I said, "If Dief's as dangerous as you say, how about Prince Albert?"

"No, no, no," he said. "That's his territory. And I'm not sure how well I'd do in a rural constituency."

I got in touch with Keith Davey, knowing that he would be interested in any move that might help attain that majority government he sought for Pearson. Pearson did speak to Hees, and in April, 1964 – although I can't say unequivocally that the one flowed from the other – Hees was named president of the Montreal and Canadian stock exchanges. Pearson wanted him in the cabinet and was planning to appoint him if he ran successfully in the next election. But Pearson faced strong opposition from members of his cabinet and others who had done battle with George in the Commons over the years.

More than two years later, during Holy Week 1965, I had a telephone call from Hees. He would be in Toronto on Good Friday and would like to meet for lunch at the Granite Club. There he asked me to evaluate the likelihood of his being given a cabinet post. I was candid. I told him that opposition to the move had hardened and that there was little chance of it happening.

I then said, "George, you're a political animal. You'll never be happy out of politics and you are by temperament a Conservative. You have most of your life invested in the party, ever since you were president of the Young Tories. Forget the Liberals. It isn't going to pan out. Rejoin your own party."

He seemed to emerge from beneath a cloud. As lunch continued, he decided to make the move almost immediately. I suggested that he call John Bassett and tell him first about the decision. He returned from the telephone to say that Bassett would be delighted to meet him. Within the week there was a front-page story in the *Telegram* in which Hees announced his return to the Conservative party and a lead editorial welcoming him back.

There were a host of important and exciting stories during the years I was at the *Star*, but none so dramatic and momentous as the ascendancy to the presidency and the assassination of John F. Kennedy. He stirred an extraordinary admiration and affection among Americans, but no more, I think, than among Canadians, who were not so much influenced by partisan political factors.

He was the scion of a wealthy family, young, handsome, brilliant, cultivated, a war hero, a Pulitzer prize winner and married to a woman as beautiful as and more stylish than any beauty queen. He transformed the presidential press conference into a *tour de force* of wit and incisiveness. He was a phrase-maker and a skilled debater who had bested Richard Nixon by a whisker. He launched the New Frontier, defended the Freedom Riders in the southern states, founded the Peace Corps, accelerated the space program and promised a man on the moon within the decade. And in the Cuban Missile Crisis, he stared down Khrushchev. A spangled excitement trailed him.

Few Canadians gave ear to Kennedy's critics, even though they made a strong case: the Bay of Pigs *was* a tragic blunder; the Berlin wall *had* been erected; the missile crisis *was* dangerous brinkmanship; and American involvement in Vietnam had, through Kennedy's actions, deepened to commitment.

To a Canadian journalist, Kennedy was, beyond all else, news. Compared to Diefenbaker's bombast and Pearson's fumbling, Kennedy was a fresh breeze. The world suddenly became more exciting. I remember most vividly the sense of foreboding in the newsroom as that Soviet ship bulled through the waters toward a blockaded Cuba, nuclear missiles clearly visible on her deck. We were publishing pictures of lights burning late at the White House and of graphs depicting the northernmost range of the Cuban-based missiles. The air vibrated with tension. With every other North American, I held my breath until the word came that Khrushchev had backed down.

And then, on November 22, 1963, the thousand days ended and Camelot crumbled. My wife came pounding up the stairs to my bedroom. In the doorway her face was grey, disbelieving, distraught. "Val Sears just called from the newsroom," she said. "President Kennedy has been shot!"

I was in bed recovering from the flu. Gathering clothing as I went, I ran for the car.

The tension surrounding the city desk was incredible. Overarching it was a bizarre sense of unreality. It was not possible that Kennedy was dead. Nor were we certain he was; the news was changing every few minutes. There were reports from a dozen sources, most of them tentative and contradictory. In addition to the tumult of the newsroom and the chatter of the newswires, a radio and a television set were blaring at the groups surrounding them.

As the news changed, we rewrote our lead story and the headlines. We remade the front and inside pages to accommodate new photographs. Honderich, unable to remain in his office, was in the chair opposite mine at the news desk. Since the arrival of television and radio, newspapers no longer print "extras" – editions other than those regularly scheduled – but Honderich changed that that Tuesday afternoon and a fleet of taxicabs joined our trucks to rush fresh bundles of papers to every available outlet.

Then, finally, confirmation: President John Fitzgerald Kennedy was dead, and we were all bereft. The heavy black headlines had already been prepared. The story needed only a new lead. I nodded to Andy Lytle, the news editor, always a locus of strength, and he left for the composing room to lock up the front page. We could relax for a moment before beginning the preparation for the following day. I brought a cigarette to my lips to light it. As I did, I saw another, freshly lit, lodged between my fingers and a third in the brimming ashtray.

Beyond its tragedy, the assassination of John Kennedy was a great continuing news story. And it developed, it seemed, every hour: the beautiful young widow with blood and brains on the skirt of her modish suit; the capture of Oswald in the darkness of a neighbourhood movie theatre; the swearing-in of Lyndon Johnson aboard the plane that would return Kennedy's body to Washington; Caroline and John-John kneeling with their mother by the casket; the leaders of the Western world marching down Washington's broad avenues to the mind-numbing pulse of the drums; the infinite sadness in the eyes of Bobby Kennedy; the riderless horse following the cortège. . . .

It was a television story, but it was no less a newspaper story. We strained for every detail; we culled from the files of every news service, omitting no item of significance; we ran page after page of pictures. It was the kind of story newsmen curse under the pressures of reporting but from which they draw pride and satisfaction when they are done.

I slept in Sunday morning, slept as though drugged, not stirring until just short of noon. I came down the stairs, bone weary and not fully awake, relishing the knowledge that the day ahead had no demands on me. But if you are a journalist, news is a narcotic. I turned on the television set. A crowd was milling about the hallway of a Dallas police station. A voice informed that Lee Harvey Oswald was about to be moved to a more secure prison. I sat down to watch. I wanted to see the wretched little thug who had snuffed out the life of the man whose vitality had energized millions.

There was a sudden jostling of bodies, a flashing of cameras, and there he was: the thin ferret's face, the puny nondescript dwarfed by his bulking Texas escort. A man pushed forward from the right side. His arm reached out. There was the sharp sound of a gunshot. Oswald grimaced.

Two images had been burned into my mind: Oswald's contorted face and the face of a man standing within arm's length of the wounded Oswald – Peter Worthington, a reporter on the Toronto *Telegram*. There could be no mistake about it; there he was again. I leaned forward, searching among the crowd. Where was our man, Rae Corelli, the man we had dispatched to Dallas post-haste the day of the assassination?

The telephone rang. It was the city room. Did I know Oswald had been shot? Yes, I'd been watching television. What was more, I'd just seen Peter Worthington at the scene. "God, no!" was the response. "Where's Corelli?" I asked. "Was he on the scene? Get on the phone and find him. I'm on my way in."

I learned when I arrived at the newsroom that Corelli had been asleep in a motel, exhausted after a series of eighteen-hour days of scrambling competition with hundreds of the best reporters in the world. But there was no time to sort that out now. Tomorrow the *Telegram* would have Worthington's first-person account splashed on the front page. I could imagine the bold, black headline: "I WATCHED OSWALD DIE!" I could see the photograph taken from the television screen with Oswald's and Worthington's heads encircled and the sub-head: EXCLUSIVE: TELY MAN THERE AS OSWALD FELLED BY AVENGER'S BULLET! What could we do to match it?

I called in staff, got people talking on telephones, checking with every possible news source as to who might have eyewitness accounts. Perhaps we could counter the Worthington story by tracking down someone else who had been in that crowded hallway. Perhaps we could get an exclusive interview with the policemen who had been leading Oswald by the arms. Perhaps. . . . Perhaps. . . . In the end we did well, but when the first edition of the *Telegram* landed on my desk, I looked at it and ground my teeth.

A week went by. I was in my office when someone on the city desk called to tell me that Corelli was back in the city and would be in the newsroom within the hour. I left instructions that he be sent to see me as soon as he arrived. In the meantime, I would have to decide how to discipline him. It was unforgivable that he hadn't been on hand when Oswald was transferred. True, it hadn't been widely publicized, but Worthington had been there. So had the television cameramen. So had the wire services and other reporters. It was Corelli's job to know that Oswald was going to be transferred and to be there when it happened no matter how deep his exhaustion. It was an unforgivable lapse.

Yet when I had been named features editor and three men were assigned to me, Corelli was my first choice. He is a solid, experienced journalist with a gift for vivid phrases and succinct statement. In later years he would become entertainment editor of the *Star* and then go into television with Global and the CBC. The telephone rang: "Corelli's on his way to your office."

I heard his footsteps, heard him greet my secretary and steeled myself to do what had to be done: I would assign him to night rewrite for a month, an onerous job. No, I would dock him a week's pay. No, I would sit him down for a month to update our standing obits (obituaries). I would give him hell. . . .

But as he approached the doorway, I realized that nothing I could say to him would match what he had already said to himself a thousand times. The greatest story he would ever cover had slipped through his fingers. No upbraiding by me could match the reproach he had already heaped on his own head. As he put his head through the doorway, I said, "Welcome back. Go home and get some sleep. We'll talk tomorrow."

I fretted about what should be done by way of discipline and finally consulted with Ray Timson, now the *Star*'s managing editor and Andy Lytle, the news editor. There was agreement that Corelli should be laid off for a week without pay. The Newspaper Guild objected, and in the end his pay was restored.

Only once in my years as a newspaper editor did I get to run into the newsroom and shout, "Stop the presses!"

It was late on a quiet Thursday afternoon. I was in my office, awaiting the All Star final edition. Ron Lowman, an assistant city editor, was on the desk. He alerted me that a good story was breaking and gave me the essential details: the RCMP, operating with a search warrant granted to the department of National Revenue, had raided the offices of New Era Appliances Limited, seizing a large amount of cash and all the company's records – enough to fill a moving van. I instructed him to run the story across the top of the front page under what we called "the Red Line," a single 36-point headline printed in red ink.

A boy brought me the first copies off the press. I had already approved the headline but, because the story was breaking as we went to press, had not read the copy. Now, scanning it, I came to the second paragraph. "Police said two of the firm's officials are Jack and Murray Bluestein. They are relatives of gambler Max Bluestein, who recently testified at Ontario's Royal Commission on crime."

It was as though I had been struck on the head with a hammer. For some months, the Ontario Provincial Police had been investigating allegations that organized crime had infiltrated the province. Their investigation had been stimulated in part by a *Star* column by Pierre Berton. Max Blustein, a small-time hood who lived off the avails of gambling, had been beaten up inside a Yonge Street restaurant and bar known as the Town Tavern. Although Blustein had been savagely punched, kicked and beaten with iron bars, and although the Town Tavern had been filled with customers at the time, no one would admit to having seen anything. Berton described it as "the greatest case of mass blindness in history." The political brouhaha stimulated by his revelations had led eventually to a crime probe at which Blustein had testified and to which our story referred.

What galvanized me into my run to the newsroom was the second paragraph. By identifying the owners of New Era as "relatives of gambler Max Bluestein," and by making reference in the same sentence to the crime probe, we were implying that the owners of New Era were connected in some way with organized crime. If no more, we were implying guilt by family connection.

I skidded to a stop at the city desk. "Stop the presses!" I shouted – undoubtedly melodramatically. Someone called the press room while I went to the composing room. It was too late to rewrite the story and to replate the front page – the early press run was already on the trucks – so I had the offending paragraph chiselled out of the metal plate and set the presses to rolling again.

Alex MacIntosh of the law firm Blake, Cassells was the *Star*'s legal counsel. When the problem was reported to him, his immediate response was, "You'll probably receive a libel notice within forty-eight hours." We did.

The situation quickly worsened. We learned that not only were Jack and Murray Bluestein *not* related to Max Blustein, they didn't even spell their names the same way: Max omitted the "e." We ran an immediate retraction.

There was more bad news. In writing the story, someone had carelessly referred to the raided company as New Era *Home* Appliances, a business having no connection with New Era Appliances Limited, and we were required to print a second retraction, clarifying that point.

The Bluesteins subsequently sued, claiming that the *Star* story was false and "had brought the plaintiffs into public scandal, odium and contempt." We had "seriously injured their character and reputation and had caused and would cause them losses of business, income, profit and credit as a result." They sought damages of two million dollars.

Our only possible defence lay in the unlikely chance that, despite the denials and the difference in spelling, the Bluesteins and Blustein might be distantly related. We set reporters to digging but came upon an immediate roadblock: the New Era Bluesteins had been born in Europe and we were unable to trace their birth certificates.

In the meantime, Ray Timson, then an assistant city editor, kept after the story. Under pressure from Timson, a staffer went one afternoon to the neighbourhood in which the Bluesteins lived. A women's tea party was in progress. There were cars parked up and down the block. As only an old-fashioned reporter would do, he copied all the licence plates and ran a check on them at OPP headquarters. Encouraged, he kept digging.

Timson came to see me. "The Bluestein libel suit . . . " he said.

"Yes?"

"Isn't their case based on the fact that we identified Murray and Jack Bluestein as relatives of Max Blustein, and that they are not, in fact, related?"

"Yes."

He grinned at me. "Well, they are related. Murray Bluestein and Max Blustein married sisters!"

The case was dropped.

Late one afternoon Honderich asked me to sub for him at a dinner at the Toronto Club arranged by Ron Todgham, president of Chrysler Motors of Canada, for Lynn Townsend, then the company's American president. It was to be a small affair, with the only outside guests being the heads of the three Toronto papers. I donned black tie and went along.

James Cooper, then the publisher, represented the *Globe and Mail*. He was a taciturn man who appeared ill at ease and said little through the lavish dinner. Shortly after the cigars and cognac were served, he excused himself and left. But not John Bassett. He had arrived late in a mood of elation; that very hour he had averted a strike at the *Telegram* by negotiating an agreement with the typographical union. It was a pleasant dinner with much boisterous talk and extraordinary food and drink. Bassett and Townsend jousted in friendly fashion about Canadian-American relations. I talked mostly to Todgham and the three Chrysler executives who had accompanied their bosses.

As we rose from the table, Bassett declared that it was too early to end the evening and insisted that we all be his guests at the Oasis Room of the Barclay Hotel, a night club of which he was an habitué. Seven of us piled into Bassett's Rolls-Royce and headed for the club on Front Street. For all its virtues, a Rolls is not a spacious car. I found myself in the back seat with Townsend on my lap. We were so many that it was impossible to get the doors closed, and pedestrians were brought up short by the sight of an overloaded Rolls-Royce careering down University Avenue, its doors hanging open, while the president of Chrysler USA complained at full voice about "the lack of space and the lousy air-conditioning in these goddamn European imports."

As we arrived, a table – dead centre and immediately below the stage – was being cleared. Bassett ordered champagne. It was showtime, and a comedian-master of ceremonies was in the middle of his routine. No one at our table paid any attention; all were engaged in boisterous and convivial conversation. The comedian soon surrendered to the inevitable and brought on the first of a series of belly dancers.

Bassett summoned the manager and told him to get rid of the paying customers. "Hurry them up. Give them their checks." The manager made a feeble protest but went to do as he had been bidden. About half an hour later the club was empty, and Bassett called for a private show.

Back came the M.C. to introduce, with ill-concealed resentment, a series of belly dancers. As a Princess Nadia began her routine (it seemed that all the dancers were Middle-East royalty) Bassett pre-empted the M.C. and took over the stage. To the tumultuous acclaim of the Chrysler brass and myself, he matched Princess Nadia as she divested herself, only copping out when it came to his boxer shorts.

I got home shortly after three.

On April 16, 1964, Toronto lawyer Barry Pepper requested that Mr. Justice Dalton Wells cite *Star* reporter Blaik Kirby for contempt of court. He held up the final edition of the previous day's *Star* and read aloud a paragraph. Kirby, Mr. Pepper argued, had written his story in a manner that was "arrogant and insolent." Mr. Justice Dalton Wells called Kirby to stand before the bench and sternly warned that, if he continued to report matters not given in testimony, he would indeed be cited. As would the Toronto *Star*.

It was a serious matter. Not only Kirby but I, as managing editor, and possibly the publisher might be charged. The penalty could be a large fine, even a jail sentence.

The warning was part of the climax of one of the longest-running scandals of the early 1960s. In the building of the natural-gas pipeline from Alberta to the Quebec-Ontario border, a sub-contract was granted to a company called Northern Ontario Natural Gas (NONG). The distribution franchise in Sudbury was the key to the success of the NONG pipeline, for International Nickel was then probably the world's biggest customer for natural gas.

Ralph K. Farris, president of NONG, offered the then mayor of Sudbury, Leo Landreville, an option on 10,000 shares of stock. Subsequently, Landreville was active in supporting the company's bid for the Sudbury franchise. Acting with caution, Landreville did not exercise his option until after he resigned as mayor and had been appointed to the Ontario Supreme Court. He then sold

2500 of the shares to pay for the stock and finally sold the remaining 7500 for a profit of $117,000.

He was charged with municipal corruption and conspiracy, but was acquitted. However, a Royal Commission headed by the late Ivan Rand found that his acceptance of the shares had "odours of scandal," and that his conduct at the securities hearings into the affair was "unworthy of a judge."

The involvement of Landreville and other prominent public figures, including a minister of the Ontario government, in the NONG scandal had been uncovered primarily by the persistence and assiduous digging of a young Sudbury reporter, Blaik Kirby, who later joined the *Star*. One of the results of his reporting was a charge of perjury against Ralph Farris, and it was during his trial that Barry Pepper, who represented Leo Landreville, asked that Kirby be cited for contempt.

The problem grew out of the fact that Kirby was familiar with every aspect of the case. Listening to the testimony, he began to fear that men he knew to be guilty were going to escape judgement. In his zeal he included in his news reports data not given in testimony. On the first occasion, the judge made a general statement to the press, warning them not to report evidence that hadn't been presented in testimony. When Kirby erred again, Mr. Justice Wells called him before the bench and specifically warned him, pointing out that, among other things, his actions might lead to a mistrial. He would not, he said sternly, tolerate any further misreporting, and in the event that it continued, would hold not only Kirby but his employers in contempt.

I couldn't remove Kirby from the assignment; it was *his* story. But neither could I risk another problem. I dispatched another reporter with him whose sole responsibility was to see that Kirby did not include in his reports anything that had not taken place in the courtroom. None the less, Kirby slipped in prejudicial material and we had to excise it.

I took further precautions. Each day I checked Kirby's story in proof form, had it initialed by the reporter who had been in court with Kirby and then initialed it myself. I personally wrote the head, had it proofed and then initialed it. Nothing could go wrong.

Until the day the paper was running late. There was pressure in the composing room to close the page on which the NONG story appeared. So solemn had been the warnings that the story was not to be altered or cut, that when the compositor found himself short of room, he dropped the second line of the heading. The heading had read:

NONG OFFICIAL LIED
RCMP OFFICER SAYS

Without the attribution in the second line, the heading stated that Farris had been found guilt of lying.

When the edition landed on my desk, I turned up the story and saw what had happened. I immediately ran to the composing room, cut enough from the story to make room, replaced the omitted line and replated the page. By checking the counter on the presses, I learned how many copies had been printed. I sent a messenger to Mr. Justice Wells' office with a copy of the edition showing the mistake. With it, I sent a copy of the corrected page and a note stating that only 4800 copies had been printed. The fault was a grievous one, I admitted, but it had been the result of human error, and had immediately been rectified.

Awaiting his response, I sat in my office contemplating an image of myself behind bars. The prospect didn't please. Fortunately, Mr. Wells took a generous view of our foibles.

I was fond of Kirby but he had to be fired. He had been warned a number of times but had disregarded all cautions. I gave him a praiseful letter of reference and he worked for a while in London, England. I reiterated the praise when he applied to the *Globe and Mail* where he distinguished himself as a television critic until his death.

During my years at the *Star*, I maintained close associations with the Liberal party. I could not, of course, participate in party activity and was doubly careful to avoid any partisanship in the news pages. The federal Liberals had returned from the wilderness. They assumed power after the election in April 1963, and immediately executed a series of pratfalls. Among them were the disaster of Walter Gordon's first budget – in its preparation he had used outsiders and almost had to resign – and the almost farcical misadventures of the much hailed "Sixty Days of Decision," in which it seemed each sweep of the new broom created problems.

But their troubles were nothing compared to the Ontario Liberals'. They and the NDP had been rejected by the voters in the

1963 election; even their leader John Wintermeyer lost his seat. The Conservatives, led by John Robarts, were sitting on a fat majority of seventy-seven, holding eighty-five seats to the Liberals' twenty-three and the NDP's eight. In the seventeen elections of the previous sixty years the Liberals had lost all but two won by Mitch Hepburn. In the twenty-one years prior to 1963, there had been seven general elections; the Tories won them all. The Liberals were a fumbling and inept group in the legislature: leaderless, fractious and anything but an effective team. So ineffective were they that, in the most recent election, the traditionally Liberal *Star* had supported the Conservatives.

Then, overnight, the opportunity came to reverse Liberal fortunes, perhaps even to take power. There had been much talk of organized crime in Ontario. The media carried dozens of stories, arguing, without presenting much hard evidence, that Ontario had become a centre of Mafia activity. As well, there had been charges in the legislature – few substantiated – and calls for the Ontario Police Commission to "do something."

The Attorney General in the spring of 1964 was Fred M. Cass, a lawyer from the Cornwall area. He had been under pressure from the police commission – then smarting from press attacks – to provide them with the powers they claimed were necessary to hold organized crime in check. In response, Cass introduced Bill 99, an infamous and ill-conceived piece of legislation that would have granted the police far-ranging and arbitrary powers, including the authority to question suspects secretly and to jail them indefinitely without trial. The reaction was immediate and violent. Bill 99 was dubbed "the police-state bill," and the outrage from every quarter shook the Robarts government to its foundations.

The *Globe and Mail* had first shot at the story and did an excellent job on its news and editorial pages. The government had clearly been caught out, but rather than retrench, it sought with considerable arrogance to brazen it out. On the *Star*, we threw everything at them: stories, features, precedents, editorial cartoons, and with other newspapers, focussed the protests of civil-liberties groups, law societies and the churches. It was a great story and we ran hard with it.

With the first edition out of the way, I telephoned Andy Thompson, the Liberal member for Toronto Dovercourt, with whom I had done some work for the party. Andy was a young lawyer who had entered politics out of a concern for the poor and dispossessed. Of the disparate band of Liberals in the legislature, he seemed the one most likely to rise to the challenge, but on the telephone he seemed bemused, uncertain.

"Andy," I said, "you *must* seize the opportunity. It's straight from heaven. You'll never again have as good a chance to turf out the Tories."

But he continued tentative and hesitant. It was obvious that he hadn't grasped the enormity of the Conservative blunder, nor did he seem able to summon the drive to do anything about it. I pressed him to rise in the evening session of the legislature and to make a speech against the bill. "Fight it, Andy. Even if the Speaker rules you out of order. Even if you are 'named' and banished from the chamber." I almost dictated the speech for him, spelling out the salient points, marshalling the arguments. That evening he rose in the legislature, and after a slow beginning, caught fire. His speech was played large on the front pages of the newspapers.

On March 23, 1964, after five and a half hours of stormy debate, Robarts finally gave in to an incensed Opposition, widespread public outcry and the crumbling loyalty of his own party. He killed the controversial sections of Bill 99 and accepted the resignation of his Attorney General, Fred Cass.

Shortly after the tumult died, Andy Thompson came to my office. His manner was serious. "Chuck," he said, "a few days ago you told me what my responsibility was in the legislature. Now I'm telling you what yours is: it's to take over the leadership of the Ontario Liberal party. You've got to do it; there isn't anybody else. If you'll run, I'll support you, and I'm sure I can get others to do the same."

His proposal came as a surprise to me, and I immediately dismissed it. Even though my Liberal connections had gone underground during my years at the *Star*, I had maintained old friendships within the party, scrupulously keeping the two interests at arm's-length. It was no secret that I planned one day to run for political office, but as my newspaper responsibilities grew, that day had been pushed farther back. Moreover, since the debate of Bill 99, the media had been touting Andy to succeed John Wintermeyer. I advised Andy to go for the leadership, that it was impossible for me to consider it.

But he would not be dissuaded. He continued to press me, listing people he was certain would join him in supporting me if I would run: among them Walter Gordon, then Minister of Finance in the Pearson government, and Keith Davey, the federal party's chief organizer. And he was sure he could persuade a number in the Ontario caucus. "You've got to do it, Chuck," he said. "For the first time in years the Conservatives are vulnerable."

As the days passed, the possibility began to intrigue me. Each night, late, I went on long walks through my neighbourhood, examining the question. As I thought about it, the idea came alive as a possibility. Had there been anyone in the caucus able to do the job, I wouldn't have given it a moment's consideration. The only two possibilities were Thompson and Robert Nixon, the member from Brant, but Andy lacked the qualities of leadership and Bob had performed disappointingly in the debate on the police-state bill. Nor was there anyone in sight beyond the caucus. There was, it seemed, a tide to be taken at the flood.

I had known since I quit the ministry that one day I would run for public office. That was one of the reasons why on my return to Canada I had moved immediately to become active in politics and had joined the Liberal party. But my disposition had always been toward federal politics. It was, I thought, where the action was, where the potential for usefulness was greatest. But I had been having second thoughts. I was beginning to believe that the provincial government was closer to the people and touched lives more immediately.

There was another argument for serving at Queen's Park rather than in Ottawa: I would not have to be away from my family most of the week. This was important to me. Sylvia and I now had four children; the eldest, Deborah, was ten, the youngest, Tyrone, was two. At the *Star* I hadn't gone to the Press Club after working hours. I had quit playing golf when I married because I was spending too much of the weekends on the course. I owned shares in a curling club but had deliberately avoided learning how to play, knowing that I might get hooked. My young family needed me at home; more important, that was where I wanted to be.

I found myself considering what I might be able to accomplish if I were leader of the party. I was still gripped by the idealism that had led me into the ministry. What an opportunity for usefulness politics could provide!

Then, of course, there was my ego. In my naïveté, I didn't doubt that if I ran I would win. Nor did it seem impossible that one day I might be premier of the province. I decided to discuss the matter with Beland Honderich. He was deeply disturbed, and angry. "Charles," he said, "you'll be making a great mistake. You're deluded if you think you can accomplish more for society in politics than you can here. You're in charge of the largest newspaper in Canada. In the *Star* you can crusade for any legitimate cause with more effectiveness than you can in the legislature. Even if you win the Liberal leadership, which is doubtful, the possibility of unseating the Tories is slim. You can spend the next ten years of your life frustrated and powerless on the opposition benches. Years ago, I asked myself the same questions you are asking, and I decided that the best place to exert my influence was here, right here at the *Star*. It was the right decision for me. It's the right decision for you."

At the end of our discussion he said, "You must realize, Charles, that if you go after the leadership you'll have to resign. You can't be a candidate and run the paper. Even if you were to treat the news with total impartiality the public perception would be that it was slanted."

I told him that I would take three days to think it through. I locked the door to my office. My secretary took all telephone calls and sent in lunch. I ran a line down the centre of a piece of paper, and began to list the arguments pro and con, straining for objectivity. I stayed with it ten to twelve hours each day, and went walking alone evenings, pondering. By the third day I was emotionally exhausted but certain of my decision – I would seek the leadership.

I notified Honderich. He was upset but didn't try to dissuade me. Typically, he warned me that my connection with the *Star* would not necessarily mean I would have the *Star*'s support in the political wars. I telephoned Andy Thompson, notified him of my decision and told him the date on which I would announce my resignation. He agreed to hold it in confidence. I had discussed with my wife the possibility of my running for office, but when I told her of my decision, she was displeased. Nor would she, as the weeks went by, become reconciled to it.

Five weeks after Andy Thompson came to see me in my office, I resigned from the *Star*. It was a difficult time. I said a private farewell to Beland and found myself close to tears. The staff presented me with a portrait by Irma Coucill signed by everyone in the newsroom, and there was a party at the Press Club, with a number of prankish memorabilia – a ballot box to be stuffed, a large cardboard carton in which to keep my political promises and some stage-money to be used for bribes. On the final morning, as I passed through the revolving doors and emerged onto King Street, the members of the typographical union were passing out ON STRIKE placards. They waved at me and called out, "Good luck, Charlie!" I returned the wave. None of us knew what a long, hard battle lay ahead or that we would all lose.

II

At the turn of the century, when Joseph E. Atkinson was named editor of the Toronto *Evening Star*, it was the smallest of six newspapers in Toronto. It comprised eight pages, carried advertising on the front page and sold for one cent a copy. During the first half of the century – in an era when newspapers were unchallenged in merchandising the news – it prospered and grew, while three of its competitors disappeared. In 1959, when I joined the *Star*, it had become the largest newspaper in Canada and was undergoing fundamental changes. Today, not twenty-five years later, it is a very different newspaper from the one I was responsible for. By the end of the century, if there is a Toronto *Star*, it will be so changed from today's as to be unrecognizable.

In the early part of the century nearly everbody read newspapers; many read two or three a day. There were no options. Television was decades away. Radio was in its infancy and hadn't yet discovered either the importance or the revenue potential of news. Motion pictures presented weekly "newsreels," as they were called, but the items they carried were few and were more features than news. Daily newspapers had a near monopoly in reporting what was happening at home and around the world.

That day is gone. As the world became a neighbourhood and the news more complex, the media proliferated and the competition to be first and more interesting intensified. With the advent of television, newspapers quickly lost ground and credibility. Public-opinion polls consistently show that newspapers are the least trusted of the major media. In a descending order, respondents find the news most credible on television, radio, magazines and newspapers. I would reverse that order.

Television news is trustworthy, it is believed, because you are yourself witness to the event. ("Look, I *saw* the prime minister say it in the House of Commons.") The presumption is that, in electronic journalism, the event is transmitted directly to the viewer whereas in a newspaper it is received second-hand; reporters intervene and filter it through their biases. The viewer is unaware that the prime minister may have spoken for several minutes and a film editor chose three snippets from his statement and fused them into a seamless thirty-seven-second clip. Except in live coverage of an event, there is no unedited news.

These are bad times for the press. The number of daily newspapers in North America has shrunk dramatically. Nor has circulation kept pace with the growth of population. Advertising dollars are the life blood of the news media and those dollars go where the greatest numbers of bodies are. Today, they are slumped before television sets. Fewer readers mean fewer advertisers, and inevitably fewer newspapers. Let a journal falter and its competition or one of the chains will seize and kill the poor emaciated thing in order to have a clean shot at the available readers. Struggling to stay alive, many publishers have descended to offering their declining readerships a daily diet of sex, sport, crime and human-interest stories, plus the appetizer of a big-buck lottery. For many, it has been a losing battle.

I am not suggesting that newspapers will disappear. The prediction that they would be outmoded and one day made extinct by the electronic delivery of news now seems to have been fatuous. For, in addition to providing a cheap, convenient and easily retrievable "data source," newspapers are an effective medium for advertisers. Newspaper advertising has the advantage of constant availability; it delivers its message at the consumer's convenience and is not gone forever after a brief glimmer on a television screen.

Despite some of the auguries and despite recent history, I am convinced that newspapers will persevere. Their numbers will almost certainly decline. (It seems likely that one of Toronto's three newspapers will die, although it is not yet possible to say which it will be.) However, no newspaper will make it to the year 2001 in any health unless it undergoes radical changes.

The direction of those changes can already be discerned.

Reporting the news will remain fundamental but it will cease to be the dominant concern. The trend will be to more information, information explaining the increasingly complex and often baffling world we live in.

Ours is a sensate age. We are assaulted daily by sights and sounds, most of them increasingly vivid and clamorous. Inevitably, our senses deaden, and to be effective, the assault on them must intensify, the messages being driven home through techniques that simplify the facts even as they exaggerate them. Television is in large part responsible; it has magnified the importance of the picture and has diminished the text. The picture may no longer say more than a thousand words but it does catch the eye, and to gain that benefit the thousand words are made subsidiary.

In the years ahead, newspapers will become more visual and more specialized, a conglomerate of news, pictures and special features aimed at numerous audiences – only one of which will be seeking hard news. They will no longer offer only the traditional sections (Women's, Sports, Business and Classified); more specific targeting will be practised. The daily newspaper will become a daily magazine.

One can already see the front page of many newspapers being transformed into magazine covers. The tabloids have long featured one dramatic picture, a provocative headline, an index and nothing more. Others commit much of the front page to a glorified table of contents often labelled *Inside*, like a circus barker touting the attractions within. The index has become akin to what television calls "the teaser," singing a siren song of pleasures ahead.

The newspaper of the future is visible in embryo. The weekend editions of many newspapers carry little news, not only because there is less important news on weekends, but because they see themselves as more than a newspaper. They have become a package of mini-magazines designed for readers with more leisure time, readers who want to catch up on and put in context the important events of the week past and to pick and choose from among a variety of articles touching on special interests. While only beginning to realize its potential, today's weekend paper is the pattern from which the future daily will be cut.

It will be a fundamental mistake if newspapers ape electronic journalism. Television has borrowed much from the print media and is still imitative, principally because most of its news and documentary people began in print. It will improve only when the people who run it are children of the electronic medium and not print. The same is true of newspapers. The newspapers that fold will do so in part because they fail to make the most of their intrinsic advantages, which are many.

Inside Politics

INSIDE POLITICS

I

In October 1952, John Diefenbaker offered me a guaranteed seat in the House of Commons. It was my first experience of Canadian politics.

I met the man who would be the Progressive Conservative leader when I returned to Regina, the city of my childhood, to conduct a fifteen-day preaching mission for the Council of Churches. It was "home-coming week" for me and I made much of it. So did the media. Diefenbaker was not yet leader of the party but he was planning to be, and he happened to be in Regina during my campaign. On the Sunday night, with about 3,000 present, he was invited to sit on the platform. Afterwards, we went together to a small social gathering in a private home.

Dief had been much impressed by the service, and after a few minutes, he drew me aside for a private conversation. He urged me to return to Canada ("Great things are afoot") and to become active in politics. He emphasized that he wasn't denigrating the importance of the ministry – making the point that he was a Baptist and active as a layman – but he insisted that, if a man truly wanted to serve his fellows, the place to get things done was in politics.

He made me this proposition: "Return to Canada, join the Progressive Conservative party and I'll guarantee you a seat in the House of Commons." He was certainly able to keep the promise: he was in absolute control of the party in Saskatchewan, where the Tories held every federal seat. Only half in jest, I quoted Martin Luther, "God forbid that I should slip from being a priest to become a king." He laughed and clapped me on a shoulder. As the evening ended, he said at the door, "If you change your mind, come and see me."

I have been fascinated by politics since the 1930s when I watched Mitch Hepburn, then premier of Ontario, utterly entrance a crowd of about one thousand at a Liberal rally in Toronto. I was there to draw his portrait for the *Globe and Mail*. In my years in the United States, I hero-worshipped Franklin Roosevelt and especially Harry Truman. In the 1952 and 1956 presidential elections, I worked for Adlai Stevenson. (I was a resident alien and couldn't vote, but I offered my services and passed out campaign literature in downtown Manhattan.) If you cared about words and ideas, Stevenson was a particularly attractive political figure. It seemed imperative that a man with such intellect and idealism be elected president. Today I have no doubt that he would have been a disaster as president. He seemed congenitally incapable of making the tough decisions.

In 1957, only weeks after my return to Toronto, I moved to become active in the politics of my own country. I read in the newspapers that the Liberal party of Ontario was holding a leadership convention at Toronto's King Edward hotel. Knowing no one, I slipped unobtrusively into the Crystal Ballroom to watch the proceedings. I was recognized by a few delegates because of my television appearances and they shook my hand. Among them was Keith Davey. I watched as the final vote tallies were announced and John Wintermeyer was elected leader.

The following week I was invited to lunch by Paul Hellyer. He had been Associate Minister of Defence and, only months before, had gone down to defeat with the St. Laurent government. He pressed me to join the Liberal party. Their prospects were anything but prepossessing: the federal wing had just suffered its worst defeat in history and the Ontario Liberals had been out of power for twenty-seven years.

The following day I was again invited to lunch, by coincidence at the same table in the same dining room of the same hotel, the Westbury. I was the guest of Donald MacDonald, the leader of the CCF in Ontario. I'd voted CCF once; in the 1940s when E.B. Jolliffe was leader of the party. MacDonald and I talked about Norman Thomas, the brilliant American socialist-idealist, whom I admired, and about Sam Gompers, the heroic early labour organizer. We discussed Bernard Shaw and the Fabians, compared politics in the United States and Canada and talked about the hopes of Canadian socialists. I liked MacDonald but was not impressed by what he had to say.

I am not by disposition a Conservative, so I didn't contact John Diefenbaker. The following week, after an extended discussion with Keith Davey, I joined the Liberal party.

Davey was then a time salesman at a small Toronto radio station, CKFH; in his spare time, he was president of the Toronto and Yorks Liberal Association. We established an immediate rapport. We were both fascinated by the political process and liked politicians, and while we were both idealists, we relished the back-room activity of organizing and building the party. Davey was a leading member of an informal organization of Toronto Liberals known as Cell 13 who met regularly to work for the return to power of a reformed Liberal party. An untried newcomer, I was not a member of the group, all of whom had been blooded in earlier electoral battles, but none the less busied myself with party activity, mostly in association with Davey.

Together, we organized and were co-chairmen of what we called the School for Practical Politics. (The approach was later adopted nationally under the title Campaign College.) The weekly meetings of the "school" were hardnosed teaching sessions spiced by light-hearted camaraderie. "Old pols" taught party workers the fundamentals: door-to-door canvassing, riding organization, fund-raising and promotion and so on. The classes marked the beginning of the revitalizing of the party in Toronto.

Only months before, Liberal fortunes had hit bottom. John Diefenbaker's Conservative party won 75 per cent of the seats in the Commons, including a majority in Quebec, amassing the largest parliamentary majority in Canadian history: 108 seats to the Liberals' 67. The press of the nation blew Taps over the Grits' grave.

But the Liberals were not without hope, and his name was Lester Bowles Pearson. Did anyone ever come to politics whose credentials shone more brightly? He had taught history at the University of Toronto. He had been Canada's senior advisor at the Dumbarton Oaks and San Francisco conferences that led to the formation of the United Nations, and he had headed Canada's delegation to the new peace body. In 1947, as chairman of the United Nations Political and Security Committee, he had played a decisive role in mediating the Palestine crisis. No sooner was he elected to the Canadian parliament than he was appointed minister of External Affairs and was instrumental in the formation of the North Atlantic Treaty Organization in 1957. That same year he was awarded the Nobel peace prize for his work in resolving the 1956 Arab-Israeli war. Beyond all this, he was an unpretentious, warm, gregarious man who freely confessed that he would rather coach a major-league baseball team than be Secretary General of the United Nations.

And yet. . . . When he rose to speak at a public function, one's soaring expectations were suddenly earthbound. His self-deprecating wit fell flat. His lisp, barely noticeable in private conversation, was accentuated by tension. Speaking in public, he had a way of closing his eyes, and of lolling his head back and to one side that appeared almost spastic. Ringing phrases became prosaic on his lips. Often, when he summoned indignation or reached for outrage, his sentences collapsed in boneless ineffectuality. Pearson didn't sound like a politician because he wasn't a politician. His genius was as a conciliator, solving problems, working with people. Loyal Liberals covered their dismay, and tried to reassure themselves: Pearson's sure touch would soon be evident; his lack of slickness would become an advantage as people grew accustomed to him and were able to measure him against the overblown bombast of John Diefenbaker. "If the Canadian people could only meet Mike face to face in small groups," we used to say, "he would carry the country by the largest margin in history."

No one believed this with greater conviction than Keith Davey. Davey is given to hero worship. (For the past twenty-five years he has committed himself unswervingly to Pearson, Walter Gordon and Pierre Trudeau – although in the latter case, one suspects there is more loyalty than affection in the fealty.) Beyond all that, Davey was a dedicated Liberal and it was inevitable that he be summoned to Ottawa to use his exceptional skills as an organizer on behalf of the party.

I was at a small luncheon for journalists and Mike Pearson was doing what he enjoyed doing: telling stories, especially stories about great events or great men in which the unexpected and, ideally, the humorous happened.

I had asked him to describe the difference in dealing with John Kennedy and Lyndon Johnson.

"The first time I met Kennedy," he said, brightening (he had been listless earlier responding to questions about the problems of his government) "was at Hyannis Port. The Kennedy clan summered there. It was an official meeting, a putting on the table matters of concern and areas of conflict between our two countries.

"Kennedy arrived at the appointed time with a dozen aides, each of them carrying a fat attaché case, and we sat down in a sunny place to talk. The Americans had prepared an agenda and Kennedy had been very carefully briefed. The interesting thing was that he had it all in his head. He knew more about some of the issues than I did and had some facts about Canada that were news to me." Pearson chuckled. "I'd only been in office three weeks – at any rate, that was my excuse. Kennedy was cordial and witty, but all business. We accomplished a lot.

"Lyndon Johnson," he said with a laugh, "was the antithesis. This time the shoe was on the other foot; he'd been in office only two months. We met at the White House. He had his aides, too, a lot of them. But we'd no sooner sat down than he said, 'Look, Mike, let's you and I slip into the next room for a few minutes and leave these guys to get started.'

"The next room," Pearson said, "was a small sitting-room. We pulled up comfortable chairs. Lyndon poured some coffee. Very relaxed, very informal. He said, 'Now Mike, they tell me you're not too happy about certain things, certain problems between our two countries. I don't know a hell of a lot about the problems, whatever they are, but why don't we do this: you tell me what you would like to see done that I can do without doing a disservice to the American people, and I'll see that it's done.'"

Pearson tossed back his head and laughed at the memory. "We were having serious problems on the Great Lakes at the time – rivalries in the Seafarers' International. There had been a number of shootings and some violence. I wanted to see it stopped. At seven the following morning, I was told later, Johnson picked up a telephone and called Paul Hall, head of the Seafarers' union. 'Paul,' he said, 'I'd like to have breakfast with you here at the White House this morning. I'm sending a car around.' Hall came to breakfast, of course, and LBJ told him of our conversation. 'Paul,' he said, 'I'd like you to put a stop to all this – you hear me now?'" Pearson laughed again. "And it stopped," he said.

When you interviewed Pearson, he would frequently seem disconcertingly vague and withdrawn, but in private conversation he exuded great warmth. Once, late in his life, we talked sports in his suite at the Inn on the Park for the better part of an hour. (The early part of the hour had been spent talking about his exasperation with some aspects of Methodism; his father had been a clergyman.) He had extraordinary recall, especially about baseball, and we traded recollections. When it was time for him to leave to make a speech somewhere in the hotel, he seemed almost poignantly reluctant to drop the subject.

Among Pearson's ministers I knew Paul Hellyer best, although we were not close friends. I saw him often, worked for him in Trinity riding when he sought to be returned to parliament, and in later years, did a weekly television show with him for five seasons. For all our frequent association I have never felt close to Paul. He is an earnest Christian and is, I think, offended by my unapologetic agnosticism. He is a contained man, not given to easy camaraderie, and is certainly not the affable glad-hander politicians are thought to be.

When he was Minister of Defence, Hellyer was asked to speak at a testimonial dinner that the late George Ben, a feisty and aggressive Toronto alderman, decided to hold for himself. I acted as master of ceremonies. The locale was the Palais Royale on the Toronto waterfront. At one point in his speech, Hellyer, extemporizing, was making comparisons between Canada and the United States.

"The United States," he declared, "is a melting pot. People have emigrated there from all over the world and have blended in one whole. Canada, too, has grown through immigration, but we are not a melting pot. We are . . . " He paused, seeking an appropriate analogy. "We are more like . . . more like . . ." And now he had it. "Canada is more like a Christmas cake; you put in the fruits and you add the nuts." He stopped, sensing that something had gone amiss but not quite sure what. A woman at the head table loosed a guffaw, and the rest of us, who had been restraining it, exploded with laughter. After a moment, Paul joined in.

II

Having made the decision to leave the *Star* and seek the leadership of the Liberal party in Ontario, I was immediately confronted by the fact that it was not welcomed by the party brass. Inevitably, word of my decision leaked to the press and, although I had not yet resigned, my impending entry in the leadership stakes made news; there were stories in all the papers. Opposition within the party to the "outsider" was soon manifest, and my initial backer, Andy Thompson, began to lose his zeal. He continued to reiterate his support but reported to me more often than was necessary his friends' insistence that he himself become a candidate.

He pressed me to meet secretly with a group of prominent Toronto Liberals. They included, as I recall it, Senator Dan Lang, Richard Stanbury, president of the Toronto and Yorks Association, David Anderson, treasurer of the Ontario party and others. It was soon evident that the purpose of the meeting was to dissuade me from running, and failing that, to convince me that I should release Andy from his commitment. Each of them made it clear, even if obliquely, that he would not support me, and all advised me that I could not possibly win the leadership.

As the days passed, it became obvious that Andy wanted out. He might have stayed loyal, despite the pressure, but I could see that if I insisted he keep his pledge – the pledge that had stimulated my entry into the race – he would be a reluctant champion. In Ottawa on business, I had time to kill and found a secluded corner on the mezzanine at the Château Laurier. After an hour or so reviewing the situation, I found a pay telephone and told Andy that he was released. He wasted little time, announcing his candidacy the following day, three days before my scheduled press conference.

The press conference was a disaster. The suite I had rented at the Royal York hotel was jammed with reporters and cameramen. I was very nervous and stumbled in my responses. I fudged on tough questions, and there were plenty of them. A former managing editor, I was a tempting target. Asked, for instance, whether, having become an agnostic, I still went to church, I said yes. But when asked where, my mind drew a blank, and after stalling and dodging about for a minute or two, I had to turn to my wife for an answer. It was a hostile grilling, but not unfair, and I went from it in despair, certain that I had done my candidacy irreparable harm.

On my final day at the *Star*, I received a telephone call from Elmer Sopha, the member of the legislature for Sudbury, asking to see me in my office. I had never met him, but knew him to be a

maverick in the Liberal caucus. He arrived with his coat collar up
and a hat pulled over his eyes. He began by informing me that he
had changed taxis twice on his way from Queen's Park and had
left the cab three blocks from the *Star* building. Bemused, I waited
to hear the reason for his visit. "I've decided," he said in a conspira-
torial whisper, "that I'm going to support you for the leadership." I
was grateful: a poll of the Liberal caucus taken by the *Telegram* had
shown that no one else would. He put his coat on, pulling up his
collar, set his hat low over his eyes and skulked out of the office,
warning me to say nothing to anyone. The following day I picked
up a newspaper to see that, not an hour later, he had himself
broken the news to a reporter at the legislature.

Discouragement bottomed out ten days later at the annual
meeting of the party. The most important matter on the agenda
was the setting of a date for a leadership convention. Prior to the
meeting, the consensus was for a date in the late fall 1964 or
spring 1965 to give the riding associations time to elect their delegates and the candidates sufficient time to tour the province.
But the party brass moved in. The management committee recommended that the convention be held September 17 to 19, leaving
only the difficult summer holiday months for campaigning. In the
debate over the date, there were frequent references to "so-called
messiahs" and comments about the dangers of personality cults.
The vote wasn't close and the recommendation was adopted. The
newspapers saw it as a victory for the establishment and as the
sounding of a death knell over my chances.

Overnight, the contest for the leadership became a major continuing story in the press. The prize had not seemed a desirable one,
but it now became evident that there would be a number of con-
testants. The Toronto papers, especially, provided detailed coverage, and I received more than my share. I make no complaint
other than to note that the stories tended to focus on me rather
than on what I was advocating. In every report or feature I was
tagged in the lead paragraph as "a former evangelist" or as a
"television personality" – often with the addendum, "married to
television singer, Sylvia Murphy." Almost never was I referred
to as "a former newspaper editor." There was frequent reference
to the fact that I was divorced. All these were facts, of course, and
it is standard media practice to identify people with convenient

catch phrases. Unfortunately, for a candidate running for political office in the 1960s, they all had a pejorative ring.

Late in the campaign, I said to John Bassett, "Why in hell does your paper invariably describe me as a former evangelist?" "Do we?" he said. "I'll soon put a stop to that."

The contest began to attract national attention, and from far-off Newfoundland Joey Smallwood got into the act.

I had stated in a speech that the last time Ontario Liberals had been in office was during the Depression, and that it might take another such crisis to return them to power. Somehow, this was reported in the press as an expression of hope that Canada suffer another Depression so that the Liberal party might get in. A week or so later, I received a telephone call from a radio station in St. John's.

"The premier has just attacked you in the Throne speech."

"Attacked *me*? What about?"

"Apparently you said you hoped there'd be another Depression so the Liberals could get back in power. Mr. Smallwood said that, if you're a Liberal, he's not, and so forth. He really got hot about it."

Joey, ever the political opportunist, I thought.

"He went on to say that when you were here in St. John's, there was a lot of talk about what a great speaker you were, so he went around to Gower Street church to hear you. He said he stood at the back and he wasn't much impressed. I was wondering if you'd like to reply."

They love political controversy in Newfoundland, more perhaps than anywhere in Canada, even controversy so obviously made of whole cloth as this one. "Yes," I said to the reporter, "I'd love to play Joey's game."

He switched on the tape recorder. "I'm interested to hear that Mr. Smallwood found it useful to attack me on what he knows must be a misquotation," I said. "No Liberal, not even one of the Newfoundland variety, would want to see another Depression, for any reason. I can only think that, if the premier took the time to attack me in the Throne speech, it must be a pretty thin speech, with not much in it for the people of Newfoundland.

"I'm interested to learn," I continued, "that Mr. Smallwood

attended one of my meetings in St. John's. He says he wasn't much impressed. I've heard Mr. Smallwood many times and have *never* been impressed."

I hung up knowing that they'd love it in the outports, and that Joey would love it, too.

There were seven candidates finally but only four of us were taken seriously. In a blaze of publicity we began to criss-cross the province speaking to riding associations, in search of delegate votes. The leading candidates were Andy Thompson, the front runner and the man with the support of the party brass, and Bob Nixon, a big-handed, gregarious Brantford farmer whose father had briefly been premier of the province in the 1930s. Their most serious rival was Joe Greene, the federal member of parliament from Renfrew-North, a clever and witty speaker who would play a decisive role in the convention. The others were Eddie Sargeant, an MPP from Owen Sound, Vic Copps, the mayor of Hamilton, who didn't campaign much and seemed to be in the race for the notoriety it might provide in his forthcoming bid for a federal seat, and Joe Gould, MPP for Toronto-Bracondale.

I had begun to win delegates, but not many, and I went to Ottawa to see if I could gain the backing of someone who would give substance to my campaign. I went first to see Paul Hellyer, and asked him outright for his support. His response taught me something about political debts.,

"Charles," he said, "I think you're the best man for the job – although I worry about your lack of experience. But I can't support you; I'm committed to Joe Gould." (Gould had no chance to win and would finally garner only 13 of the eventual 1,370 votes cast.)

"But isn't that a waste of your vote?" I asked. "Gould hasn't a snowball's chance. You agree that the party urgently needs strong leadership and that it won't come from any of the other candidates. So if, as you say, I'm the man for the job, support me. I need someone's advocacy."

"I'm sorry," he said. "I *have* to support Gould."

"But why waste your vote?"

"Because," he said, "Gould's provincial riding overlaps my federal riding and he has worked for me at election time. I owe it to him."

Judy LaMarsh, the Minister of Health and Welfare, was

equally direct. "I think you'd make a good leader, but I can't support you. I don't know who I'll vote for – Thompson probably. Maybe Nixon, although I don't think either of them will do much. Davey thinks Andy's the right choice and wants me to back him. He doesn't impress me as a leader, but he's worked hard for both Mike and Walter [Gordon]."

One of the rewards of junketing about the province was picking up the trail of Mitch Hepburn, the St. Thomas, Ontario, onion-farmer who had been the Liberal premier in the 1930s during the Great Depression. What astounded me was the vividness with which he was remembered. Old-timers would talk to me about him, about his skills as an orator and about the controversial things he did, and their faces would be illuminated by the memory:

> Like the time Mitch came to this little one-horse town and stood on the steps of the town hall. And all the shy people from out in the boondocks came to the edges of the square and wouldn't move in closer. And how there was no sound-system and everybody was worried that nobody'd be able to hear him. And how, instead of shouting, Mitch began to talk in a normal voice, all the while with his hands held out and the fingers moving, moving in a sort of beckoning way. And as he talked, the people slowly drifting in until they were crowded all around him. . . .

> When Mitch was on tour, he would get in the car in the morning, all bright-eyed and bushy-tailed, and put a little bag, like a doctor's black bag, in the back seat and tell whoever was driving him, "Now look here" – he'd be laughing and full of ginger – "don't let me touch that bag back there until I've finished what I've got to do today." And then, after the first meeting, he'd come back to the car, all bouncy and excited at the way he'd had the crowd in the palm of his hand, and so on. And he'd get in the car and reach back for the bag. "Maybe we'll just have one. A little one. I think I earned it, don't you?" And it would go that way from town to town until Mitch was snoring in the back seat and somebody had to sub for him.

> There was the time when Mitch was coming here to speak and it had been advertised for weeks and people were planning on

coming from miles around. And the man who owned the hockey rink was a Tory and he wouldn't rent out the rink. And somebody told Mitch the meeting was going to have to be cancelled and Mitch said, "The hell it is!" and got a big circus tent from somewhere – God knows where in the summer on short notice – and the word went out and he had about three times as many as he'd of been able to get in the rink anyway.

Mitch used to blame the whole damn Depression on the Tories in general and poor old George Henry, the premier, in particular. The Depression was happening all over the world, but when Mitch got through you'd've thought it was something the Tories invented over at Queen's Park.

Believe me, there was nobody anywhere could talk like Mitch. He'd take a crowd that had been sitting waiting in this hot, sweaty hall for more'n an hour and inside five minutes he'd have them splitting their sides or sitting with their mouths open like a dying fish. He could go on for more'n an hour and nobody'd move. Even the babies quit crying. . . .

It soon became obvious that I couldn't win unless I made a move that would counter the strongest argument against me: I had never run for political office, and if I did win the leadership, I wouldn't have a seat in the legislature. I decided to make a move that couldn't be gainsaid. I picked up a telephone and called John Bassett at the *Telegram*.

"John," I said, "I have a marvellous Machiavellian idea and I want to talk to you about it."

"Machiavellian?" he said. "That's the best kind. Come on over."

John had already proven himself a friend. When I had announced my resignation from the *Star,* he immediately called me.

"Why are you leaving the *Star*?" he asked.

"Because it's Honderich's view, and mine, that I can't continue to run the paper while seeking the leadership of the Liberal party. It would make everything I do here suspect."

"Nonsense," he roared. "I ran for parliament in Spadina while I was publisher of the *Telegram.*"

"Nevertheless, that's Beland's feeling."

"Come and work at the *Tely*," Bassett said. "It won't bother me. If you win, okay, you can quit."

I thanked him but said no. He immediately ran an editorial advocating my election, arguing that it was the only sensible choice for a party in deep trouble – a gesture much appreciated by me but making me even more suspect to some Liberals.

"Well now," he said, "what's this Machiavellian plan of yours?"

"I want you to use your influence to get John Robarts to call a by-election in Riverdale prior to the leadership convention. If he calls it, I'll run. If I win, I'll have proven myself a vote-getter and I'll have a seat in the legislature. Otherwise," I said, "I'm dead."

"But you can't win Riverdale," he said. "It's a Tory riding."

The evidence was certainly there. Robert Macauly, who had resigned the seat only six months earlier, had won the previous election by a 3800-vote majority. The Tories had held the riding for the past thirty years, usually winning easily. When they had been beaten it had been by the NDP, but each of those victories had been aberrations as quickly overturned. The Liberals had won once, but usually finished a distant third. The odds against were great but I had decided that my only chance was to go for broke.

"If I lose, I lose," I said. "I'm going to lose the convention anyway. The only hope I have is to demonstrate what I can do, and the only way that can be done is in Riverdale."

John was pondering. "I'd certainly love to see you kick the Grits in the ass," he said, "but I'm a loyal Tory. I've got to satisfy myself that calling the by-election doesn't do a disservice to my party." He suddenly brightened. "I've got it: Robarts is worried about you being across the floor in the legislature, so I tell him we knock you off in Riverdale. I *like* it!"

He told his secretary to get the premier on the phone. In a moment, his telephone buzzed.

"John," he said, "I know you people are worried about the possibility of Templeton taking over the Grits. I've been thinking: the best way to make sure that doesn't happen is to call the by-election in Riverdale, and call it before their leadership convention. Templeton's on the record that if you do, he'll run. You can throw in the troops, knock him off and he'll be finished."

Bassett winked at me. It was obvious that Robarts was warming to the suggestion. Within a week he announced by-elections in Riverdale and in Windsor-Sandwich, which was also vacant. The date chosen was September 7, ten days before the Liberal leadership convention.

My introduction to Riverdale was sobering. There was no organization. The riding was run as a holding operation by an amiable innocent of grade-school education and no political skills who wasn't sure he wanted me in the riding. Nor did the one Liberal with any political organization – Fred Beavis, a long-time "old-guard" member of Toronto's city council. He greeted the announcement that I was going to seek the nomination by saying to the press, "We don't need Templeton here." Nonetheless, I won the nomination after a fight and set out to win the by-election.

Running concurrently for the provincial leadership and in the by-election, I had to divide my time. The combined tasks led to sixteen-hour days. I was up mornings before six in order to be at the street-car stops, shaking hands with people in the riding as they went to work. The remainder of the day was spent trudging the streets knocking on doors, "mainstreeting" or doing some of the multitudinous tasks that are part of running for political office. Money had to be raised. Speeches had to be prepared and delivered. Campaign literature had to be written, printed and distributed. Door-to-door canvasses of each house in the riding had to be organized and carried out. Our small and valiant band had to be divided in two: one group to work in Riverdale, the other to pursue the leadership. Such time as I could spare from the riding was spent in driving or flying to all-candidates' meetings across the province. In addition, at home there was the unremitting opposition of my wife, who viewed the decision to run for office as an abandonment of our family.

The pressures intensified. The Conservatives nominated Ken Waters, a pleasant fellow born in the riding, living in the riding and doing business in the riding. (He was a florist.) The Tories assigned their best organizer to the campaign and sent in the troops. John Robarts came into the riding twice as did a covey of cabinet ministers. Bob Macauly, the former member for Riverdale, added his considerable influence. Overnight, a forest of "Vote for Ken Waters" signs sprang up on lawns throughout the riding.

But the real heat came from the New Democrats. They mounted a campaign that was a model of political action, headed by Stephen Lewis. New Democrats flocked to the cause from across and beyond Metro Toronto. Before they were finished, they had completed three canvasses of the riding and knew exactly where the vote was. The candidate, Jim Renwick, was tireless. He had been at work months before the by-election was called and, in the course of the campaign, had knocked on every door. On election day, workers poured in from across the city to deliver the vote to the polling stations. Labour unions sent workers and provided transportation. It was a brilliant campaign, the plan for which subsequently was incorporated in a handbook and used in other by-elections in other places.

My campaign began to founder. The local organization was virtually non-existent. Those who came from outside the riding worked with admirable zeal but they were few. Many Liberals who might in other circumstances have come in to help were loath to do so; they were backing other candidates and didn't want to see me get the leg-up that a win in Riverdale would give. Some of the candidates made token appearances (Nixon worked hardest) but little more than that. Andy Thompson knocked on a few doors.

I didn't realize how badly I was trailing. Two things misled me. My high profile in the media led people to greet me warmly on the street and on their doorsteps, and a sampling purchased from Elliot-Haynes, a professional polling organization, showed me well in the lead. (Their figures indicated the exact reverse of what would happen on voting day. When, after the campaign, I paid my bills, I sent them a note saying, "Any reputable company does business on the basis of 'Goods satisfactory or money refunded.' You were so utterly wrong, I refuse to pay you a dime.")

The auguries were there, plainly to be read. Waters and Renwick lawn-signs outnumbered mine five to one. We had planned two canvasses of the riding but had been unable to accomplish one. We wasted money on a great picnic, with clowns and balloons and fireworks and free hot dogs. Three thousand came – 80 per cent of them children. Daily, our campaign headquarters was jammed with people laughing, talking and drinking coffee. Waters' and Renwick's committee rooms were empty; their workers were out canvassing.

The newspaper coverage dealt principally with personalities and with peripheral issues. Much was made of the fact that I was divorced. My leaving the ministry also received disproportionate attention. Both the *Star* and the *Telegram* devoted a full page to a discussion of the subject, asking whether an agnostic should be the leader of a political party. So much was made of it that Al Forrest, then the editor of the United Church *Observer* and a syndicated newspaper columnist, made a spirited defence on my behalf.

Early in the campaign, the *Globe and Mail* called for a full discussion of the issues, warning that the leadership race should not be a mere matter of different personalities. But neither the *Globe* nor the other papers made any serious attempt to report the discussion of the issues. In Riverdale, neither Renwick nor Waters dealt with the issues or specified what they would seek to do if elected. I held three public meetings, addressing myself to problems in the riding and in the province. The halls were crowded – mostly with the converted, I fear – but the press didn't report a line of what was said.

Nor was the electorate interested in the issues. The one lively concern I encountered as I went about the riding was the introduction by the Pearson government of a new Canadian flag – a federal issue. The question most asked of me when I knocked on doors was, "What are you goddamn Liberals doing to our flag?"

I record all this not because I resent it or believe it was the reason I lost. It was not. It is worth noting, however, because it illustrates how unimportant issues are in contemporary politics and how swift is the change of standards in a modern society. Nowadays, many candidates for public office are divorced. There are a number of men in politics who have left the ministry or left the church. Little or no attention is paid.

I was only just abed one night when the telephone roused me. It was Phil Givens. Givens is now Metropolitan Toronto Police Commissioner; he was then mayor of Toronto. During my early years in the Liberal party, he and I had become friends. We shared a love for politics, for words and for the techniques of public speaking. Later, when I was at the *Star*, he often telephoned, usually to talk about some knotty problem he was facing at city hall. Evenings, I often went to his home for a late snack or a drink. When he brought Henry Moore to Toronto for the installation of his "The Archer" in Nathan Phillips Square, he invited me to a private lunch with him and Moore.

Now, on the telephone, he sounded depressed. "Chuck," he said, fatigue in his voice, "let me tell you what I've been doing tonight. I've attended three public functions, the last one a community picnic. All evening long I've been making inane conversation, grinning like a fool and laughing at bad jokes – in other words, being mayor of Toronto. As I was leaving the picnic, absolutely bushed, I was stopped three times by three absolutely certifiable idiots. They wanted to talk to me – about sewers and pot-holes and noisy neighbours – I'm so tired I can't even remember what they said. I was standing there, nodding and smiling and making responses, dying to get home to my wife and family, talking to people who – and God knows I'm no snob – to people who, if I weren't in politics, I wouldn't spend five seconds with."

"While this was going on," he continued, "I was thinking: get on the phone and call Chuck Templeton. He's doing the same thing; nodding and smiling and shaking hands with those fringe people whose one mission in life seems to be to bug politicians. Chuck, what I'm saying is this: they're going to beat you – the party, I mean. You're going to lose."

"No Phil," I said. "I'm going to win."

"No you're not," he said flatly. "The deck is stacked against you. Regardless, the reason I called is to tell you I'm not sure it's worth it. The one thing I don't want to see happen is for the party to wipe your nose in it. Okay? Now go back to sleep."

The tension on voting day was intolerable. I had announced that if I was defeated I would withdraw from the leadership contest, so everything was at stake. I was too taut to hang about the campaign headquarters and went for a walk along the Danforth. The people passing in the street smiled in a friendly fashion, but even as they did, I noticed that most of them averted their eyes. I said nothing to my workers, hoping against hope, but knew in my gut that the day was lost.

We gathered that night in Player Hall for the vote. There was a buffet and drinks and much convivial excitement. I was surrounded by reporters and cameramen. Minutes after eight o'clock the votes began to be tallied on a blackboard. Renwick went immediately into the lead; I fell quickly behind. Thirty-nine minutes later, I conceded. My two eldest children, Deborah and

Michael, were in tears, as were many of my workers. The victory party became a wake. My political career was over before it had begun.

There was a *coup de grâce*. The following morning, I went by my campaign headquarters to pick up some personal belongings. I was greeted with the news that a dozen heavy-duty staplers (used to post campaign signs) had been stolen, as had a radio, a large coffee urn and other valuables. My treasurer was busy at an adding machine. He gave a rueful shake of his head and said, "It's an estimate, of course, but it looks like, here in Riverdale alone, you're about sixteen thousand dollars in debt."

Within days, the picture changed. I had formally withdrawn from the leadership contest, but a group of my supporters, headed by Clem Neiman, a Mississauga lawyer and my campaign chairman, refused to accept the decision. A Draft Templeton committee was formed and found an extraordinary manifestation of commitment: delegates from across the province telephoned or sent wires insisting that I remain in the race, vowing that if I did withdraw, they would vote for no other candidate. I had no knowledge of what was happening; I had retreated to a cottage on Georgian Bay "to lay me down and weep awhile." Neiman telephoned to tell me that, when I returned, he would present me with a list of more than 250 delegates irrevocably committed to me.

I was astonished. Thompson and Nixon hadn't been claiming more than three hundred to four hundred first-ballot votes. I told Neiman that if he could provide me with specific names and concrete evidence that they intended to vote for me, I would reconsider my withdrawal. But, I cautioned him, no pretense, no engineered draft.

Three days later I returned to Toronto. The following morning I met with the Draft Templeton committee at my home. Outside the house, the media milled about, some lounging in their cars, others gathered in groups on the lawn. Neiman and the committee presented the evidence: a stack of telegrams, a record of more than two hundred telephone calls and a list of 234 bona fide delegates pledged to support me.

I wanted very much to re-enter the race. I had campaigned for two and a half months. I had criss-crossed the province, working from dawn through the late-night hours. My weight had dropped from 208 to 186 pounds. I was in debt for thousands of dollars. (At the end of a political campaign, a candidate is legally responsible for any debts assumed in his or her name and cannot write off the indebtedness as an income-tax deduction.) In those weeks of intense effort, I had developed strongly held convictions about the state of the party. I wanted very much to put those views to the convention. I no longer believed I could win, but I did believe I had earned the right to speak to the party.

Neiman went out to invite the press into the house. My wife, who had been listening to the discussion with the committee, signalled to me, her face grim. I went with her to a small room off the kitchen.

"Are you back in the race?" she asked.

"Yes," I said. "I owe it to the people who are backing me. But more than that, I want the opportunity to address the convention. I can't do that if I'm not a candidate."

"Then let me warn you," she said. "If you go out there and announce that you are again a candidate, I will tell the press, the moment you're through, that I have an announcement to make. I will announce publicly that I'm suing you for divorce, and that you are a poor husband and father." Her face was contorted with anger. "Believe me, Chuck, I mean it!"

Neiman was banging on the door. "Charles! They're waiting."

In the dining room the floodlights were dazzling. The room overflowed with reporters and cameramen and equipment. I went to a chair set at the head of the table. Sylvia came and stood to my immediate right. I made a statement, giving my reasons for returning to the fray.

The report in the *Telegram* read:

> Sitting at his dining-room table, tense and rarely smiling in front of more than a dozen newsmen . . . the man who has inspired thousands from the pulpit and has showed that he can generate a similar enthusiasm at political meetings was strangely subdued. . . .

After a few questions and answers, I said, "Well men, that's it. That's all I have to say."

There was a momentary silence. I held my breath, waiting for

Sylvia to speak, envisioning the headlines. Nothing happened.

The convention broke new ground and was given unprecedented coverage by the press. It borrowed the hype and hoopla, the hi-jinks and zany, boisterous celebration of American presidential nominating conventions. There were costumes and funny hats and badges and balloons, roisterous singing and late-night drinking – and, of course, wall-to-wall politicking.

My re-entry into the race changed things. When I withdrew, there had been a scramble for my delegates and various claims as to where they had gone. But now we were back to where we'd been ten days earlier, with Andy Thompson claiming a first-ballot victory, Bob Nixon saying he would take it in three and Joe Greene arguing that, inasmuch as he was now the only man who could win against the Tories, he would finally emerge on top. There was agreement on only one thing: because I'd been defeated in Riverdale, I was a spent force.

The first opportunity the fifteen hundred delegates had to assess us together came on the opening day. The Liberal University Association invited the seven candidates to address them. When the session was over, the press made soundings and concluded that I had made gains. Seven of Thompson's delegates had switched to me, as had four of Nixon's. My people estimated that I had probably picked up eighteen votes.

At least I wasn't being counted out.

Several senior cabinet ministers and party officials were much in evidence – as the saying has it, twisting arms. Keith Davey moved about the hotel arguing Andy Thompson's case. Walter Gordon, Mitchell Sharp, Paul Martin and others were buttonholing delegates. Judy LaMarsh was interviewed on radio. "Ontario needs a leader not tied up in Ottawa or at Queen's Park," she said. "Somebody who's free to travel the province and build up an organization." That could only mean me or Vic Copps and Copps wasn't a contender. There was consternation in the Thompson camp and Judy went back on the same station a few hours later to say, "Thompson's my choice."

On the Saturday morning, I held a press conference. In the midst of answering questions, surrounded by a group of perhaps a dozen reporters, one of my aides broke in to hand me a telegram.

It was from René Lévesque. He had heard, mistakenly, that I had won the leadership. His message read: CONGRATULATIONS. ONTARIO LIBERALS EVEN DUMBER THAN I THOUGHT. NOW GO ON AND THROW OUT THE TORIES. I folded the telegram and put it in my pocket. Lévesque was a member of the Liberal government in Quebec but was already an outspoken separatist. The reporters sensed something in my smile and badgered me to tell them whom the message was from. "A friend," I said.

Each of the candidates had extensive convention headquarters and hospitality suites. I had none, having cancelled the Alberta Room and our suite after Riverdale. Nor had we money to spend on signs, posters, badges and all the other paraphernalia. My supporters made do: they blackened beneath one eye and wore hand-lettered badges reading, I'D RATHER FIGHT THAN SWITCH! Signs from the Riverdale campaign were recycled. Someone contributed a batch of simulated-straw boaters, with a paper band encircling the crown with the words, TEMPLETON FOR LEADER! They seemed a rag-tag bob-tailed group, but their enthusiasm was kinetic.

I spent much of my time holed up in a room working on my speech. It would be my one opportunity to express the thoughts that had been seething and yeasting as I had observed the provincial party close up during the previous ten weeks. I had decided that I would present an unadorned and specific analysis of our problems and weaknesses with concrete proposals for solutions. Riverdale had made evident my own lack of experience and my political naïveté, but it had taught me certain lessons and had helped make clear the nature of the party's major problems. I would speak to them.

I wrote and rewrote and polished the speech. I read it to Neiman and to the late Mark Gayn, the brilliant foreign correspondent on the *Star*, who had offered his help. I incorporated some of their suggestions and honed the result.

Lots had been drawn for the order in which each of the seven candidates would speak to the convention. Nixon was first. He came through as the essentially decent man he is, but there was no spark of excitement. The organized demonstration that followed his speech was extraordinary, though: hundreds of bobbing signs, a marching band, Indians from the Six Nations Reserve. Nixon stood on the platform, entranced by it all, smiling his characteristic lop-sided grin.

Joe Greene was next. His pitch throughout our campaigning had been that he and I were the only candidates with the presence and the platform ability to overturn the Robarts government. He was indeed effective on the platform. He had a slickly homespun style, a sense of his audience and an exceptional wit, and it was generally assumed that he would be at his best in his address to the delegates. But for some reason he came up flat. At the end, straining, he said, "I hereby release my delegates. Let everyone else do the same and let's make this a democratic convention."

I began by seizing the opportunity Greene had handed me. "I *did* release my delegates," I said. "But they wouldn't go!" There was a roar from the crowd.

In highly partisan meetings, it is standard practice for factions in the audience to interrupt the speaker they favour with cheers, chanting and applause. I reminded my delegates that I had only eighteen minutes, that there were things I wanted to say and that I would appreciate it if they didn't interrupt with applause. Moreover, I said, there will be no organized demonstration after the speech. The strategy was that, having no money and having made no preparation, it was better to do nothing than to do something poorly.

This was the report in the Hamilton *Spectator*:

> Charles Templeton reactivated his political career last night with a dazzling speaking performance which completely overshadowed those given by the other six candidates. The former evangelist and newspaperman changed his tack from one of glamour and slick professionalism to serious business and may have altered the future course of his party as a result.
>
> Unlike his opponents, Mr. Templeton did not personalize. He dealt with the real issues at stake, and his audience of more than 2,000 loved it.
>
> He was interrupted by applause 28 times during his speech and received an ovation at the end.
>
> Gordon Blair, who was chairman while the candidates were nominated, had to call repeatedly for order after Mr. Templeton spoke as a growing buzz of comments filled the room.

Andy Thompson had drawn the unenviable last spot. The audience was tired and restless. He made a wise decision; he threw aside his prepared speech and, in a brave show of contained Irish anger, lashed out at the criticism some of the others had levelled at him – that he was the organization's man, the lackey of the powers in Ottawa. "Are these men not Liberals?" he asked. "What's wrong with having the support of the men and women who know the party best and want the best for the party?"

It was a strong and effective response.

The speculation as to what would happen in the first ballot was unanimous: Thompson, Nixon and Greene would lead in that order, and I would head the also-rans. The Thompson camp, reassured by Andy's fighting speech, were declaring victory on the second ballot, perhaps even the first. Nixon was predicting that he would lead on the first ballot and win on the third. Greene's scenario was that, after the first ballot, my supporters, having satisfied themselves in a losing cause, would join his group to put him over the top.

The first ballot was a bombshell, surprising everyone, no one more than me:

> THOMPSON — 379
> TEMPLETON — 317
> NIXON — 313
> GREENE — 236
> SARGEANT — 61
> COPPS — 51
> GOULD — 13

The announcement was greeted with a collective gasp and then a wild roar of triumph from my supporters. Thompson had greatly overestimated his strength. He was nowhere near the 686 votes needed to win. After my failure in Riverdale, I had made an unexpected recovery and was only 62 votes back of the leader. After a twenty-minute interval, the bottom man was eliminated and the second ballot followed.

> THOMPSON — 408
> TEMPLETON — 356
> NIXON — 351
> GREENE — 211

The excitement mounted. A major upset seemed possible and the convention was seething with speculation. I had whittled Thompson's lead to 52 votes and had maintained a slim lead over Nixon. Everywhere on the floor, workers were button-holing delegates, pleading their individual causes. Walter Gordon and Keith Davey were on their feet, moving through the crowd wooing votes. Mitchell Sharp stood with a paternal hand on Nixon's shoulder. The third ballot:

> THOMPSON — 462
> TEMPLETON — 396
> NIXON — 356
> GREENE — 149

Greene's support was fading fast. He left the convention floor quickly. One of his workers went to Keith Davey. "Joe's looking for you," he said. "I'm looking for him," Davey replied.

Upstairs in their hospitality suite, Greene's dispirited supporters met in an emergency caucus, unsure, looking for guidance. But Greene didn't appear; he was nearby, closeted in a room with Keith Davey and Walter Gordon. One of my workers, Mel McGinnis, was outside the room, an ear pressed to the door. Davey, Gordon and Greene emerged from the room, walking quickly; Davey and Gordon returned to the convention floor while Greene went to meet with his caucus.

As he stood before them, he was clearly disheartened and ill at ease. He had predicated his entire campaign on the premise that neither Thompson nor Nixon had the qualities needed to challenge the Conservative government: "Thompson has had five years in the legislature to show his strength and has done nothing. Nixon is Mr. Nice Guy, but he'll never follow in his father's steps." Now he stood before his supporters, mopping his brow.

"They want me to put on a Thompson button," he said apologetically.

There were cries of, "No! No!" Tom O'Neill, a Toronto lawyer and Greene's floor-manager, shouted, "I'm going to work for Templeton and take as many Greene supporters as I can," and was immediately involved in a heated debate with Jim Palmer, a seven-foot giant from the Ottawa area. O'Neill broke away and ran for the convention floor. The delegates, confused and arguing among themselves, straggled into the hallway.

On the floor, the word spread: "Greene's going over to Thompson." O'Neill seized a Templeton hat from a nearby delegate and jammed it on his head, muttering about betrayal. Another Greene supporter, Kevin Martin, pushed through the crowd, trying to get the chairman's eye so that an announcement could be made from the platform that Greene wanted to withdraw from the fourth ballot. "Too late," he was told.

THOMPSON — 520
TEMPLETON — 422
NIXON — 387
GREENE — 37

Thompson had picked up a majority of the Greene votes and had increased his lead to almost a hundred. My eight-year-old son, Michael, put his lips to my ear. "Hey, Dad," he shouted over the din, "when are you going to pass him?"

"Good question," I said.

Clyde Batten, my floor manager, slipped into a seat behind me. "Let me talk to Nixon," he said. I shook my head.

What he was proposing was what is known in politics as a "deal." He would confer with the Nixon people and make an arrangement: whoever – Nixon or I – remained in the race after the next ballot would immediately and conspicuously go to the other, shake his hand and accept the other man's button, thus signalling to his delegates where he wanted them to transfer their support. If the transfer of votes was successful, the winner would be in debt to the loser and at some future time would find a way to repay the debt. (For instance, not long after the convention, Greene was named federal Minister of Energy.)

But when I re-entered the race, I had pledged that I would make no deals, and I wasn't going to change my mind now. Beyond that, it was clear to me – if to no one else on the floor but the professionals – that even if Nixon agreed to a deal it wouldn't be possible for him to transfer enough support for me to win. His delegates were mostly from non-urban ridings and tended to be more conservative in their attitudes. Too much had been made of the fact that I was a minister who had lost his faith, a divorced man who had remarried.

Batten continued to press me. To get away from his importunities and to release some tension, I got to my feet and went into the aisle. Nixon's campaign manager, David Anderson, approached me, a question in his eyes. "What do you say, Charles? You can't win, you know. But you can be the king-maker. Let me give you a Nixon button. Come over and talk to Bob." I shook my head. The fifth ballot:

THOMPSON — 539
TEMPLETON — 419
NIXON — 392

Nixon had been eliminated. It was now a two-man contest. Delegates and spectators were on their feet, shouting, jumping up and down, waving signs, standing on chairs, chanting the names of their candidates. The convention was suddenly two camps.

Scott Young wrote in his column in the *Globe and Mail*:

At the end, for the sixth and final ballot, only the two names remained on the big ballot board: TEMPLETON, C. THOMPSON, A.

Never in memory had two men fought for a major political position in this country with more dissimilar weapons. Thompson had the army, the navy and the air-force gun positions on high ground, enfilading fire, a headquarters full of generals. He sat throughout the afternoon directly in front of the Liberal leadership convention chairman. Beside him with a walkie-talkie sat a university student who, just before the final vote, was droning into his radio: "Number 22 to Master Control. Do you read me? Would someone bring some sandwiches and coffee to Mr. Thompson in the front row?"

Templeton had the guerrillas. He operated from well back in the forest at the south end of the room. The bandages from his defeat in the Riverdale by-election the week before were invisible but there. He had come limping back into the leadership fight only three days before. Drifting in and out of the underbrush to join up had come some of the men and women who had been with him before, until by voting time, he too had something to fight with; lame but game.

My supporters had come to the convention merely wanting to put on record their support of the candidate they believed could turn the party around and return it to power. They wanted also to register their disapproval of the control being exercised from Ottawa. Their opposition to Thompson had turned bitter. They saw him, unfairly, as a puppet who would be manipulated by "the establishment." But now the picture had changed. David might beat Goliath. They could *win*!

They surrounded and broke over me like a giant wave, picked me up and bore me on their shoulders into the aisles; chanting, shouting, waving signs, clapping each other on the back. In all my experience, I have never seen a moment to match it. A forest of hands reached up to be touched or shaken. Women hugged my legs and kissed them. Thompson supporters saw what was happening and quickly matched the action, putting Andy on their shoulders and moving into the aisles. As we passed, we reached out and shook hands.

Riding above the crush I was oddly detached and entirely calm. I knew I could not win. I felt a momentary sadness in the realization of the disappointment my supporters would feel when the final tally was announced. In the meantime, there was nothing to do but to clasp hands above my head in the boxer's salute. The sixth ballot:

THOMPSON — 772

TEMPLETON — 540

I went again to the solitude of the cottage on Georgian Bay. A day or two later, the telephone rang. It was Walter Gordon.

After some talk about the success of the convention, he said, "Charles, I'm told you'll be pretty deeply in debt as the result of the two concurrent campaigns. Do you have an estimate as to how much?"

"I'm not sure," I said. "I had a word with my treasurer and I gather it's worse than I'd thought."

"Do you mind my asking how much? I'm not prying?"

"More than twenty thousand dollars."

"Well," he said, "I've been talking to Keith. It's his view and mine that the party is indebted to you. We don't mean to minimize the contribution of the other candidates, but it was your presence that caught the interest of the public and the press and helped make the convention. We thought we would like to organize a dinner at one of the downtown hotels. Perhaps charge $125 a plate – $25 to pay for the dinner, the rest to diminish your indebtedness."

I had come to know Walter Gordon but not well. Shortly after

I joined the party, he invited me to dinner at his Ottawa apartment and we'd had a long conversation. We'd met informally a number of times. I knew the depth of his commitment to the party. I knew of Keith Davey's admiration for him as a man and mentor. I, too, liked him — it would be difficult not to.

I didn't understand then what I do now: that Walter was making more than a gesture of kindness. In effect, he was saying: Charles, you fought a tough but fair fight. You didn't attack the party or your opponents. But there's something you need to understand: we who are sometimes called the establishment have a stake in the party. Some of us have put years into it. We have worked to revive it and to make it an instrument of reform, and we simply could not permit you to walk in and decamp with the family jewels. But now that we have the measure of you we'd like to invite you to join the club.

I had a problem. When I made the decision to run, I made a vow to myself that I would not be in anybody's pocket. I would, insofar as was possible, avoid political debts. That was why I had refused the suggestion that Nixon and I join forces for the last ballot. To avoid being beholden, I accepted contributions to my campaign of one hundred dollars or more under two conditions: that the money be paid to my treasurer and not to me; and that the contributor understand that he was buying no present or future advantage. When George Metcalf, then president of Loblaws and an old acquaintance, gave me a cheque for (as I recall it) five hundred dollars, I thanked him but added, "Before I accept it, one thing should be clear: if at any time in the future I'm in a position to be helpful to you or to Loblaws, I can guarantee you only one thing, a fair hearing. And it's entirely possible that I might find it necessary to act in a way opposed to your best interests."

Now, Walter Gordon was making a generous offer to help with my financial debts. Yet, I still had hope that I would one day lead the party; when that day came, I wanted to be my own man.

"Thank you, Walter," I said. "I appreciate your thoughtfulness. I really do. And Keith's. But I'll work it out myself."

When all the bills were in, they amounted to some $24,000. It took three years to pay them off.

Within two years, I was offered the leadership of the Ontario Liberal party on a platter.

Andy Thompson had been involved in an automobile accident

in which two elderly women were seriously injured. With his concurrence, it was decided that he should resign the leadership. Bob Nixon came to see me. He told me that a leadership convention would be called, and wanted to know if I would stand for election. If so, he said, he would like to nominate me. Since it was unlikely that there would be any other candidates, he would move that I be elected by acclamation. It was a generous act. He made it clear that he was expressing not only his own wishes but those of the party brass. I told him I would need some time to consider it.

It was a knotty problem. My run for the leadership had left my marriage precarious at best. A revival of my political ambitions would undoubtedly destroy any hope of rapprochement. Moreover, I had four young children, each of whom I was determined to see through university and, if they wished, graduate school. I was working as president of a struggling advertising-display company called Technamation Canada, my moderate salary being paid by a company owned by my brother, who also had an interest in Technamation. And I had only begun to pay off the debts incurred during my foray into politics. If I were to assume the leadership, I would need to work at it full time and I would be without income. The salary and benefits normally paid by the legislature to the leader of the opposition would not come to me since I did not have a seat.

I pointed out my financial problem, and it was proposed that an ad hoc committee of the federal Liberal caucus meet with me to resolve the matter. We met in the office of Edgar Benson, then Minister of Finance. Present were Benson, Mitchell Sharp, Judy LaMarsh, Paul Hellyer and half a dozen others. The press got wind of the meeting and camped at the door.

It was an informal gathering. Drinks were poured. Someone ran down the specifics of the financial dilemma. It would not be a short-term problem: there were no by-elections due and a general election was not likely for two or three years. There was general approval of a suggestion that the caucus commit itself to raise an amount sufficient to pay a moderate salary, but when Benson asked that a sum be specified and a concrete plan laid out, the meeting fell back on vague expressions of assurance. "Don't worry," they all said, "it will be taken care of." But no one would specify how.

I raised a second problem. As leader, I would want to wage an aggressive, province-wide campaign, but the provincial organization was deeply in debt and I had been told that there weren't enough funds even for gasoline money. "Don't worry, Charles," was the airy response. "We'll look into it."

There was one memorable moment. Late in the discussion, when we had all put back a few, Judy LaMarsh addressed herself to me. She was wearing, after the fashion of the time, a mini-skirt and black mesh stockings; legs crossed, she was seated opposite me on an overstuffed sofa.

"Charles," she said "we're talking about backing you. But how do we know you'll look good to the people of Ontario?"

I shrugged. "I don't know. Maybe I won't."

"I will say this," she added with a grin, "you look damn good to me right now."

By the end of the meeting it was evident that no one was prepared to make concrete the good intentions expressed by all. In Toronto, a few days later, I called a press conference to announce that I would not be a candidate. Bob Nixon was chosen leader.

During the campaign, I'd had a telephone call from Roy Thomson, not long afterwards to become Lord Thomson of Fleet. He came quickly to the point.

"What are you going to do if you lose?"

"I'm not going to lose."

"Every candidate believes that," he said, "but more lose than win. What are your plans if you don't win – are you going back to the *Star*?"

"I really don't know. I haven't given it any thought."

"Well, I have," he said. "If you lose, give me a call."

I had known Roy Thomson for years, not well but well enough to like him. Like most journalists, I was critical of the way he ran his newspapers; his principal concern was not their performance as news journals but their viability as business investments. But I had found him an interesting and complex man. Interviewing him once for television, I referred to a news item in which it was reported that his net worth was thirty million dollars but that his goal was to turn that into three hundred million dollars.

"What's the point?" I asked. "Look at the suit you're wearing. It must be ten years old. Look at your shoes. And that tie! So what's the difference between one million and three hundred million? You can wear only one suit at a time and eat only one meal at a time and drive only one car at a time – and on the evidence, none of those things matter to you. What's the point of this drive?"

He looked at me through the thick lenses of his glasses. "Charles," he said, "if I were an actor, there would be an Academy Award to testify that I was the best actor. If I were a physicist or a chemist there would be the Nobel prize. If I were a writer, there's the Pulitzer. Each says, 'You're the best among your peers.' Well, I'm a businessman. Money is the evidence of how good I am at what I do. It's my Oscar."

A few days after I lost the convention, I called him as promised. He came on the line in his usual direct way. "So, you lost."

"No doubt about that."

"I'll put the question to you again — what are you going to do?"

"I don't know yet."

"How'd you like to work for me?" he asked. "I've been watching you over the years and I'm prepared to offer you a job. Are you interested?"

"I'm interested."

"Okay," he said. "As you probably know, I've begun to extend into Africa. I have some pretty exciting plans there: television, newspapers, other interests. How'd you like to run it for me?"

I don't remember how I responded; I was caught by surprise. We talked for a few minutes and I told him I'd be in touch. There was a brief moment when it was a tempting proposition, but having returned to Canada only a few years earlier, I had no desire to leave again.

There were other political opportunities. David Crombie, who was at the time a teacher at Ryerson Polytechnical Institute, and Tony O'Donohue, a Toronto alderman, took me to lunch and tried to talk me into running for mayor of Toronto. They proposed to introduce party politics to Toronto, not through the traditional parties but with an organization called Civic Action, a coalition not unlike Fiorello La Guardia's fusion party in New York City. But municipal politics didn't interest me; the mayor has little power and too few options. Crombie himself later became Toronto's "tiny perfect mayor" and graduated to the House of Commons and candidate for leader of the Conservative party. O'Donohue's two tries for the mayoralty failed.

During the leadership campaign I had received a note from Morton Shulman enclosing a contribution. Shulman was the former

coroner for Metro Toronto who was only beginning his controversial career as a tilter at establishment windmills. His note read:
"Off the record: if you win the leadership I'll join the Liberal party
and run with you in the next election."

Some time after the convention, Morty's allegiance precipitated a momentary awkwardness. He had decided to enter politics
but hadn't decided with which party. He had been an active
Conservative, but for his own reasons had become an avowed foe
of the Tories. Morty, a self-confessed millionaire, is the antithesis
of the conventional socialist so the NDP didn't seem a likely home.
The Liberals were the logical option and he had talked at length
with Bob Nixon, the new leader. Nixon wanted him in the party,
but some of the small-minded men in the caucus — of whom there
were a number — were afraid Shulman would steal the limelight.

Shulman telephoned me late one evening in a quandary as to
what action he should take. Finally, well after midnight, having
checked the situation with Nixon and Stephen Lewis, the leader
of the NDP, I advised Shulman that he really had but one option,
the New Democrats.

The following day he called a press conference and announced
that he would join the NDP. In his statement he said, "I made the
decision to become a member of the New Democratic party after a
long conversation with one of my closest friends, Charles Templeton." Which hardly seemed appropriate — I was a vice-president of the Liberal party at the time.

III

The leadership campaign behind us, I became one of Keith
Davey's trouble-shooters. Keith relishes his role as the party's
national organizer and performs it with a happy exuberance. I
visited him frequently at his Cooper Street offices in Ottawa and
enjoyed watching him play political manipulator with what can
only be described as zest. As many as a dozen times during an
hour's visit he might break off a conversation to take "important
calls," quickly becoming immersed in the specifics of a particular
problem or catching up on local political gossip in Sudbury or
Saskatoon or Fredericton or Revelstoke, or in his beloved

Toronto. He is a man wedded to his work, exultant in his niche.

You have to guard against Keith's enthusiasms. In each general election he likes to set up scenarios in three or four ridings that will attract the particular attention of the media. I sometimes had to remind myself that Keith's and the party's interest might be inimical to my own. He made a number of more or less serious proposals that I run as a candidate in various elections; the most fanciful of these kamikaze missions had me being parachuted into Burnaby-Coquitlam to "knock off" the then leader of the NDP, Tommy Douglas.

In the 1963 general election I was dispatched to Algoma East "to rescue Mike Pearson." Like all political organizers, Davey, despite his essential level-headedness, is subject to unreasonable panic. Joel Aldred, a Conservative entrepreneur and sometime television-commercial spieler, decided to challenge the prime minister in his own riding. Algoma East is a sprawling, sparsely inhabited section of mid-northern Ontario. Pearson had first run there because it was a safe Liberal seat. He only occasionally visited the riding, despite which it cheerfully returned him each election with thumping majorities.

But now the mellifluous and personable Aldred was on the scene, working hard, taking his best shot at the absentee landlord and "getting lots of ink." There was a sudden flurry of alarm at Cooper Street. Pearson's other responsibilities made it impossible for him to visit the riding, so I was sent. I flew in to the Manitoulin and immediately challenged Aldred to a debate on the issues. He didn't respond. I made a couple of speeches in hastily arranged rallies – not so much for the people who attended as for the press – and for a few days junketed from place to place, showing the flag and dampening whatever Tory brushfires there might be.

It was all unnecessary, of course. The people of the riding weren't buying Aldred's pear-shaped tones, and the PM was returned with a sizeable majority.

In 1965, in his first bid for office, Robert Andras was in trouble, trouble not of his own making, and I was sent to see if I could help out. Andras, who would later hold a number of important cabinet responsibilities and end his political career as president of the Treasury Board, was the Liberal nominee in Fort William, now incorporated into Thunder Bay, Ontario. I went directly from the airport to a downtown hotel, where I met a very depressed candidate. He was fighting an opponent he couldn't grapple with – the series of political scandals that had dogged the Pearson government's steps during the previous year. Most notable among them was the so-called Rivard affair. It was a complicated and sorry tale.* Enough to say that the Liberals had been targets of the press and the opposition over a series of unsavoury goings-on in which they had been bumbling, insensitive, imprudent and slow to act. With the calling of the election, the Conservatives and the NDP had revived the mess and, while the tactic had not been all that successful elsewhere, Andras told me lugubriously that it was about to defeat him in Fort William.

I thought he was exaggerating. (It is astonishing how irrational normally sensible men can become in the pressure cooker of an election campaign.) To sniff the political atmosphere, I went for a two-hour stroll in the downtown section and, in the course of a number of conversations, discovered that Andras' reading of local sentiment was accurate.

Back at campaign headquarters, I asked the candidate if he could buy time on the local television station. He checked. By a stroke of luck, a half hour was available at ten the following evening immediately after *The Man From U.N.C.L.E.*, the highest rated show on the station at the time. I arranged for a simple set – a desk and an artist's easel against a black backdrop – and notified Andras that I was going to talk about the so-called scandals.

He shook his head. "We've had specific instructions from Ottawa that only the prime minister is to speak to the charges. No candidate is to discuss it publicly."

"I'm not a candidate," I said.

The Rivard scandal was at that point a phoney issue and could be shown to be so. At the television studio, I came on the air cold, occupied in making a lightning-fast caricature of a fulminating John Diefenbaker. When it was finished, I turned to the camera, introduced myself and said straight out that I was going to speak candidly and without histrionics about the various scandals. For half an hour, I perched on the edge of the desk, moved to the easel to make swift sketches, or spoke directly to the lens of the camera. I had spent years learning how to use television and now it paid off. As the program ended, Andras was so excited he ran onto the

---

* Best told in Richard Gwyn's, *The Shape of Scandal* (Toronto: Clarke, Irwin and Co., 1965).

set, threw his arms about me, lifted me into the air and swung me around. He was elected by a small majority.

Next stop was my native province, Saskatchewan, where politics is fought bare-knuckles. My task was to tour the province – the Tories held every seat – and to give particular aid and comfort to Hazen Argue, the Grits' one, long-shot hope. I found Argue an introverted, diffident man, given to preoccupied silences. He had been for eighteen months the national leader of the CCF party before defecting to the Liberals, and was passionately hated by the NDP. In 1965, he was trying for election in Assiniboia, having been defeated in 1963.

I was chauffeured about the province by a madman assigned by then premier Ross Thatcher. The entire tour of five cities was driven with only one hand; the other was occupied in gesturing as we rocketed along the straight-as-a-string Saskatchewan high-ways at ninety miles an hour. Often, I was tempted to return to prayer.

As recompense, I was told wonderful tales of local politics. They played for keeps in Saskatchewan: you left someone to guard your car when you made a speech if you didn't want to find your tires flat or water in your gas tank when you returned. I heard of meeting-hall doors nailed securely shut; a candidate's car fastened to a telephone pole with a length of heavy chain; and of obscenities added to campaign posters so that the candidate him-self had to destroy them.

Bully-boy hecklers were sent to meetings to frighten away women and the timid. They would feign fist fights in the midst of the candidate's speech and flee before the police arrived. A woman brought her hungry baby to a meeting and sat in the front row so that the infant's crying drowned out the candidate's speech. At another meeting, a man brought an enormous German shepherd on a leash. He, too, sat in the front row. Throughout the candi-date's speech, the dog lunged toward him, straining at the leash, teeth bared, snapping and snarling. It didn't make for oratory.

There were, of course, the common tales of election-day chicanery: of ballot boxes stolen and of dead men voting, some many times. In turn, I told him horror stories I'd heard about the Toronto-Dovercourt riding in the 1930s. Such skullduggery as when a scrutineer for one of the parties lodged a piece of lead beneath a fingernail when unfolding ballots for tallying, and managed to mark those cast for the opposition in such a way as to make them invalid. One party organizer perfected a brilliant scam. Early in the day, a voter entered the polling station. Having been given his ballot, he substituted a folded piece of paper and voted it. The unmarked ballot was then given to the organizer. He marked the X for his candidate and gave it to an indigent or a rummy whose name was on the voters' list. The man deposited the marked ballot and returned with the unmarked one he'd been issued, whereupon he was rewarded with a couple of dollars or a bottle of cheap liquor. The system was repeated throughout the day.

My efforts in Saskatchewan didn't achieve anything tangible. Once again, the Liberals lost every seat.. Hazen Argue was defeated but was rewarded by "being summoned to the Senate of Canada."

I was scheduled to go next to Victoria but was diverted to the Northwest Territories by an urgent telephone call from Keith Davey. It seemed there was a chance to capture the seat and that all that might be needed was an extra push.

I flew from Edmonton to Yellowknife aboard Pacific Western Airlines. The initials PWA, I was told by fellow passengers, stood for "Please Wait Awhile" and "Pray While Aloft." The centre of the cabin was occupied by an enormous piece of crated machinery, lashed to the floor. The few seats that hadn't been removed were occupied mostly by stolid and silent Inuit and Indians. They had brought lunch, and as soon as we were airborne, unwrapped it. I passed when a steward offered me a squashed box lunch.

In Yellowknife I was informed that I couldn't meet the candidate, Bud Orange; he was campaigning at the eastern end of the riding. I looked at a map: I was closer to Toronto than I was to Bud Orange.

Yellowknife looked as a picture-postcard wilderness city should: scrub, rock outcrop and water. Most of its residents dressed in clothes suited to the setting; in my light topcoat and white shirt and tie, I looked like the prototypical city slicker. There were, of course, most of the amenities of a southern city, but the feeling was of being at the end of civilization's reach.

I did all the things you do when you are beating the political drum. I was interviewed by the local paper and on radio, was photographed shaking hands with the shy and inscrutable men introduced to me as the leaders of the native peoples, was taught a few words in Dog Rib, addressed a public meeting in an inferno-hot hall, was presented with an Inuit bone knife and spoke to a group of wives of engineers, accountants and other "southerners" who were doing a limited stint at the Pine Point mine. The conversation afterwards consisted of stories about the various manifestations of cabin fever.

The entire flight across Great Slave Lake was accomplished with my heart palpitating. We were just out of sight of land when the single engine of the bush plane began to catch and occasionally to falter. The pilot opined that there might be a little water in the gas line and that it must be freezing. Nor did my trepidation subside when he reassuringly pointed out that, if the engine did quit, we would last no more than four minutes in the cold, grey waters below.

There were two memorable moments during a two-day stay in Hay River. On the drive into the dust-mantled town, we passed an extensive fenced area, every square inch jammed with gigantic earth-moving machines. My driver told me that, at the end of the Second World War, the United States Army engineers who had been building and maintaining the Canol Pipeline simply abandoned their equipment. The cost to ship it home was prohibitive, and they were forbidden by law to sell it in Canada. A citizen of Hay River, a middle-European as I recall it, slipped out of town with the usual prospector's equipment – a sleeping bag, a gun, an axe and some matches, along with some flour, salt, beans and tea – and living off the land, followed the pipeline. He had taken with him a can of paint, and he laid claim to millions of dollars worth of abandoned equipment by simply painting his name on it.

The editor of the newspaper in Hay River was an intense, narrow-jawed young man. He sat at his overburdened desk at one end of a long and very narrow office, every square foot of the floor heaped with stacks of yellowing back issues. I tried to talk politics while he talked about the development of the north – two zealots, we held simultaneous conversations about entirely different subjects.

As we spoke, he picked up a chunk of rough rock and looped it across the intervening distance. I reached for it but dropped it. Picking it up, I was surprised at its weight and noticed that flakes had fallen from it to the floor.

"Lead and zinc," he said. "From the Pyramid mine. Have you heard of it?"

"No," I said, and tried to get back to the Liberal party.

"Do yourself a favour," he said, "get yourself some shares. It's going to be bigger than Pine Point."

The following morning, killing time at the Edmonton airport, I checked Pyramid shares in a newspaper. They were listed at eighteen cents. I was unimpressed – I'd been touted on penny stocks before. A few months later, Pyramid was selling at thirty-two dollars.

It wasn't a total loss: the Liberals won the seat.

Lester Pearson was in Winnipeg for a major rally and I was flown there to "warm up" the crowd for ten minutes before introducing the prime minister. I was well known in the city – some eighty thousand had attended my preaching mission there in 1956. But we had reckoned without the NDP.

They lined up before the doors opened and immediately occupied the front three rows in the auditorium and all the front seats in the gallery. As I was introduced and made my way to the lectern, they sent up a cacophony of whistling and booing, and the moment I started to speak, began to heckle. My every statement was challenged with hoots and jests and shouted questions. The badgering was not ill-tempered, the jibes were mostly attempts at humour, but it was impossible either to ride over it or ignore it. Things grew worse when the Liberals in the crowd began to boo the hecklers, for it sounded as if the increased uproar was directed at me.

I soldiered on, perspiring, shouting to be heard above the mêlée and swiftly growing hoarse. As there was no option, I quickly moved to my conclusion and returned to my seat. The booing immediately switched to applause. Mr. Pearson got a respectful hearing.

Something like the debacle in Winnipeg happened some years later when I was asked to speak prior to Pierre Trudeau at Maple Leaf Gardens in the 1974 campaign. The Gardens was jammed; the proportion of teenagers was much larger than would normally be the case because of the presence of The Guess Who. In the wake of their incredibly amplified rock music, I rose to speak, my brain numbed by the uproar. The frenetic din that followed the music didn't diminish by a decibel. In mid-speech, my mind was elsewhere, vowing never again to accept an invitation to such an occasion.

Pushing through the crowd five minutes later, I passed an old friend. "Hi, Chuck," he shouted. "When are you on?"

In November, 1965, Lester Pearson's government was returned with its second straight minority. Having counselled the prime minister to go to the country, assuring him of his longed-for majority, Walter Gordon, political head of the party, and Keith Davey, the national organizer, resigned. Four months later, Davey was appointed to the Senate. In 1968, Pierre Trudeau ascended to the leadership and, in setting up his election apparatus, passed over Davey and appointed Robert Andras anglophone political organizer. Jean Marchand was made responsible for Quebec.

I had never been enthusiastic about Trudeau and had been publicly critical of him on radio. Nonetheless, I continued to work for the party. In the spring of 1972, the prime minister began to make noises about an election and the requisite organizational structure was set up. Clem Neiman, who had been campaign manager in my bid for the Ontario leadership, was named Ontario chairman. He persuaded me to act as Chairman of the Candidates Committee, my task being to find suitable candidates and to talk them into running.

The weeks dragged on. Summer came and a half dozen election alerts passed without a writ being issued. It was obvious that Trudeau was unable to make up his mind. I was growing restive. The idea for a novel was yeasting in my head and I was anxious to get to the daily routine of writing. By mid-July, I'd had enough and asked to be released from my responsibilities. Neiman wouldn't hear of it. As the dwindling days of summer revealed more indecision in Ottawa, I saw a way out of my dilemma.

Although he had been set aside by the prime minister, Keith Davey was loyal to the party and he was filling a relatively minor role in the Ontario organization. I told Neiman I was adamant about resigning and proposed that he replace me with Davey as candidates chairman. As I recall it, he passed the task to Keith and Dorothy Petrie, Neiman's co-chairman. Incidentally, they subsequently married, although not as a result of this joint assignment. When Trudeau finally called the election for October 3, his majority was reduced to a slim, two-seat advantage. In August 1973, Davey was summoned to serve again as national organizer.

I have not since worked for the party. There was no rupture; it was simply that I was growing increasingly critical of the Trudeau government and was voicing my criticism on the air in my daily dialogue with Pierre Berton. Liberals do not attack their leader, so I severed my connection.

It was also the beginning of the end of my marriage to Sylvia. Such warmth and mutual commitment as there had been was destroyed when I decided to run for public office. Early in 1975, after fifteen years, I left home. We were divorced in February 1976. On December 21, 1980, I married Madeleine Helen Leger. Happy day.

IV

I like politicians. Not all of them, of course, but the breed. If pressed to say why, I would be at a loss. I know many of them, some well, but I have no illusions about them and take such characteristics as self-absorption, overweening ambition and pretentiousness as essential to their trade. That they have king-size egos should not surprise; anyone who runs for political office *must* believe that he is superior to his fellows to want to be set over them. (I use the masculine gender here because of the awkwardness of he/she and because politicians *are* preponderantly male.)

It is, of course, facile to speak of politicians as a group. In personality and talent they range the spectrum and vary as widely in their ambitions. Some lust for power (the most unlikely see themselves as *numero uno,* their improbable dream hidden from even those closest to them until the time comes to declare themselves as candidates in a leadership convention), some aspire to little more than to represent their neighbours in parliament. Some are compassionate, realizing themselves through service, others do little that won't serve their own ends. Some are honourable men, some are mountebanks.

The largest vocational group among politicians is lawyers, which fact is neither surprising nor regrettable. The reasons for their disproportionate representation are obvious: lawyers are trained in law; government has mostly to do with the making of laws. Happily, their number is leavened by accountants, clergymen, farmers, businessmen and what have you. A few are academics. A very few are women.

There are reasons why few women occupy seats in the federal or provincial legislatures. Principally, it is because political parties are of the nature of men's clubs, and women are not readily admitted. Male politicians — and I'm speaking here of those who work at the job year round rather than spasmodically when there is an election — like to get together to "talk politics." They meet in "smoke-filled back rooms," in hotel rooms, in each other's homes. Theirs is an easy camaraderie, a jackets-off, collars-open, shirt-sleeves-rolled informality, with feet on the table and a drink in the hand. The conversation is "man talk," the language is forthright and occasionally raunchy. Expletives go undeleted. It is a habitat in which males feel at ease only in the company of other males. Not many women are at home in this environment, and while the political pros will accommodate to the presence of women, the old ways are cherished and protected.

The situation is changing but not very rapidly. Most of the women active in politics are relegated to secondary and tertiary tasks and have not yet begun to realize their potential. Women are more numerous than men in the population, and if they were to emphasize their solidarity, they could elect more than their share of members. But there is no evidence that women vote for women because they are women. If anything, the contrary is true. This will surely change, however. Women will make their way in politics as they are doing in every other activity, and one day — but probably not in this century — the Canadian head of state will be an extraordinary human being addressed as Madame Prime Minister.

To an outsider, it must seem odd, almost masochistic, that anyone would offer himself as a candidate for public office. There are rewards, of course, but the price exacted can be excessive. Public-opinion polls reveal that politicians are not highly esteemed by their fellows — the very word is spoken with a curl of the lip. The stereotype is a pompous, unctuous, garrulous and self-serving extrovert who "rides the gravy train" and "fattens at the public trough." He is a target of abuse for his fellows and the press, is maligned in editorials and cartoons, is criticized in letters to the editor and is commonly the scapegoat in matters over which he has no control.

When in 1964 I ran for a provincial seat, the demands made of me most frequently were that I "do something about that damned new Canadian flag" (a federal responsibility) and about property taxes (an affair of the municipal government).

The stuff of daily politics is tedious, exhausting and without glamour. The successful candidate immediately loses his privacy. He is subject to being called upon at any hour of the day or night and on weekends. His constituents expect him to solve problems as varied as finding a job for someone's layabout son-in-law, improving the mail service, filling a pot-hole or halting the nuclear-arms race. In responding to these and other appeals, a politician must move with circumspection. If he uses his influence unwisely, he may be charged with influence peddling. Innocent of wilful impropriety, he may find himself pilloried in the House and by the news media and end with his good reputation besmirched.

Some politicians become wealthy through politics, others are beggared by it. The pay in the House of Commons may not be princely, but it is adequate. The pension – if the member can stay around long enough – is more than generous. If he has served the party loyally, even defeat can be rewarding – a seat in the Senate may secure the future. The contacts and experience gained in political life can put a man in the way of lucrative opportunities. Despite these rewards, many backbenchers pay for their years in politics with debts incurred in campaigning, in maintaining two households, in the mandatory contributions to every "worthy cause" and in the thousand and one expenditures for which there is no recompense.

The heaviest cost may be a broken or gutted marriage, a result of the neglect of a wife and children and frequent and prolonged absences from home. The sexual temptations are many; a politician is a celebrity of sorts and there *are* politicial groupies. The loneliness and discouragement of the political arena and the tenuousness of the future can lead to heavy drinking. Let that man count himself among God's favourites who has a supportive family, a private income and a safe seat.

But the candidate is only the focal point of the political process. Behind him, unnoticed and usually unheralded, are the volunteer workers. Many have a dedication akin to a missionary's. They work sweat-shop hours without pay or hope of tangible reward, simply to see their man win. They are satisfied with a handshake or an arm about the shoulder or a word of commendation, and for this they will canvass strange streets in good or bad weather, climb narrow stairs, knock on every door, accost passers-by, solicit votes. They endure insults, hot rebuke and massive indifference with few complaints and undiminished vigour. On election day they drive the infirm to the polls, babysit so that mothers may vote and, at the end, agonize or exult with the candidate as the results come in.

Part of their recompense is, of course, an identification with celebrity, the sense of being part of Something Big. But political workers are prepared to do more than bask in a reflected spotlight; they are givers as well as takers. Many are lonely people who find companionship among their kind. Some are social misfits and a few are intolerable one-note bores, but the political process wouldn't work without them. Those who sit on the sidelines and scorn all politicians and their followers owe these "foot-soldiers" more than they know.

7

Inside *Maclean's*

INSIDE *MACLEAN'S*

In May 1969, a spotlight picked up a singer perched on a high stool against a black backdrop. He struck a single chord on his guitar, and to the melody of "Where have all the flowers gone?"sang:

> Where have all the good jobs gone . . . ?

Another chord:

> Gone to Charlie Tem-ple-ton.

Blackout!

Thus did the CBC program *Nightcap* react to the announcement by *Maclean's* magazine that I had been named editor-in-chief. The singer didn't know, nor did I, that it would prove to be anything but a "good job."

At the time, the Maclean-Hunter vice president with particular responsibility for the company's flagship publication was R.A. McEachern. He had called the previous Friday to ask if I would join him for dinner Sunday evening at the Rosedale Golf and Country Club. He preferred not to say why. At the table, he greeted me by saying, "I suppose you've heard I'm a pretty tough customer to get along with." I hadn't. In fact, I knew nothing about him except that he was the man involved in the mass resignations of *Maclean's* senior staff in 1964.

McEachern was a short, skinny man, stooped from a chronically bad back. He was in his late sixties, had thinning hair, a cadaverous face and an abrupt manner of speaking. When he wished to be, he was warm and companionable. He had an eclectic mind, was more widely read than anyone I had encountered in business and was a skilled organist who had worked his way through the University of Toronto by playing in Toronto churches. Unfortunately, he was utterly lacking in supervisory skills.

He came immediately to the point. He had invited me to dinner, he said, to offer me the job as editor of *Maclean's*. The magazine was in trouble. It needed an infusion of fresh ideas, a sense of direction and a firm editorial hand. Having examined my work at the *Star* and at CTV, he was certain I was the man needed.

He held out tempting incentives: a salary well above what I was earning at CTV, a leased luxury automobile, free gas, oil, parking and washes at the company garage, a paid-up pension, and if I wanted it, a five-year contract.

I made soundings with some friends, among them Pierre Berton, who had been managing editor at *Maclean's,* and with whom I was doing a daily radio show on CFRB. He and others expressed concern about the Maclean-Hunter management. Yes, I should take the job, they said, but only if I could ensure that I would be free to run the magazine without undue interference. I notified McEachern that I would accept but only if I was given an unequivocal commitment that I would be free to develop and pursue my own directions. If *Maclean's* did not have sufficient confidence to grant that assurance, I said, I would stay at CTV. The guarantee was given.

I went to *Maclean's* intending that it be the job at which I would spend the remainder of my life. As "Canada's National Magazine," it certainly offered scope and challenge, and it provided the opportunity to fashion a journal that would be important in the life of the nation. I said a reluctant and affectionate farewell to friends at CTV, selected from the list of available cars a new Mercury Marquis, expressed pleasure when McEachern told me he was having a drop-leaf rosewood desk made for me (I had admired the one in his office) and, at his suggestion, took a two-week vacation with pay before beginning the new job. It would give him time, he said, to enlarge and completely refurbish my office. "We want you happy here."

I very much needed a vacation; the pressures at CTV had brought me to the edge of exhaustion. But rather than recoup on a Caribbean beach, I bought a suitcase full of magazines and withdrew to my cottage on Georgian Bay. I had much to learn and I began my education with a crash course. The process revived me and my head began to hum with projects and possibilities. I could hardly wait to begin.

There were early auguries of trouble.

Three days before I was due to start, I received a telephone call from McEachern: could I delay coming for an additional week? The new office, he explained — at which workmen had been toiling around the clock — would not be ready on time. He didn't tell me that when the office was almost completed, someone noticed that it was six inches larger than the office occupied by Donald Hunter, the company president. One of the walls was immediately torn down and moved in eight inches.

I arrived at work the first day to find the magazine being picketed. A group of feminists were circling outside the main entrance to the building. They were protesting an article in the current issue, an excerpt from a new book, *Men in Groups,* by Lionel Tiger.

I was no sooner seated at my desk than the telephone rang. It was McEachern. "Go down and talk to those women," he urged.

"I don't know what they're unhappy about," I said. "I haven't read the article."

"Don't worry about that. I've just had a call from a friend at the *Star*; they're sending over a photographer. Great publicity for your first day on the job."

I wasn't overjoyed at the prospect but agreed to go. As I emerged from the building, one of the women recognized me and I was immediately surrounded, all twenty protestors shrilling at me at once. I tried to respond but they weren't interested in explanations. The tumult mounted. As I turned to flee, one of the ladies brought her sign down on my head. At that moment, the *Star* photographer arrived. The caption under the front-page picture read: PROTEST GREETS NEW EDITOR.

Back in my office I found two nurserymen staggering under the weight of a magnificent *ficus benjamina.* Setting it in position, one of the men said he hoped the tree would do well. "They're very sensitive," he said. "If it doesn't like the atmosphere here, it'll die on you." Within a week it was dropping leaves; within six weeks the branches were almost bare, the leaves shrivelled.

Having hired me, McEachern didn't neglect me. There immediately began a stream of memoranda, as many as half a dozen a day, offering suggestions and drawing my attention to items and articles in various publications. Galley-proofs arrived with negative comments scribbled on the margins about the articles or writers. It became immediately evident that McEachern was not enamoured of the magazine's staff. His sharp comments pictured them as lazy, untalented, pseudo-sophisticated and guilty of moonlighting on company time. For the first few weeks I responded to the memoranda but soon found this time-consuming and unrewarding; but even dropping them in the waste basket didn't stem the flow.

When McEachern hired me, it had been to replace Borden Spears. I had known Spears at the *Star* where he had been managing editor, and later when he was managing editor of the *Financial Post*. When I joined *Maclean's,* he had been editor for five years, during which time the magazine had moved from the red into the black. McEachern had pressed me to try to induce Spears to stay on as associate editor. It would make the transition smoother, he said. Spears was a good man and I was happy to do so.

Not three months later, a memorandum from McEachern instructed me to fire Spears and to reduce my staff by two. I was troubled. I had urged Spears to stay and he had done so against his better judgement. During the break-in period, his help had been invaluable and his commitment was without reservation. When I discussed the matter with McEachern it became obvious that he had planned from the beginning to dump Spears; the only reason he had been kept on was to avoid trouble with the staff and public criticism. McEachern's claim, however, was that the budget had to be trimmed and, now that I was in command, Spears was redundant.

I believed in the right of management to manage and had no quarrel with the decision to cut the budget by reducing staff. I did feel, however, that *Maclean's* had an obligation to Spears and was not meeting it. I suggested that, rather than being dismissed, Spears should be offered a post elsewhere in the extensive Maclean-Hunter organization. He had certainly demonstrated his competence while at the *Financial Post* and *Maclean's*. But McEachern was adamant: fire Spears and the others.

I pressed him further. If it was necessary to dismiss Spears, surely some recognition should be given for his contribution to the magazine – at least give him extended severance pay. The answer was a flat no. A day later, he telephoned to say that he had decided to extend Spears' severance pay, and that I should postpone firing the other two staff members. It was essential, he said, to avoid public criticism about "more firings at *Maclean's.*"

As the weeks passed, my problems with McEachern worsened. I had not been on the job a month when his attitude went through a metamorphosis; it became one of master and scholar and his comments were often insulting in tone and content. Overnight, he instituted a weekly meeting with one evident purpose: to question and cavil about what was in the works and what long-range plans were envisioned. I learned that he had asked Doris Anderson, the editor of *Chatelaine,* to provide a report on what was required to improve *Maclean's.* He summoned John Peters, a New York magazine consultant, to scrutinize my plans and to make recommendations to him – despite the fact that Peters came to Toronto once a month for regular consultation. McEachern instructed me, contrary to my recommendation, not to bid for publication rights to excerpts from important books; he made changes in a cover I had approved; he vetoed changes I had proposed for the format of the magazine and then, as he often did, reversed himself a week later.

And the daily memoranda kept flowing, some of the suggestions bordering on the ludicrous: begin a monthly feature on "The Best Joke I've Heard on TV," paying readers ten dollars for each submission used. Do an article on a man in South Carolina who imports dragonflies to combat a mosquito problem. . . .

I could not believe what was happening. I had planned to devote an entire issue to a critical analysis of the news media: radio, television and newspapers. The lead article had been assigned to Peter Gzowski, a former *Maclean's* managing editor. McEachern ordered me to cancel the feature and to pay Gzowski off. Although he had not seen Gzowski's piece, he was certain that it would make trouble. He said he had received a telephone call from someone (he wouldn't say who) who had threatened that, if we carried the article, he would sue for libel. This despite the fact that it hadn't yet been written.*

---

* A reader may find the above account incredible, doubting that such things could happen on a magazine as prestigious as *Maclean's*. The facts were documented at the time of my leaving the magazine and have never been challenged.

Serious problems arose related to *Le Magazine Maclean,* a French-language monthly published by Maclean-Hunter in Montreal. As *Le Magazine* was losing money, McEachern decided that it was to be reduced to simply a translation of the English-language *Maclean's* and that I was to be its editor. The staff would be reduced to Mario Cardinal, the present editor, and one assistant; the entire operation was to be moved to Toronto.

I had no quarrel with the decision to cut losses and was willing to assume the added responsibility. I did point out that, with the growing nationalism in Quebec, the decision might be a mistake, a mistake that could be bad for the company's image and for anglophone-francophone relations. I did a study and suggested changes that would put *Le Magazine* on at least a break-even basis, urging that the maximum French-Canadian content be maintained. A week later I was instructed to proceed with the original plan, but to implement it in stages in order to avoid repercussions in Quebec.

Cardinal flew to Toronto. As we talked it became clear that, although he was being urged to stay on as associate editor, he had been told nothing about *Le Magazine* becoming a French-language echo of *Maclean's*, or that the operation was to be moved to Toronto, or that his staff was to be cut to one. He had been told only that *Le Magazine* and *Maclean's* would carry no more editorials – something *I* hadn't been told. (McEachern told me later that he hadn't liked the political tone of the editorials in *Le Magazine,* which voiced Quebec aspirations, albeit moderately, and that there would be less criticism if I dropped *Maclean's* editorials at the same time).

An impasse was reached. So many differences had arisen that McEachern and I had come to the ridiculous situation where we were no longer speaking to each other. Such communication as was unavoidable was done through memoranda. I had appealed to McEachern to let me run the magazine, telling him what I had told Beland Honderich: if I am capable, leave me alone. If I am incompetent, fire me. The plea was unavailing.

Each magazine at Maclean-Hunter has what is categorized as

a "publisher." His responsibility is to supervise all aspects of the magazine other than the editorial. *Maclean's* excellent publisher, Gerry Brander, came to see me.

"Charles," he said, obviously not relishing his task, "we've got a ridiculous situation here. Two grown men – a vice president of the company and the editor-in-chief of our most important publication – and you're not speaking to each other."

"Like two little boys," I supplied.

"Exactly," he said. "Look, we've got to straighten this out. If I can get Mr. McEachern to agree, will you agree to a face-to-face meeting, with me present to resolve the problem?"

"I'd welcome it," I said.

In his office, McEachern was seated behind his desk, apparently at ease. I took a chair to one side, not at all at ease. Brander cleared his throat nervously and began.

"Now, Ron and Charles, we find ourselves with ... with a problem. That problem is making the production of the magazine exceedingly difficult. Without apportioning blame or responsibility, I would like to try to get it resolved here and now. Perhaps each of you would like to say what you think needs to be done. Ron ... ?"

McEachern was all reasonableness. "I really don't know what the problem is. *I* don't have a problem. From the day Charles arrived, I've done everything in my power to help him. I've consulted. I've forwarded suggestions. I've worked with him to solve his problems." He turned to me. "I'll be candid – and I don't say this in a critical manner, Charles – but I'm at a loss to understand what your problem is."

Brander responded. "Charles is of the opinion that he is not free to put out the magazine."

McEachern shook his head, an aspect of sad bemusement on his face. "I really don't understand it. My purpose – and I'm sure it must be Charles' – is to produce a first-class magazine. Everything I've done is to that end."

Brander turned to me. "Charles?"

I shook my head slowly. "I don't know what to say. Ron sees it as a non-problem. Why are we meeting?"

"No, no," Brander said. "The point of our getting together is for each of us to speak his mind, to clear the air. Ron has said what he thinks. Now you say what you'd like him to do."

"In a sentence – " I said – "to do what he promised to do when he hired me – to get off my back."

McEachern was asked if he had anything further to say, and so was I. Nothing was added and I left.

We were now at the point of no return. I had no option but to resign. The situation was deteriorating daily. There was seething unrest among the staff. I had not discussed my problems with them but there are few secrets in an office filled with reporters. McEachern's interference had been obvious. The treatment of Spears rankled. The eviscerating of *Le Magazine Maclean* and the cavalier treatment of Cardinal had stirred anger. The arbitrary cancelling of the in-depth examination of the news media because of outside pressure had inflamed. The office was awash in rumours and little work was being done.

I decided to take the matter to the president of the company, Donald Hunter. He was in Calgary at a convention and I reached him at his hotel. I gave him a swift rundown of the events of the past five months and told him, regretfully, that unless changes were made, I could not continue as editor of the magazine. "You can't have two editors," I told him. "Mr. McEachern wants to decide the content of the magazine and its tone. That's his prerogative, but if he continues to do so, I will have to leave."

Hunter promised to look into it and call me back within the hour. A day passed. After leaving half a dozen messages, I finally reached him. He was oddly diffident. I told him that there was a swiftly burgeoning revolt and that *Maclean's* was about to have another mass resignation of staff. "The problem is," I said, "exactly what it was in the earlier firings and resignations: Mr. McEachern is, for all his undoubted ability, temperamentally unable to supervise journalists." I suggested that, in the interests of the magazine, a change be made at the level of the board of directors, with someone else being made responsible for *Maclean's*.

His only response was to gloss over the problem. I offered to fly to Calgary for a meeting. I suggested a three-way conference telephone call with McEachern. He preferred to wait until he was back in the city the following week. It became evident that he was stalling, trying to paper over the rift. He again promised to call me the following morning but didn't.

It was now obvious that I would be fired at a moment convenient to the company – I had observed that this was the way *Maclean's* often dealt with staff problems. But I had never resigned from a position in anger. I had gone to *Maclean's* planning to stay, and I very much wanted to. And there was, of course, the question: where would I go?

There was another larger concern: *Maclean's* is "Canada's national magazine," but another internal row and staff walkout might deal it a mortal blow. If that was followed by the resignation of Cardinal and his staff, it might be impossible to find a journalist of stature to save the magazine. And that would be Canada's loss.

I pondered the matter long and painfully and finally decided on my course. I would resign but would simultaneously release to the media a statement detailing my reasons. It was important to do so: the issue was editorial independence and the survival of the magazine. By making public the details of the impasse, the board of directors would be forced to deal with the essential problem — the inability of the vice-president to work congenially with the editor and staff of the magazine. McEachern's disdain for journalists and his arbitrary actions had led to irreconcilable differences and resignations by other senior staff. Now it was happening to me. It must be dealt with. I drafted a detailed press release.

A delegation of ten staff members came to see me, asking if it was my intention to resign. I told them it was. They then informed me that they had decided to resign en masse. Cardinal added that he, too, would leave, as would his staff. I argued that their leaving would not be in their own best interest or in the best interest of the magazines, and I elicited a promise that they would postpone any action.

I made one last attempt to save the situation. I wrote my resignation to Hunter but left it unsigned. It was on his desk on the Monday morning when he returned from Calgary. I waited through the day for a response. There was none. With a profound sense of sadness, I instructed my secretary to issue the press release. As I did, she handed me a press release that had been prepared by the editorial staff:

> In the considered judgement of the undersigned *Maclean's* staff, Mr. Templeton and Mr. Cardinal are justified in their resignations. Mr. Templeton has been subjected to destructive harassment for several weeks. Mr. Cardinal, editor-in-chief of *Le Magazine Maclean*, was misled into believing that the company would retain a measure of French-Canadian expression. Both men handled an impossible situation with dignity and

principle and stand high in the esteem of their colleagues. In the interests of the magazine, Mr. Templeton has asked his staff to remain at their posts. Members of the staff will make their individual decisions on his request; those decisions will depend largely on the degree of editorial independence accorded by management to Mr. Templeton's successor.

The statement was signed by Philip Sykes, managing editor, and by Alan Edmonds, Walter Stewart, Douglas Marshall, Marjorie Harris, Jon Ruddy, Courtney Tower and others.

Late in the day we all repaired to a nearby Chinese restaurant on Elizabeth Street and held a wake.

Inside Inventing

INSIDE INVENTING

T he man seated opposite appeared every bit the successful tycoon. There was authority in his speech and command in his presence. He exuded energy. We had been chatting during the meal but I had been reluctant to ask his name, certain that he was known to everyone but me.

The occasion was an elaborate dinner at the York Club given by John Bassett to honour Gavin Astor, later Lord Astor, son of the publisher of the London *Times.* I was one of perhaps eighty guests. The tables were arranged in rows, and the man across from me had dominated the conversation around him, speaking spiritedly and informedly on a number of subjects. After a brief lull in the conversation, he addressed himself to me.

"Well now, Mr. Templeton, you left *Maclean's* because of a dust-up with management. What are you doing now?"

"Inventing," I said.

"Inventing?" He was dubious. "You mean you're working at it full-time?"

I was, except for the daily radio show I did with Berton. After I left *Maclean's,* I decided to commit two years of my life to something I had long wanted to try – inventing. I knew something of the difficulties, having for years tinkered off and on with various devices. But more pressing matters had always intruded and I hadn't followed through. In this I was like ten thousand basement tinkerers (patent attorneys holiday in the Caribbean on us) who believe that, one day, we will come up with the ultimate gadget and live out our days hailed for our ingenuity and up to our wallets in royalty payments. (The odds against that happening, incidentally, are at least ten thousand to one.) Regardless, I decided to take the gamble. At fifty-four, I was young enough to risk the time.

I rented a hole in the wall over the Toronto-Dominion bank on Yonge Street at Hayden. It was a tiny cubicle with only one window and it was barred. The floor was made of reinforced concrete to prevent access to the vault immediately below; exposed water and sanitary pipes ran across the ceiling long before it became fashionable. Perfect for my purposes. I moved in a draughtsman's table, a second-hand metal desk and a borrowed chair, purchased the necessary draughting materials and was ready to begin.

But at what project? You don't say, "Well now, it's Tuesday. I think I'll invent something." Inventions meet needs, but first the need must be perceived. But how do you go about devising a solution to a perceived need? Observing that none of the available mousetraps are satisfactory, you decide to build a better one and begin by learning everything you can about mice and mousetraps. Then, for days and weeks and months, you puzzle to the point of obsession over ways to ensnare the tiny rodents. Early on you learn that, before you, other minds have asked the same questions. You carry on normal social intercourse, but much of your mind is off somewhere thinking mousetraps, to the frequent exasperation of those about you. You live mousetraps, you dream about mousetraps, your life revolves around mousetraps.

In the meantime, you test various approaches to the problem by making sketches or, if the idea seems promising, by making a model. A dozen times a light bulb may turn on in your brain and you utter the time-honoured "Eureka!" only to follow it with the "Aaargh!" of disappointment. The course becomes trial and error. Idea after idea is conceived, then developed, then rejected.

Then one day, out of the blue, usually without warning, an idea will present itself, fully articulated and often surprising in its ingenuity. The sudden illumination is not the result of chance; it is the product of a gestation period in the unconscious. The process is so normal you come to depend on it. Set a question loose in your mind and keep asking it in different ways, and your unconscious will toil for you, independently, even as you sleep, and finally present you with a not unreasonable answer.

There follows the refining process: the making of detailed mechanical drawings, the fabrication of a model, consulting with patent attorneys. These are exciting days: the world is about to beat a path to your door. They are followed usually by a prolonged, disheartening search for a manufacturer or for someone who will help you market your realized dream.

(It is often said that the novelist's is the loneliest craft. I would argue that the life of the inventor is lonelier. Both seek in a solitary place to fashion something from nothing but thoughts. But the writer's study becomes populated by characters. They are real people and they often become more real than family or friends as the book takes shape. The inventor works entirely alone. He lives with amorphous ideas, with inanimate things, and there is no companionship in them.)

Shortly after moving into my hideaway over the bank, I chanced to read in the business section of the *Globe and Mail* an article based on an interview with the federal deputy minister of mines and resources. He was bemoaning the lack of development in the north and appealing to Canadians to demonstrate the ingenuity through which this part of the nation could be exploited. Among the problems, he said, was the development of a system to transport the oil and gas believed to lie beneath the frozen wastes and waters.

I was intrigued and went to work.

The man across the table at the York Club was asking what I had invented.

"A system for transporting oil from the far north," I said.

He looked at me from beneath lowered brows. "Do you know anything about the north country? Have you ever been there?"

"Not the far north," I conceded. "The Northwest Territories, Yellowknife, Great Slave Lake. Not in winter," I added, "and only for a few days. But I've read a good deal."

"What are the major problems of constructing a pipeline in the north?" he asked. There was challenge in his voice.

"The weather, of course. The terrain. The permafrost. The fragile ecology. The migratory habits of the caribou."

His frown deepened. "And you've worked out a system for transporting oil south?"

"Such as it is."

"Tell me about it," he said. "But wait a minute. Before you do, have you protected it – your system, I mean? With the patent office."

"Not yet."

"Then don't give me any details. Just the general principles."

I described the system. His manner grew serious. He put a series of questions to me, repeating the injunction not to reply in specifics. Finally, he said, "Here's what I'd like you to do: talk to a patent lawyer, get yourself some protection and then come and see me."

Embarrassed, I said, "I'm sorry. I don't know who you are."

"Bill Twaits," he said.

Of course: W.O. Twaits, president of Imperial Oil of Canada.

I met with a patent attorney and a few weeks later called Twaits. He asked me to come to his office the following morning at ten. He laughed and said, "I'll have my northern vice-president with me."

His office was what I expected: a penthouse; expansive, masculine, with a massive desk and deep leather chairs. He introduced me to three men: one his "northern vice-president" (there seemed to be an in-joke there that wasn't explained), another I took to be a lawyer and someone else. I had been working for months on the system, drawing every detail of the structures and devices. I spread a dozen white-prints on a large coffee table and, for perhaps twenty minutes, explained what I had been up to. No one interrupted. When I was finished there were questions.

Twaits didn't mask his enthusiasm. He drew the others aside for a brief conversation and then returned to me.

"Harry Waste," he said, "he's president of the Bechtel Corporation. Do you know anything about Bechtel?"

I shook my head.

"Bechtel is the largest builder of pipelines in the world. Their headquarters is in San Francisco. They work for us and nearly everybody else in the oil business. Right now they're involved in enormous projects in Saudi Arabia and in other Arab countries. And in our north. Waste and some of his people will be here next week. I want you to meet him. I'll set it up."

The following Monday morning I sat alone and nervous in a suite in the Royal York hotel waiting for Harry Waste. I'd been told by the man who left me there that Waste would see me when he was able to break from a meeting elsewhere in the hotel. But time was running on and I knew he had another appointment at noon. When he entered, flinging aside his jacket and shirt and tie while he said hello, he seemed unhappy to find me in his room. He was brusque and preoccupied. I got the impression he was seeing me because Twaits had pressed it on him.

"Okay," he said, glancing at his watch, "you've got ten minutes. Let's see what you've got."

I went though my drawings, making the necessary explanations. He changed his glasses to see better. When the time was up, he asked, "Can I keep these?" I said, "Yes." "Good," he said, heading for the door. "I'll get back to you."

The following day, I received a telephone call from a Ray Christopherson in Bechtel's San Francisco office, and later in the day from Bruce Wilson, Bechtel's Canadian rep. He wanted some basic information – mailing address, telephone number, and so on. In the course of our conversation, he asked if I would like to try my hand at a particular problem the company was facing. Apparently, in laying pipeline to Europe from Saudi Arabia and other Arab countries, it was necessary to avoid rounding the eastern end of the Mediterranean. (Although he made no reference to it, I presumed that the object was to stay clear of Israel.) A decision had been made to cross the Mediterranean to Italy but great difficulty and many delays were being encountered laying pipe in bad weather. In an oddly offhand way, he suggested that I might want to give it thought.

I spent weeks working on the problems, and devised two systems to stabilize the "mother ship." I was directed to be in touch with German-Milne, a shipbuilding company in Montreal, and flew there to confer with their senior people. The meeting was cordial and encouraging but nothing came of it.

Nor did anything come of my meeting with Harry Waste. Five months passed before I heard from John Lynch, vice-president of Bechtel's pipeline division. They had examined my proposals carefully, he said, but had decided that they were too costly to implement.

It was the first of a series of near misses – although on a grander scale than my others. As I would learn, it was typical of the inventor's life.

In 1970, as now, most smokers were worried about the risk of emphysema and lung cancer. The report by the Surgeon General of the United States had frightened many, but the initial alarm had diminished and most of the addicted had temporized by switching to filter cigarettes. The emphasis at the time was on longer cigarettes, one brand boasting that its greater length "travels the smoke farther on its way to your throat." I set myself to inventing a filter that would be more effective than those on the market.

I finally settled on a system that replaced the usual filter with a plastic helical coil, three-quarters of an inch in length. The principle was this: the smoke, on reaching the helical coil, would be carried around the circumference in descending circles until it emerged. In travelling three-quarters of an inch, it would thus traverse approximately nine inches. During that time, it would be cooled and, at the same time, would deposit a considerable proportion of the tars and nicotine on the walls of the coil.

I made the necessary drawings and prepared a three-foot long model of the coil carved from a cylinder of insulating foam and covered with clear plastic so that the action within could be observed. When smoke was blown in one end, it could clearly be perceived moving in descending circles until it vented at the end. The effect was dramatic and impressive.

I called John Devlin, president of Rothman's, and made an appointment. He agreed to see me as a courtesy, I'm sure, but when I laid before him the drawings and demonstrated the movement of the smoke through the model, he became visibly excited. He asked if I had done a patent search. I hadn't – it's an expensive process, and in 1970 cost between three hundred and one thousand dollars. He told me not to concern myself about it; he would have the search made in Washington and in The Hague, where most patents related to the tobacco industry are registered. In the meantime, he would have a number of filters hand-made and tested at Rothman's research facility in Quebec City. He impressed on me the need for total secrecy in the meantime.

As I was leaving, Devlin escorted me through the Rothman's packaging plant. Once again I was high on the roller-coaster ride of anticipation. As I watched the tens of thousands of cigarettes being packaged, I added a Templeton filter to each one, paying myself a royalty of a fraction of a penny for each one of course.

All new ideas are not patentable, of course. To be granted a patent, a device must meet three criteria: it must be novel, it must be inventive and must have a practical application.

A patent search is an interesting if tedious process. There are men and women who spend their days questing through the multiplied thousands of patents on file in the various capitals of the world. The object of their search is to discover if some previous invention incorporates any or all of the principles used in the proposed device. If in this search a previous patent is discovered, there is little you can do about it. You have been pre-empted by some inventor who, years or decades earlier, hit upon the idea you thought you had been first to grasp.

When your patent attorney forwards copies of the few or many patents that incorporate principles or systems similar in some way to your device, you examine them with a combination of trepidation and fascination. If you find that your concept is not original, your work has been wasted and the money spent having the search made is gone. The fascination derives from examining the work of other inventors. Some of the devices are brilliant, of course, but the vast majority are gadgets which any amateur can see are of no practical use.

But now the report from the search in Washington was in, and the news was bad. In 1894, in a day before cigarettes were commonly mass-produced and most smokers rolled their own, a man in Wyoming patented the idea of passing cigarette smoke through a helical coil. He proposed in his application that the filter be made of wood or clay (plastics were unknown), inserted at one end of the hand-rolled cigarette, and at the end of the day, washed with soap and water. Impractical as it may have been, it pre-empted my idea. Moreover, with the passage of more than seventeen years, it was now "in the public domain," and any manufacturer who wished to use the idea was free to do so.

There was further bad news. The coils that had been tested on smoking machines at the Rothman's laboratory demonstrated that, while the idea seemed valid in theory, it was not effective. The first puffs of smoke were indeed cooled by their extended passage through the filter but, once the filter was heated, the smoke emerged hotter than would normally be the case. And the amounts of nicotine and tar precipitated on the walls of the coil were negligible.

To help me market an invention with a military application, I turned to, of all unlikely people, Billy Graham. Billy's influence opened doors at the Pentagon in Washington, D.C., and provided access to the senior research and development people in the United States military establishment.

The war in Vietnam was at its height. In my reading, I came upon an article delineating the plight of American pilots downed in the jungle or behind enemy lines. Some were captured, some starved, some died of their injuries. Common to the incidents was the fact that search-and-rescue aircraft often flew nearby but the downed pilot had no way to signal his whereabouts. So I devised a system that would allow a downed pilot to signal to his rescuers without betraying his presence. Seeking the opportunity to demonstrate it to the United States military, I wrote the Pentagon. There was no reply. A number of telephone calls was fruitless.

Billy Graham was a close friend of the incumbent president, Richard Nixon, and a frequent visitor at the White House. I took advantage of Billy's and my long friendship to telephone him, reaching him on vacation at a resort in Huntington Beach, Orange County, California.

"Billy," I said, "I have an invention that I'm convinced could be useful to the American forces in Vietnam. It will save lives. I'd like to demonstrate it to you and, if you feel that you wish to do so, I'd like you to see if you can arrange for me to show it to someone at the Pentagon."

Billy responded in his typically friendly way by inviting me to fly to California and to stay with him at his hotel. I didn't accept the offer of hospitality, but did fly to Los Angeles, registered at the Beverly Hilton, and the following day, drove to Huntington Beach.

Billy was tanned and looked fit. I had brought bathing trunks and for a couple of hours exposed my Canadian winter-pale skin to the California sun. We swam, ate by the pool and talked about old times. Away from the public area, I demonstrated the device.

Billy said, "Chuck, I have no talent for mechanical things, but it looks like a sensational idea. I'll be glad to talk to somebody about it."

He picked up the telephone. "Operator, I want to talk person-to-person to Mr. Melvin Laird in Washington, D.C. Yes, Melvin Laird, the secretary of defence. Try the White House first and then the Pentagon."

Within minutes the operator called back. "Hello, Mel? It's Billy Graham. How are you?" His voice exuded cordiality. "I'm fine, thank you. Yes, Ruth is fine — I'll tell her you were asking. . . . Mel, I want you to know I pray for you every day. And for the president and the other members of the cabinet; that God will bless you in your tremendous task . . . . Thank you, I appreciate your prayers. Mel, I'll tell you why I'm calling. I have here with me one of my oldest and dearest friends. He's a Canadian and his name is Charles Templeton. The best way I know to describe him is to tell you he's the Walter Cronkite of Canada." In a chair nearby, I flinched. "In addition to his broadcasting," Billy went on, "he's an inventor. He's flown here from Toronto to show me something designed to save the lives of our boys in Vietnam. Now Mel, I'm not qualified to judge whether it's a good idea or not, but it certainly impresses me. I really do think somebody should look at it. But I wouldn't want him to get passed off on somebody who wouldn't do anything — you know what I mean. Could you speak to the right person . . . ?"

He came from the phone to tell me that someone from the Pentagon would be in touch. Three hours later when I arrived back at my hotel, there was a message to call, as I recall it, a Mr. Janssen at the Pentagon. My contact was businesslike but deferential.

"Mr. Templeton, perhaps we can set up an appointment now."

"I can pretty well suit your convenience," I said.

"At *your* convenience, sir," he said. "Just let me know when you'll be in Washington."

"How about Thursday at ten?"

"Yes sir. If you give my office a call when you arrive, I'll send a staff car to your hotel."

The system I would demonstrate incorporates a six-foot by six-foot sheet of reflecting material, so polarized that when it is viewed through a compatible rotating disk, it alternately flashes black and white. I wanted to stage my demonstration as dramatically as possible, so I had the driver show me where Mr. Janssen's office was and laid out my material on the lawn beneath his window.

Janssen was dressed in a jacket and slacks and greeted me without military stiffness. I gathered that he was the civilian head of the Pentagon's research and development branch. We talked for a while, then I led him to one of the windows. Three storeys below, on the lawn, he could see the nondescript gray square of polarized material.

"Imagine a downed pilot, at sea in a raft or in a clearing in the jungle," I said. "He is without power and doesn't dare show a light. He unfolds a sheet of material like the one you see down there and places it on the ground or floats it on the water. And that's it. Search-and-rescue aircraft then merely sight through a rotating spinner like this, and here's what they see."

I passed the spinner to him. He looked through it, peering at the polarized area three storeys below. "Jesus Christ!" he said.

He experimented with the spinner, asking me a series of questions. Then he went to a telephone, punched a number and we were joined by another man in civvies. He was introduced as the head of a research department. The two of them went to the window and for perhaps five minutes examined and discussed the display below.

After an extended conversation, I went with the research head to his cluttered office. We were joined by two other men, obviously scientists, both in civilian clothes. One of the men questioned me about my technical training and, learning of its sketchy nature, seemed vaguely resentful, and said nothing further. An hour later, I was returned to Mr. Janssen.

"I'll be in touch soon," he said.

A letter came the following week informing me that a series of tests would be made. I heard nothing further for three months and then received a detailed report. The material I had left with them had been experimented with and tested in various locales under a variety of conditions: on the roof of the Pentagon, with flights of Grumman fighter aircraft doing air-to-ground studies; floated on the surface of Chesapeake Bay, its effectiveness tested by planes from an aircraft carrier; and so on. Other experiments were conducted over both open and forested land areas. In all, more than $200,000 was spent.

In the end, rejection. There had been high expectations at first, but finally the project was abandoned. Two reasons were given: new sighting devices were being introduced that could perceive body warmth night or day, and from great heights, and the problem I had sought to meet had been largely resolved. Additionally, viewed from the air, the great amount of polarized light reflected from bodies of water or after a rainfall diminished the effectiveness of my device. It was a great disappointment.

In the meantime, I had been working at devising a child-proof safety closure for containers holding dangerous substances. Again, my interest had been stimulated by an article in a newspaper. A child of three had drunk from a bottle of household bleach and had only been saved by prompt action at Toronto's Hospital for Sick Children. Not many days later, another child downed a bottleful of aspirin and almost died. I would try to design a cap or closure that would make such accidents unlikely.

Researching the problem, I was astonished to find how many children swallow harmful substances and how indifferent government and manufacturers were to the danger. The poison centre at the Hospital for Sick Children alone receives forty thousand calls a year, and in 85 per cent of the cases something hurtful has been swallowed.

The initial question was, of course, why does a child try to ingest such substances as bleach or aspirin? The taste of either is abhorrent to an adult. I learned that there are only four kinds of taste buds on the tongue — sweet, sour, salt and bitter — that they mature at various times and that they are not all fully functional until a child nears four years of age. The sweet-sensitive buds are concentrated on the tip of the tongue, sour flavours are detected at the sides of the tongue and bitter flavours at the back. Thus, a young child eating aspirin will not be deterred by the taste.

There was an ingenious closure on the market. It could be opened only if downward pressure was exerted while it was being turned. This foiled children, but it had disadvantages: it was difficult for older people and arthritics to operate; early models did not effect a tight seal, and were therefore unsuitable to contain liquids. I set out to circumvent both of these problems.

After three months of experiments and trying dozens of options, I found a solution. I refined the basic idea, worked out adaptations for various applications and constructed a crude working model. It met all the basic requirements: it was tamperproof for children, yet relatively easy to operate for the old and the infirm. It sealed tightly, did not present problems in fabrication and was inexpensive.

I have an advantage over most independent inventors. Because of my public activities I am well known, and this usually enables me to reach the president or some senior officer in a Canadian company, at least to arrange an appointment. My first contact was with Anchor Cap and Closure, a Toronto firm. The president showed immediate interest. I left him a set of white-prints and a textual description and was assured that he would be in touch soon. Weeks passed. When I reached him he was full of excuses for failing to contact me. He had, he said, held meetings with members of his staff, had checked the design with manufacturers of moulds and was now ready to introduce it to two of his largest customers. However, when weeks passed and I received nothing but vague responses, I notified him that I was withdrawing my submission. At that point he told me that the companies he had showed the closure to were definitely interested but had decided not to proceed.

"Are they satisfied with the concept?" I asked. "Are they convinced it will provide the protection?"

"Absolutely. No problem there."

"Then what's the problem?"

"Cost. Not that the closure would cost more per unit once it's in production, but there would be development costs. There would have to be some changes on the assembly line. And they would want to do some market testing and follow that with an ad campaign. They think they'll stay with what they have for now."

I was astounded. "Are you saying that, knowing their product is hazardous to children, and with the opportunity to make a change in packaging that would effectively end that possibility, they're unprepared to act?"

"They prefer to wait until the government requires everybody to make a change," he said. "That way they won't be at a competitive disadvantage."

I went next to Crawford-Birrell Inc., a manufacturer of plastic containers in Rexdale; I was becoming impatient with Canadian corporate conservatism and Crawford-Birrell had an association with Owens Illinois, one of the largest manufacturers of glass and plastic containers in the world. Birrell, the president, was enthusiastic and, on his next trip to the United States, took with him the specifications for my closure. I received a letter from Owens Illinois inviting me to their Toledo, Ohio headquarters.

The plant was impressive. Modern in design, it sprawls over acres of land on the outskirts of the city. A vice-president of the company took me on a tour of the bustling premises and introduced me to half a dozen officials. I spent the remainder of the day in discussion with two of their engineers and returned to Toronto buoyed by the energy and drive of the Americans.

A sudden roadblock: a letter came from Owens Illinois informing me that their legal counsel had done a patent search and was
of the opinion that my design might infringe on an existing
licence. I'd had a search done earlier and had turned up the patent
in question. My attorney had advised me at the time that, while
there was one aspect of similarity, there was no infringement.
Moreover, the other device was too complex to be technically
feasible. And too costly. I so informed Owens Illinois, but their
attorney counselled them not to proceed until the possibility of
infringement had been ruled out.

After days of sleuthing, tracking him through three cities, I
found the inventor in Washington, D.C. He was the executive
officer of the United States Airline Pilots Association. I flew to
Washington.

He was quite open with me. He had spent months of time and
thousands of dollars obtaining a patent and then seeking to interest manufacturers and had finally written off the entire experience as an adventure. Now, seeing an opportunity to recoup his
losses and make a profit, and realizing that without him I was
forestalled in my negotiations, he asked half of any royalties that
might accrue. I agreed, and he assigned his rights to me.

I met immediately with Owens Illinois, to tell them that the
infringement problem had been resolved. They were enthusiastic
about the project; I returned to Toronto, hopes high.

I never heard from them again. Telephone calls went unre-
turned. I wrote, but there were no replies. I don't know why. I
know only from other inventors that it is not uncommon behaviour. I had heard horror stories (some of which are true) about
great corporations stealing ideas and devices and I became convinced that this was what was afoot. So far as I know, my suspi-
cions were groundless.

After two more attempts to sell the closure, I put it aside. As a
change of pace, I turned to simpler tasks, and spent some weeks
trying to devise children's toys. One day, after changing the
ribbon on my typewriter, I tossed the empty metal portion into
the waste basket. After a moment's reflection, I retrieved it. It
consisted of two metal disks joined by a central axle. Experimenting, I placed it on the edge of a yardstick, let it roll down the slope
and, as it approached the end, lofted it spinning into the air. It
behaved as I hoped it would – the torque produced by the rotation

kept it upright. Good, I thought: a properly designed spinner (the ribbon-holder) fitted to a wand (the yardstick) would produce a spinning disk that could be flipped into the air and, with some practice, caught again on the wand. Two players could toss it back and forth like a vertical Frisbee. I worked on the design and had a model made at a cost of $180.

Watching my children play with a bolo-bat – whacking a tiny rubber ball to the length of an elastic and striking it again and again as it returned to the bat – I asked myself: what if I were to remove the face of the paddle, leaving only the rim? Would it be possible, instead of striking the ball, to have it pass back and forth within the rim? I fashioned a crude model from a coathanger and practised. It took some perseverance, but as I got better at it, it was fun.

I called the first game "Spinaroo" and the second "Hoop Ball," and took them with other concepts for children's games to the Ideal Toy Company in Toronto. They were taken by the first two and rushed samples into production in order to be ready for showing at the annual Canadian Toy Fair. Both are "action toys," and need to be demonstrated to be appreciated. (Who would buy a hula hoop hanging on a wall?) Ideal had agreed to hire teenagers to demonstrate both "Spinaroo" and "Hoop Ball" to passersby, but didn't. Orders were few.

A Canadian Armed Forces training aircraft went down in the Ungava region of Labrador. According to newspaper reports, the only equipment for signalling to search-and-rescue planes was a small hand mirror, a standard part of the survival kit stowed aboard aircraft flying over uninhabited territory. The mirror was a circle of chrome-plated metal with a hole in the centre. A downed airman peered through the peep-hole at an aircraft passing overhead; while sighting on the plane, he was to attempt to reflect the sunlight on it. It was obvious even to a child that it was a totally inefficient system, its effectiveness depending almost entirely on chance. It angered me that a downed pilot's chance of being sighted might rest on such an amateurish device.

I set to work to improve it and came up with a heliograph sighting device that would enable the user to direct the sun's rays at a target. (Incidentally, in developing an early model, I sustained a macula, a permanent opaque scar on the retina of my left eye.)

The device was small enough to be included in a survival pack, simple to operate and cost less than ten dollars to manufacture. I took it to the Canadian Armed Forces base in Toronto, demonstrated it to a Captain Kemp and, at his request, left it with him so that tests could be made.

There were the usual delays. Tests were conducted by personnel at the base. The report confirmed that the device was practical and a major improvement over the system being used. But nothing happened. After four months and many evasions, Kemp confessed that, "We don't have the budget to proceed. It's as simple as that."

He was chagrined over the enforced inaction and sought to be helpful. He referred me to two officers at the United States Air Force at Wright-Patterson Field, Dayton, Ohio. I didn't follow through. The two years I had committed to inventing had expired, and I was driven by necessity to work at a job offering a greater likelihood of remuneration.

This was not my first disappointment at the hands of the military. I had demonstrated a number of polarized signalling and training devices to Air Vice-Marshall F.W. Ball, Deputy Chief, Plans at the Department of Defence in Ottawa. The meeting with Ball and a group of half a dozen senior officers had been arranged by Paul Hellyer, who was then Minister of Defence. Not all the devices were mine; some had been developed by an American company with which I had a connection. I submitted the proposals, evaluations of them made by the Sheppard Technical Training Center at Sheppard Air Force Base in Texas, and a detailed analysis of the use of the processes by both the U.S. Army's Birdie Air Defence System and the Royal Air Force's technical staff in England.

The officers present at the two-hour demonstration were gung-ho, but as months passed, I found myself shifted from one department to another. No one, it seemed, had the authority or the wit either to conclude the discussions or to move them forward. No one said no, but neither did they say yes, and after a while I wearied of the game.

A system for joining plastic pipe (PVC) in the field was of interest to Dom-X, a Toronto firm. With my participation, they conducted several months of experiments. The end result? – "I'm sorry, Mr.

Templeton, we would like very much to proceed but, quite candidly, we don't have the money for R and D" (research and development).

A bed-chair for invalids or for people who simply like to laze abed went to Liberty Ornamental, a manufacturer of tubular chrome furniture. The president asked for the right to develop it and promised to make a prototype. Months passed – "The furniture business is slow right now." It took two months to get the drawings back.

A twelve-pack canned-drink dispenser went to the Canadian subsidiary of Continental Can. It was a corrugated cardboard container; it was light and portable, and dispensed individual cans. After three meetings, the response was, "Sorry. Most of our new-product research and development is done by the parent plant in the States."

An expandable wrench with increased leverage was shown to Aikenheads, the hardware people. The response was, "Ingenious. We could sell that. I suggest you take it to Crescent Tools in Jamestown, New York."

In two years I invented and made detailed working drawings or models of twenty-seven devices. In developing them I spent in excess of sixteen thousand dollars. I did not make five cents. (Oddly enough, while concluding this book, I sold two games to Waddingtons – the House of Games.)

I have talked to other Canadian inventors, some of them men of virtuoso ingenuity, and their experiences are akin to mine. I found one common complaint: Canadian companies lack imagination, daring and aggressiveness. Most are reluctant to allocate money for the research and development of new products; many are indecisive; too many depend for innovations and new products on parent firms outside Canada. Almost without exception, the inventors I met were frustrated and discouraged. The federal and the Ontario governments have each set up organizations to counsel with and help inventors. I contacted both of them. There was much talk and some encouragement but little practical help.

My experience showed me that there are literally thousands of Canadians working alone in basements and home workshops. The majority are tinkerers, but there are many others with genuine talent who have become frustrated and discouraged and, as I did, finally, give up. And Canada is the loser.

In *Ideas in Exile,* his massive study of Canadian inventors and inventions, J.J. Brown writes:

> Canadians have made contributions to world science and technology out of all proportion to their small number. Some Canadian inventions made possible major world industries, but we have ended up importing from England, Belgium, Italy and the United States billions of dollars of equipment invented here. This is our basic problem as a nation: a conservatism carried to the extreme of idiocy. If not corrected soon, it will leave us unable to compete as an industrial nation in the modern world.

The problems and discouragements faced by the Canadian inventor are many and forbidding. Usually years go by between the conception of a new idea and its sale to a manufacturer. But the amateur inventor is a valuable resource, and if Canada is going to increase its manufacturing, its productivity, its exports and its balance of payments – even as it creates jobs – it is going to have to resolve this particular problem of waste.

In the meantime, anyone interested in the rights to a simple device that enables even the unskilled to drive a woodscrew without having it twist away beneath the screwdriver . . . or a revolutionary typewriter table that eliminates backache . . . or a system to shield the operator of a computer terminal from emissions . . . or even a new form of chess, simple enough to be enjoyed by a child yet complex enough to challenge a "master" . . .

Inside Radio

INSIDE RADIO

I

The voice of the station manager at WGR/Buffalo was tinny on the intercom. "Okay, we're ready to go. On my cue, please." He raised his hand, jabbed a forefinger in my direction and I began to read: a news bulletin, a weather report and a commercial for a bank.

"Okay," he said. "Now, I want you to look out of the studio window and extemporize for three minutes on what you see."

My mouth dry with fear, I described the people on the street, the traffic, the flags in the wind and the skyscape. All the while, flashing quick glances at the sweep hand on the studio clock and wondering what I would do when I ran out of things to say. I made it, but barely. Afterwards, the station manager and I chatted for a few minutes while he gave me his version of "Don't call us, we'll call you."

I have occasionally wondered what would have followed had I become an announcer on an American radio station. I was twenty. It was during that hiatus early in my ministry when I briefly lost my faith and returned to Toronto. To earn some money, I sold four political cartoons to the Toronto *Telegram* and decided to try to get into radio. No Toronto station would give me an audition, so I tried Buffalo. Fortunately, I wasn't hired.

During the Avenue Road Church and Youth for Christ years, I did hundreds of radio broadcasts, mostly on CHUM. Monty Hall, host of the television show *Let's Make a Deal*, and Larry Mann — who these days berates his staff in television commercials for not using the telephone to do business – were staff announcers. Robert Saunders, whose *Mayor's Report to the People* preceded my broadcast on Sunday afternoons, would frequently go past his allotted half hour. When he realized that he was about to run over, he would say something like, "I need another minute or two to finish. I know my good friend Charles Templeton won't mind if I take a little of his time. Incidentally, go hear him preach. It'll do your heart good."

In 1958, shortly after I returned to Canada from the United States, All-Canada Radio, a syndicate serving stations across the country, asked me to produce ten one-minute news commentaries five days a week. Over the next six months, I ended each day wearily hammering out ten pages of editorial copy and taping them for transmission to stations subscribing to the syndicate.

Pierre Berton was providing a similar service and we often crossed paths. One late night after we had recorded our commentaries, I said to him, "Pierre, this is crazy. The two of us should simply sit before a mike and extemporize a dialogue on the news." He nodded agreement, but before anything could be done about it, we both left All-Canada.

In the spring of 1966 I received a telephone call from Jack Dawson, station manager at CFRB Radio. "I hear through the grapevine that you're considering doing a newscast for CFTR. If you're prepared to do a newscast, why not do it for the biggest and best?"

I was in fact weighing an offer from Ted Rogers, who owned CFTR, and I had mentioned it to my brother, who was a neighbour of Dawson's. Three days later, I met with Dawson in the office of W.C. Thornton Cran (friends called him Winkie), president of CFRB. Also present was Don Hartford, then the treasurer and now president. Although nothing specific was said about it, it was evident that they were concerned about Gordon Sinclair's health and were thinking about an eventual replacement. (Seventeen years later Sinc is still going strong.) They wanted me to begin with a noon newscast and see how the cards fell.

I pointed out that a newscast would take hours of preparation and that I didn't have that much time available. As we talked, my mind flashed to the night when I suggested to Berton that we combine our editorial efforts. On an impulse, I said, "Double the money and I'll get Berton. We'll discuss the news in an opinionated way and you can call the program *Dialogue.*"

After some discussion, Cran and Hartford withdrew for a few minutes. When they returned, Hartford said, "Get Berton and you've got a deal."

I reached across and picked up a phone. "Pierre," I said, "I'm at CFRB. They'd like to do *Dialogue.*"

"Fine," he said. "What's the money?"

It was the beginning of an association on radio that has continued for almost eighteen years. Pierre and I have discussed the news five days a week on almost four thousand broadcasts – for four years on CFRB and thirteen years on CKEY, syndicating the program across Canada, first on Standard Radio and later on Maclean-Hunter's Newsradio. In that time, *Dialogue* has been nominated three times and, in 1978, it won the ACTRA award for Best Radio Program.

Within weeks of beginning the program I ran into trouble. Berton and I have always spoken bluntly on *Dialogue,* never hesitating to criticize or praise any organization or individual from the prime minister down. On this occasion, I had been outraged by a small rump of Conservative backbenchers in the Ontario legislature. They had badgered in an exceptionally crude and cruel manner a member of the opposition while he was trying to make a valid point – a point made, coincidentally, on the previous day's *Dialogue.* I described the noisy backbenchers as "ignorant boors who were often asleep or drunk in their seats."

There was an immediate uproar. I was attacked in the legislature and received word via the grapevine that I was going to be summoned before the bar of the legislature and charged with contempt. It was a serious matter. The legislature is in effect a court and, even though the charges I had made were factual, they would be difficult to prove under formal questioning.

I let it be known through friends in the chamber that, if I were hauled before the bar, I would defend my statement that some backbenchers were drunk in their seats, by raising questions about what was known as "the biggest blind pig in Ontario" – the Members' lounge at Queen's Park. Though unlicenced, it served liquor. There was also a custom, now ended, that when the premier was scheduled to visit the lounge, a banquet licence would be obtained so that he would not be compromised. It was an innocent bit of official hypocrisy but a political buzz-bomb.

The issue died.

The question most asked about *Dialogue* was "Do you and Berton decide in advance of a discussion which side you'll take?" The answer is no, but with one exception.

During the first week the show was on the air, we were at a loss for a subject – a not uncommon problem. Henry Moore's magnificent sculpture known as "The Archer" was about to be installed before Toronto's City Hall, and there was controversy over its appropriateness. Pierre and I held the view at the time that each of our discussions should be controversial, so I volunteered to speak in opposition to the Moore. On the air, Berton demolished me. I was arguing a case I didn't believe in and was ineffective and unconvincing. We resolved that day never to take a position we didn't hold and have never deviated from that decision. That we so often differ stems from the fact that our basic philosophies are so different.

My life has touched so often on Berton's and his on mine that it seems appropriate to say something about the association. Through a series of choices and coincidences we have worked together for more than a quarter of a century. For eighteen of those years we have met most weekdays to discuss the news. Before that, we performed on CBC radio and television. We were at the *Star* together, although I seldom saw him there as he wrote his column at home. As well, we have been thrown together in many other ventures.

Over the years we have become friends, although not intimate friends, for we see little of each other socially. Listeners who hear us assault each other on *Dialogue,* where occasionally the sparring degenerates to a verbal slugging match, say, "Surely, at times, you guys must hate each other." There *are* times when anger flashes. We may even descend to name-calling, some of the milder epithets being, "naïve Philistine" (directed at me) and "knee-jerk socialist" (at him). Sometimes at the end of the program there is tension in the air and a bristling between us, but invariably one or the other will say something like, "That was a hairy one," the other will grin and that is the end of it. It would not have been possible to sustain the program over eighteen years had we not each developed a profound mutual respect, a respect tempered in the daily jousting. My wife Madeleine's view is that we have endured because we are both "blessed with an imperturbable egotism."

The fact is that we agree on many issues, but we differ as

frequently as we do because we are very different individuals. We are unlike in our political philosophies, our attitudes to work and play and in our reactions to public notoriety. Both of us would resist being labelled, but Pierre is by disposition if not affiliation a socialist. I am a liberal. We both work hard but very differently. After the research has been completed, he writes his books over a few months in a sustained burst of concentration. Working seven days a week, I may take as long as a year and a half. He plays as hard as he works, taking frequent breaks to distant places. I seldom go out of the country, and withdraw each weekend to my home on Georgian Bay, where I spend each morning at the typewriter. This baffles and exasperates him. Many times he has fumed at me, "For God's sake, Chuck, take a break! Go out and get drunk. Fly to Paris or Jamaica or somewhere and do absolutely nothing." I pay no attention.

Pierre is gregarious. He enjoys parties and public functions. He doesn't seek attention but gets lots of it and relishes celebrity. I am no misanthrope but I am bored at parties, ill at ease in public, self-conscious when recognized and slightly resentful when approached. He seems never to worry about his health (he has a high pain threshold and actually finished one of our *Dialogues* while passing a kidney stone); I am given to occasional hypochondria. Pierre pretends not to be concerned about the reception given to his books by the press, but is. I fume and fret unduly, and before publication day suffer greatly from the Dreads. At Christmas I give him a bottle of champagne; he gives me a bushel of birdseed.

We are not entirely unalike. We're both birdwatchers, both fascinated by politics, both love cats (I introduced him to the Himalayan breed) and wouldn't be without at least one. We are both cartoonists (although Pierre is a comic-strip fan and I am not), both love books and couldn't exist without newspapers. A fundamental similarity is that we both love life, live with zest and are interested in everything.

Berton is not thoughtful but he is generous and loyal to his friends. Years ago, he urged me to buy the house next to his in Kleinburg (Jack McClelland now owns it) and often proposes that Madeleine and I join him and Janet on a vacation. We have not yet been able to. Before I married Madeleine and was, for a few years, alone at Christmas, Pierre insisted that I join the Berton family for their celebration. On those occasions when I have been very much in need of the good counsel of a trusted friend, I have turned to Pierre.

Twice, Berton and I just missed carrying our working relationship to the ownership of a newspaper.

In February 1965, after having resigned from the *Star* and been defeated in my bid for the leadership of the Ontario Liberal party, I was for a brief period president of Technamation Canada, a small company manufacturing polarized advertising displays. One morning, I received a telephone call from George Monteith of the Montreal law firm Monteith, Hamilton, Holbein Ltd. He informed me that, while the *Globe and Mail* was not on the market, R. Howard Webster, the chairman and publisher, would consider an offer to purchase it.

A month earlier, Phillip Givens, then mayor of Toronto, had gotten in touch to inform me that the *Globe* might be available for purchase and wanted to know if I would be interested. I told him I would. Givens passed on the information but did not disclose my name. Now the opportunity was moving closer.

I got in touch immediately with Martin Goodman and we met for lunch. I had met Goodman when I first joined the *Star*. Beland Honderich had gathered a small group to bid him farewell as he left for Harvard University on a Neiman Fellowship. After his sabbatical, he was posted to Washington and then to Ottawa as bureau chief. Now he was back in Toronto on the path that would not long afterwards make him publisher. At lunch, Goodman and I formed an informal partnership and divided our responsibilities: I would do the negotiating and prepare the presentation; he would raise the money. The asking price, according to Monteith, was $15.5 million.

It developed that, because of my association with the Liberal party, there was concern that I might move the paper in that direction. I had already decided that, if we acquired the paper, I would eschew partisanship and follow an independent editorial policy. In response to a request, I wrote a six-page letter outlining my view of the directions the *Globe* should take and the specific objectives I would set. I put together a board of directors that included Donald Fleming, the former finance minister in the Diefenbaker government, Dr. Davidson Dunton, president of

Carleton University and the former president of the CBC, André Laurendeau, vice-chairman of the Royal Commission on Bicultu- ralism and Bilingualism and the former editor of *Le Devoir,* Walter Harris, chairman of the board of Victoria and Grey Trust and former finance minister in the St. Laurent government, Pierre Berton and others. I also specified that the asking price of $15.5 million would be met through the raising of $3 million in equity, with the balance in bank loans and privately placed debentures.

Over a period of a few weeks, the negotiations began to cool. It became obvious that there were concerns over my political views. Overnight, conversations ended, and not long afterwards I learned that the *Globe* had been sold to F.P. Publications.

In my final conversation with Monteith I had been asked in an offhand way, "Would you be interested instead in buying a Toronto radio station?"

"Which one?"

"CKEY."

"Thank you, no," I said.

There was another opportunity to buy a newspaper. In 1971, John Bassett decided to cut his losses and sell the Toronto *Telegram.* I was in his office on another matter and asked him if the rumours were true. Yes, he said. The paper was losing money, there seemed no likelihood of reversing its fortunes and he had decided to fold it while it still had assets.

In the midst of our conversation he said suddenly, "By God, Charles! You and Berton should buy it. The two of you have the experience, the moxie and the drive to make it work. If anybody can save it, you guys can."

I broached it to Pierre. He was immediately interested. We agreed that, first, we should learn the magnitude of the *Telegram*'s financial woes. I called Bassett. He said he would arrange for us to see the books. He added a warning. "Look," he said, "you're both friends of mine and I wouldn't want you to get hurt; the picture is forbidding. But, if you guys can make it go, nobody will be happier than I."

After meeting with Bassett the following day, Pierre and I returned to my car and drove slowly east on Front Street, talking. I pulled to the curb in front of Union Station and for perhaps twenty minutes we each put forward our views about what needed to be done. We agreed that we should convert the paper into a tabloid, radically change its style and find a new name. Pierre was disposed toward an emphasis that was politically left, making the target audience working people and members of craft and labour unions. I believed we should avoid any political colouration, convinced that that era of journalism was passing. We jousted lightly about our respective titles and our particular responsibilities.

Then, almost as though on cue, we turned in the seat to face each other. "Pierre," I said, "while we've been talking I've been thinking about the next three to five years. We both know that, if we're going to make it succeed, it's going to take twelve- to fourteen-hour days, seven days a week. Are we prepared to put aside the other things we're doing and devote ourselves to this?"

"Chuck," he said, "that's exactly the question I was going to put to you. I don't think I am."

"Nor am I," I said. And that was that.

Pierre and I had been at CFRB almost four years when I received a telephone call from Doug Trowell, president of CKEY radio, asking if he could come by and see me. I had met Trowell when I was at *Maclean's* — CKEY is owned by Maclean-Hunter — and had found him personable but oddly wary in social intercourse. Wanting to avoid a time-wasting discussion, I said, "Doug, if it's to discuss our moving to CKEY, let me simply say that we love it at 'RB and it would be pointless to talk about a move." None the less, he said, he would like to chat.

I had broadcast over CKEY in the early 1940s. Having founded the Avenue Road Church, I was anxious to extend its outreach. I walked into the studios (they were then on University Avenue) without an appointment and asked to speak to Jack Kent Cooke, the president. His secretary was getting rid of me when Cooke passed by. He knew me from my days as sports cartoonist at the *Globe,* crooked a finger and said, "Come with me."

In his office he came right to the point. "Why do you want to be on radio?"

"For the same reason Imperial Oil and Pepsodent toothpaste and Bovril want to. It's the best way to be in direct touch with the people."

"If I put you on the air, will you pay your bills?"

"Of course," I said.

He grinned at me. "I've had that promise from men of the cloth before."

Now, some thirty years later, I sat in my tiny cubicle talking with Doug Trowell, the present head of the station. After a few minutes, I said, "What's on your mind?"

He said, "I have two propositions to put before you. First, that you and Berton move *Dialogue* to CKEY. Second, that you also do our 8:00 a.m. newscast."

I said, "Doug, as I told you on the telephone, we're happy at CFRB. It has the largest audience in the country, maybe in North America. It's professionally and competently run. In the years we've been there there has been no attempt to control what we say. More than that: getting up before dawn to do a newscast doesn't appeal to me at all."

He said, "May I ask you a question in confidence?"

"That depends, of course."

"What does 'RB pay you and Berton?"

I said, "I can't tell you that."

"Trust me," he said. "I have a very specific reason for asking. I give you my absolute assurance that the information will go no further than this room."

"We're pretty expensive," I said evasively, not wanting to answer his question.

"How expensive?"

"Very."

I finally told him the figure. He put his head down and said nothing for perhaps thirty seconds. I filled the silence by saying, "I *told* you we were expensive."

"I'll double it," he said. "As well, I'll pay you (naming a figure) to do the newscast."

Now he had given *me* pause. I considered it a moment and said, "Have you discussed this with the management at Maclean-Hunter? I'm not their favourite employee."

"Yes," he said. "They understand what happened at the magazine."

"I'll pass your offer on to Berton."

"Why don't you do it right now?"

"He's in Japan."

"I'll pay for the call."

I tracked him down in ten minutes. While we were waiting, I

argued about doing the newscast. For five years on the *Star* I'd risen before dawn and hadn't liked it. An 8:00 a.m. newscast would require me to be up before five. The prospect didn't please. Trowell argued persuasively. He saw the newscast as more important to the station than *Dialogue*. There is a maxim in radio: "Whoever owns 8:00 a.m. owns the day."

"Try it," he said. "You'll like it."

On the long-distance line my conversation with Berton was guarded. He was interested. We agreed that before we could decide we were bound to give CFRB the opportunity to match the offer. Dawson responded with one increase, and then a second, but would not duplicate Trowell's offer.

On my third day at CKEY, James Cross, the British trade commissioner, was kidnapped by the *Front de la Libération de Québec*. Eleven hectic days later, the Trudeau government proclaimed the War Measures Act. The following day, Quebec Labour Minister Pierre Laporte's murdered body was found in the trunk of his car. As the news broke, I volunteered to do double duty and went on the air every half hour updating the story.

On the day Prime Minister Trudeau proclaimed the War Measures Act, Berton had been in a fury during our *Dialogue*. I had opposed his rush to judgement, arguing that we should wait until the prime minister addressed the nation. "We've got to trust him," I insisted. "He's privy to information that we don't have. The crisis *must* pose a genuine threat to the nation or he wouldn't call out the troops."

That night, I watched Mr. Trudeau on television, awaiting the promised explanation. He came on the air, steely, sombre, serious in a dark blue suit, the only visual relief the splash of colour on his lapel. It was an impressive performance, a bit of theatre. But he presented no concrete reasons for his unprecedented action, no adequate accounting for the army in the streets, for the hundreds of arrests in the night, for the suspension of civil rights.

I telephoned Berton. "I feel betrayed," I said – a bit theatrical myself.

The following day and through the week we hammered the government, disregarding warnings that our broadcasts were subject to the strictures of the Act and despite the fact that most Canadians approved the draconian steps the government had taken. So far as I know, no one else in the electronic media raised a voice those first few days. There was much adverse mail, but one heartening note – CKEY's management stood solidly behind us.

In the summer of 1971 the United States government announced that it would conduct underground nuclear tests at Amchitka, a tiny island in the Aleutian chain off the tip of Alaska. As the date approached, warnings and protests began to be heard from scientists, environmentalists and private citizens. When his chief environmental officer warned President Richard Nixon that there was the possibility of unforeseen consequences, he intervened and postponed the tests.

Across North America the protests mounted. There was a vast uneasiness among Canadians and some irresponsible speculation from both the qualified and the kooks: "The blast will trigger an earthquake." "A tidal wave will sweep onto the British Columbia coast." "Thousands of seals and millions of fish will be killed by the concussion." There were noisy protests before the United States embassies in Ottawa and Toronto. Then, after weeks of indecision, the president announced that the experiment would proceed, arguing that national security took precedence over other considerations.

Harvey Clarke, the public-relations head at CKEY, had been troubled by the issue and had been wondering if there was "some civilized way to protest." He suggested that I mention in my newscast that I planned to send a telegram to the White House registering my objection to the detonation of the bomb, and that anyone who wished to add his or her name should send it to me. The response was immediate and overwhelming. Before I had concluded the newscast, cars were pulling up at the door of the station, motors left running while drivers dashed inside to leave their names.

Berton and I expanded the theme on *Dialogue,* stipulating that anyone wishing to add his or her name to the telegram must include ten cents, the cost of appending the signature.

Within one week, 179,886 people sent in their names. The telegram we dispatched was the longest ever transmitted by Western Union and measured almost a mile in length. Using up to three circuits, it took eighty hours to transmit. The cost was $9,449.32. Berton and I flew to Washington to present it at the White House. When the wire was delivered to us at the gate to the Executive Office Building, it was in the form of eleven huge rolls of paper. The only thing we could find to carry it in was a supermarket shopping cart.

Berton and I had not intended to take the wire to Washington; we had hoped to have it presented to President Nixon or his designate through the Canadian Embassy. But they refused to have any part in it. Nor would External Affairs in Ottawa help. Almost 200,000 Canadians, speaking with one voice and paying for the privilege, wanted to lodge a reasoned protest but External wasn't interested. If anything, their reaction was negative.

In Washington, surrounded by American reporters, Berton and I tried to find some official in the American government to receive the telegram. But we would not be turned away, and when finally we trundled our creaking, overburdened shopping cart through the halls of the OEB to the furthermost end of the building, it was to meet with John Dean, special counsel to the president.

Dean, a small, neat but unimpressive man, came from his office to greet us. He seemed a timid fellow, soft-spoken and unprepossessing. I explained our mission and sought an assurance from him that the telegram would be brought to the attention of the president. He was non-committal at first, but when I persisted, murmured something to the effect that, yes, Mr. Nixon would be informed.

Finally, Berton, who stands six-foot-three, leaned over and tapped a finger on the shoulder of five-foot, eight-inch Dean. "Look, Mr. Dean," he said, punctuating the words with the finger, "180,000 Canadians paid to put their signatures on this wire. We've come all the way from Toronto as their representatives to bring this thing to Mr. Nixon's attention. We want to be able to report to the Canadian people that he will see it. Do we or don't we have your personal guarantee that he will?"

Dean bobbed his head and said, "Yes sir. Yes sir."

Two days later, on Saturday, November 6, 1971, the bomb was detonated. The sky didn't fall.

In November, 1977, I received a telephone call from a man who gave his name as Jim Lilly and represented himself as a private detective. He informed me that he had access to tax files at the Department of National Revenue and that he would reveal to me how the leaks worked if I would meet with him.

It is not uncommon in the news business to be contacted by

informants who promise to divulge inside information on some important matter or to alert you to corrupt behaviour by someone important in public life. Most such callers are kooks, and you soon learn to recognize them as such. But the man on the telephone sounded legitimate, and I invited him to my apartment. He brought with him a man he introduced as his partner.

Lilly was a fast-talking, extroverted man with overtones of flim-flam. His partner, Charles Meredith, was taciturn and seemed trigger-tense; as Lilly spoke, he occasionally interrupted to tone down or correct extravagant statements. They told me that they operated a two-man private-detective agency in Toronto, but had been informed that their licence was about to be lifted by the attorney general's office of the Ontario government.

Lilly was candid. He admitted that, in the pursuit of their work, they had sometimes bent the law, as, he insisted, did most people in the business. He insisted, however, that none of the offences were serious and suggested that I check the AG's office. He had come to me, he said, seeking a trade-off: if I would make "no more than one phone call," asking that his case be reviewed, he would demonstrate to me how private tax information could be obtained at will. Seeking to establish credibility, he said, "You have an unlisted telephone number, right? I can find out what it is in two minutes."

He picked up the telephone, dialed a number and spoke briefly into it, cupping a hand so that I couldn't hear. After a moment, he said, "Thank you," made a note and passed it to me. "Incidentally," he said, "you have four demerit points against your driving licence."

I was intrigued. If he could demonstrate with equal facility that personal income-tax information was not sacrosanct, the implications were enormous. "I'll enquire at Queen's Park why your licence isn't being renewed. If it isn't because of a serious infraction, I will ask if the decision can be reviewed. But I will make no advocacy; you understand that?" The two men nodded. "Now," I said, "how is security breached at National Revenue?"

"Rather than tell you," Lilly said, "I'll bring you the details of your tax return last year."

We met the following morning. I reported on my call to Queen's Park. There were some unspecified irregularities in the pursuit of their work as private investigators, but nothing of a criminal nature. They had been told to desist but hadn't. Consequently, their licence was going to be suspended. However, I was given an assurance, with no promise given or implied, that the case would be reviewed.

"Now," I said, "what did I earn last year?"

Reading from a pocket notebook, Lilly reeled off my tax-file number, social security number, gross income, taxable income and the amount of tax paid.

"Incredible," I said.

"And," he added, obviously relishing the impression he was making, "here is the name of your accountant, his address and telephone number." He passed me a slip of paper.

I had discussed the situation with Berton overnight and we had agreed on a plan. If there were leaks in the Department of National Revenue, we would have to establish that they were widespread. We would need evidence that secrecy could be invalidated across the country.

"Are you prepared for one more test?" I asked. Lilly nodded. "Then get me the tax returns for two people: Geoffrey Woodward, who lives in White Rock, British Columbia and a woman who lives in Montreal." (Woodward is Berton's brother-in-law. He had readily given Pierre permission to proceed. The woman was the Montreal representative for McClelland and Stewart, Berton's and my publisher. She too had agreed to let us use her in the test on the condition that her name not be made public.)

The following morning, I put Lilly in touch with Berton by telephone. He reported that Woodward's tax return had been filed on a short T-4 form at the Pender Street office of Revenue Canada in Vancouver. He provided all the basic details, including the fact that the tax had been paid by personal cheque and that Woodward had been reassessed, naming the amount. He provided the same kind of information on the Montreal woman. Berton checked his sources. All the data were accurate.

I now asked Lilly to meet an extraordinary test. "Get me the tax information on Joe Clark, the Leader of the Opposition in the House of Commons."

"I'm not sure I can do that," he said. "It may be flagged – the returns of many important people are – but I'll give it a try."

"One condition," I said. "I don't want to see the data. Put it in a sealed envelope."

He was back the following day with an envelope. I telephoned Mr. Clark's office and spoke to his executive assistant, Bill Neville, telling him exactly what had happened. He called me back to say that an accountant from Clarkson, Gordon in Toronto would come to my apartment to check the authenticity of the data.

That afternoon, a formal and very precise gentleman arrived from Clarkson, Gordon. He insisted on identifying himself with documents and insisted that I remain in the room while he opened the sealed envelope. When he had perused the contents and made notes, he placed them in an envelope, sealed it and asked me to initial it. An hour later, Neville called to say that Clark had confirmed the accuracy of the information.

Now to break the story. Berton and I were aware of the seriousness of what we were doing. The Income Tax Act guarantees by law the secrecy of the information in tax returns. The only persons permitted to have access to tax records are the head of Statistics Canada – under controlled conditions – and the minister of Health and Welfare who may ask for tax records under the Old Age Security Act and the Canada Pension Plan. Even with these exceptions, specific permission must be granted by the minister of revenue. We were aware that we had broken the law and had conspired to do so, but had convinced ourselves that the actions we had taken were in the public interest. We were prepared to face the consequences.

We were determined also that our revelations not be used for partisan political ends. So, at 8:05 a.m. November 17, on the morning of the first of two broadcasts we did on the subject, we notified all three political parties. I called the prime minister's office and spoke to Dick O'Hagan, Mr. Trudeau's press-liaison chief. He put me in touch with Jean Carpentier, the PM's executive assistant, to whom I related the entire story. Berton gave the same information to Ed Broadbent, the leader of the NDP. Mr. Clark had already been informed.

We made a further decision: we would not permit the revelations to become a media circus. We each pledged that, subsequent to the broadcast, we would not speak to any journalist, would not be interviewed on radio or television (including on our own station) and would make no statements except to such government officials as might contact us.

The broadcasts created a sensation. The story was headlined on page one in newspapers across the country. There was an immediate uproar in the House of Commons. Through some ineptitude, the prime minister's office had failed to notify Joe

Guay, the Minister of Revenue, and he was taken off guard by questions from the opposition and the press. Guay, who was Liberal patronage boss for Manitoba, and who was shortly thereafter appointed to the Senate, seemed more confused than usually. Pierre Trudeau, on the other hand, asked by the press for his reaction, snapped, "Put 'em in jail."

As expected, I heard from the RCMP. An inspector Brockbank came by appointment to my apartment to interview Berton and me. I asked a lawyer friend, Julian Porter, to join us. Brockbank was courteous and soft spoken. He asked a few questions and then asked for the names of my informants, prefacing the request by saying, "I presume you're not prepared to give the names." I told him that Berton didn't know the names and that I had pledged not to reveal them. He smiled, nodded and left.

Our informants proved to be eager beavers. I had instructed them not to be in touch by telephone because of the possibility that my line might be tapped. Nevertheless, later that day, a manilla envelope was slipped beneath my door. Within it was another sealed envelope bearing the information that it contained the tax return of the Speaker of the House of Commons. I tore it up unscrutinized. There was enough fat in the fire.

Clare Wescott, an old friend, telephoned. Wescott is executive assistant to William Davis, the premier of Ontario. It was he whom I had called to check into my informants' problems with the Attorney General's office. Westcott told me that he had just concluded a conversation with the officer who headed the OPP security force at Queen's Park.

"He's an experienced man," Clare said, "and pretty level-headed. He thinks that you may need police protection."

"Protection?" I said. "From whom?"

"Your informants are so-called private investigators," he said. "Sometimes they skate pretty close to the edge of illegality. Even more important, they have some, shall we say, unsavoury associations. They know things about some of the really rough operators in this town, enough to blow the whistle on them. These people could be worried that this information may have been passed to you for future broadcasts and they might want to keep you quiet." He paused, ill at ease. "I know, Charles, this all sounds cloak-and-dagger, but my OPP friend is convinced that you may be at some risk."

"Clare, you're kidding?"

"There probably isn't any danger," he said, "but we'd both feel better if you let him arrange to keep you under surveillance for the next few days."

It is my custom to travel each weekend to my cottage on Georgian Bay near Penetanguishene. I arrived at dusk on the Friday. Within a few minutes there was a knock on my door. When I opened it, there were two heavy-set men on the threshold, veteran OPP officers in civvies, one a senior officer from Toronto headquarters who had driven up from the city, and the other the divisional head at Barrie. I invited them in, gave them a drink and we talked for an hour.

That entire weekend, an OPP cruiser parked out of sight on an old logging road back of the cottage. When it grew dark, I walked up the road to take the officer a cup of coffee. He thanked me and asked me to leave the outside lights burning through the night. "I'll be doing a walkabout every hour or so," he said.

As I drove to Toronto early Monday morning, I spotted in my rear-view mirror an unmarked police car hanging two or three cars back on highway 400. He followed me, showing great skill in the city's heavy traffic, until I turned in at the underground garage at my apartment building.

Berton and I did two follow-up broadcasts. Another private investigator contacted me. "What you discovered is a commonplace," he said. "Accountants in recognized firms regularly call the tax department. Just by giving their names, they are given confidential information. Moreover, although you didn't ask for it, corporation tax files are also available. As well, it's a simple matter to learn the details of anyone's bank account, or if you wish, the specifics on long-distance phone calls, including the numbers called, the number called from and the duration of the calls."

We checked and reported these and other facts on the program. The opposition kept the heat on in the Commons, abetted by outraged editorials in newspapers across the country. The Minister of Revenue ordered all departments and all branches to tighten their security procedures and to clamp down on any leaks.

There is a sequel.

I fully expected, after the passage of time, to hear from the Department of National Revenue. I hadn't been audited for five years. Some senior official, smarting from the adverse publicity I had engendered, would surely order an examination of my returns. But nothing happened.

One night, abed, in the twilight before sleep, I was jolted awake by the sudden memory of a conversation five years old. I had once been a partner in a small advertising agency. When I resigned, a sizeable sum had been paid to me – salary I'd postponed taking in order to help get the company on its feet. The conversation that now thrust me bolt upright in bed had been between me and my accountant and had to do with where the income should be reported: in my personal return or through the private company I owned, each filed months apart. I remembered now that we had left the decision up in the air. Had the income fallen between two stools and been overlooked?

In the morning, I contacted my accountant. He called back in an hour, chagrined. The payment hadn't been reported.

"Declare it," I said.

He urged caution. Five years had passed, he pointed out. To declare the income now – especially after my revelations about the tax department – might lead to serious problems. Moreover, he reminded me, there would be the basic tax to be paid, plus the penalty for late filing, plus the accumulated interest over five years. And any number of other complications.

"Declare it," I said.

He argued with me. "Aren't you acting precipitately? The company that paid you the money went belly-up years ago. Its final audit has been done. At this late date there is no possible way the payment can be traced. The decision is yours, of course; I'm merely fulfilling my responsibility to point out what you're getting into."

He proposed that he call an acquaintance at the revenue department and put the case to him hypothetically. He reported that his friend had said, "If I were your client, I'd forget it. The returns from five years back are baled and stored in a warehouse. It's a dead issue. All it would be here is a headache."

I tried to dismiss it from my mind but couldn't. I owed the money. I believe people should pay their taxes. Beyond that, what if the facts were discovered? Wouldn't the department be justified in throwing the book at me? What would be more natural after the criticism I'd levelled, after the public embarrassment, after the wrangling in the Commons? Beyond that, I'd built a reputation for veracity over a lifetime; was I prepared to destroy that?

I called my accountant. "Declare it."

"Okay," he said, "if that's your decision that's your decision. But before you make up your mind let me add one more fact: after four years there is a form of limited liability; you can't be audited after four years have passed."

"Declare it," I said.

He called the following day to say that he had filed the supplementary return, explaining the circumstances. The man to whom he spoke at the tax office said, "Templeton, eh? And he claims he overlooked that much money. This looks like something for Special Investigation."

In a few days a letter came from the tax department asking me to sign a waiver, thus authorizing the department to examine my returns for the previous seven years. I signed, thinking, "I'm cooked. They're going on a fishing expedition. They're going to throw the book at me. They're going to demand that I cross every *t* and dot every *i* for the past seven years. They're going to grill me on every deduction, demand every receipt."

Weeks passed with no word. Then my accountant called to tell me that an auditor had moved into one of his offices, had asked for all my records over a three-year period and had ensconced himself behind a closed door, emerging only to send out for cigarettes or coffee. A week or so later, I was asked to attend a meeting at my accountant's office. With him were three officials from the tax department. I was asked a few questions to clarify some small details. There was an extended silence while one of the men reworked some figures with a pencil. The condemned man watched silently. He handed me a sheet of paper. I scrutinized it for a moment, beginning, of course, at the bottom line.

"Is this everything?" I asked. "Are you finished?"

There was a nod of assent.

"Then I have something to say."

My accountant raised despairing hands, shaking his head vigorously. "No, Charles. No! Forget it. Leave it be."

I disregarded his protest. "In the light of the recent brouhaha in the House of Commons," I said, "I had expected you to throw the book at me."

One of the men said, "It didn't take much of an examination to establish that you weren't a tax cheat."

"You didn't let me get away with anything," I said ruefully, "but neither did you nail me to the wall. I have no beef. You've been scrupulously fair. I intend to say so publicly." I subsequently recounted the experience on *Dialogue*.

Five years passed at CKEY and things had gone well. There had been no problems of consequence; indeed, there had been frequent commendation by Trowell. Nor had there been a word of criticism or even a suggestion of a change in the content or style of the newscast. There had been sharp differences with the head of the newsroom over facilities and back-up services but they had passed. When I requested the privilege of doing the newscast from a studio in my home, there had been immediate acquiescence. When I changed residences, I paid to move the equipment. I reciprocated their consideration by serving without remuneration as principal commentator at the Conservative and NDP leadership conventions (in which Bill Davis and Michael Cassidy were elected), during the FLQ crisis and on other occasions.

The eight o'clock newscast was achieving what had been hoped for. When I took it over in September 1970, the spring Broadcast Bureau Management ratings had shown an audience of 69,000. By November, the numbers had increased to 89,000. By the spring of 1976, they had climbed to 158,000, more than double the 1970 figure. During the Amchitka protest, CKEY logged the largest audience in its fifty-eight year history. More important, the station was much stronger at every period of the day than it had been.

I would not be so presumptuous as to claim the credit for the increase. Joe Morgan's newscast at 7:00 a.m. had a larger audience than mine but, as Trowell had emphasized when he hired me, the 8:00 a.m. spot conditions the entire broadcast day. The station was prospering.

On the Friday afternoon of the 1976 Dominion Day weekend, I received an urgent call from Stuart Brandy, the station manager. "I want to talk to you about the eight o'clock newscast," he said. "Can we meet first thing tomorrow morning?" I was leaving the city for the weekend later that evening and suggested that, if it was urgent, we meet at my home. Brandy arrived an hour later; I poured him a glass of wine.

Suddenly, without preamble, he said, "Now Charles, about the

eight o'clock newscast – we've just had a meeting and have made
a firm and final decision: we want to drop you from the newscast.
We've made different arrangements."

I stared at him for a moment, blinking, confused. There had
been no discussion, no hint of a change of plans, no intimation
that everything wasn't gung-ho for the fall season.

"What do you mean, you've made different arrangements?"

"Pete McGarvey. I've just notified him that he'll be taking over
and I wanted you to know first." (McGarvey, a long-time friend of
Brandy's, had come to CKEY from Chatham, Ontario, three years
earlier.) "We will, of course, pay you to the end of your contract."

"Well, yes," I said, "we *do* have a contract."

"We'd like the new arrangement to begin Tuesday morning."

I said, "Whoa! Hold it just a minute. I'm confused. Are you
saying that I'm off the program as of now?"

"Yes."

"That you don't want me to say goodbye to my audience or
even to commend McGarvey to them?"

"That's right."

I was at a loss. "What happens if I come in as usual Tuesday
morning?"

"I won't permit you to go on the air."

"Are you saying that you will bar me from broadcasting?"

"Yes."

"How would you do that?"

"I would have somebody do it." He paused. "The newscast I
mean."

"Stu," I said, "I don't believe what I'm hearing. Are you saying
that I'm such a poor broadcaster you can't put up with even one
more day of my services?"

"We've decided to make a change and it will be made on Tuesday," he said flatly.

"And what do I say when I'm asked why I'm not doing the
newscast – when I'm queried by the press, or by the staff at the
station?"

"You could say something like: the newscast has become an
increasing chore over the years and you've decided to make a
change. Something like that."

"C'mon, Stu, who will believe that? If I was going to drop the
newscast it wouldn't be after my vacation, two weeks into the
new season. And why in heaven's name did you have me start the

new season when, within two weeks, you were going to make a change? It's crazy."

It suddenly broke on me what was happening. Jack Dennett, CFRB's enormously popular eight o'clock newscaster, had died during the summer. Brandy and Trowell, disregarding all the established facts about listener loyalty, had leaped to the conclusion that Dennett's audience could be wooed away from CFRB. My style and approach to the news was very different from Dennett's but McGarvey's was somewhat similar. Eureka! A chance for a big breakthrough! In Maclean-Hunter fashion, once a decision had been taken, the change would be made with complete indifference to the employee involved.

But I had a problem. I was still working for the station and would be there each weekday – I had a separate contract to do *Dialogue*. Moreover, the *Dialogue* contract had an exclusivity clause that prohibited me from working for any other station in the Toronto area. Very well, I thought, if we're playing hardball, I can play that game too.

I said, "And with the newscast finished, you're proposing nothing else?"

"Well, we're going to make a change at eight o'clock but we still like Charles Templeton as a broadcaster."

"What do you have in mind? Or have you so much as thought about it?"

He looked at me in surprise. "Would you be *willing* to work for CKEY?"

"You're forgetting something," I said. "I already do. *Dialogue* – remember? But in response to your question, yes. If the program and the terms are satisfactory."

It was left that I would come up with a proposal over the weekend. I did – a three-minute daily commentary on the news, *Charles Templeton's Journal*. I did it for the next year or two. Then, at my convenience, I gave three months' notice and terminated it.

In late 1978, after eight years with CKEY, Berton and I signed a contract to provide our program, *Dialogue,* for an additional five years. There were handshakes all around, a glowing press release and stories in the newspapers. Not eight months later, Trowell called me to say that he had decided to drop the program.

He, Berton and I met for lunch. Trowell explained his decision by saying that the station had suffered two successive declines in the BBM ratings. His research had told him that the audience wanted more music and less "talk." Therefore he was going to "cut back on the talk" and drop *Dialogue*.

I attempted to summarize what was being said. "As I understand it, you have decided to drop *Dialogue* from the schedule, but you recognize you have a contractual obligation to us. The purpose of this discussion is to see if some mutually satisfactory accommodation can be worked out?"

"Right. I certainly wouldn't be happy with you fellows taping the programs and us throwing them in the can."

"So we're not here to discuss the possibility of continuing the show?"

"That's right."

Berton said, "You must have something in mind, Doug. What's your proposal?"

He proposed that the program conclude five weeks later, at the end of June when we went on vacation; CKEY would pay us to the end of the year.

"Doug, we just signed a new contract. It has more than four years to run. You're proposing to pay us for year one but to forget the the other four. That's hardly reasonable."

He said he would discuss it with his associates and get back to me the first of the week.

I heard nothing for twelve days, until I received a telephone call from the Edmonton airport, where Trowell was between planes. He had decided not to drop the program after all, but suggested that we accept a pay cut of one-third. Our response was that, inasmuch as the program was going forward as planned, and inasmuch as we had only recently mutually agreed to a new contract, we would prefer simply to fulfil our responsibilities under the agreement.

Over the next few years the station changed its pattern and its on-air performers with bewildering frequency. There was little feeling of continuity. Despite the stated intention to cut back on "talk," no talk was cut, but the style of music was changed. Then, a year or two later, there was a pendulum swing to what was called "Talk Radio," a mixture of phone-in shows and occasional music. Another six months and the talk shows were dumped.

At the conclusion of our contract in June 1983, after almost eighteen years – thirteen on CKEY – *Dialogue* ended without so much as a farewell drink or a handshake. I'm not a fan of Maclean-Hunter management.

II

Of the media, radio suffers most from arrested development. It has never realized its potential, nor is it likely that it will with the many options now being offered by its electronic and print competitors. By and large, commercial radio has become background entertainment, white noise asking no commitment of the mind, only breaking the pattern from time to time to offer such services as news, weather, time-checks and traffic reports. Its singular function is the popularizing and playing of the music of the masses – sometimes seeming to be little more than the promotion arm of the record companies.

Having begun with great promise, radio flourished in the first half of the century, changing our perception of the world. The world became a neighbourhood if not a brotherhood, and we found ourselves as caught up in events halfway around the globe as we were with happenings on our doorstep. Then television broke on the scene and radio, losing its uniqueness, began to beat a muffled drum.

Those who have grown up in the television era cannot imagine the excitement that accompanied the advent of radio. It came to flower, an evident miracle, in the 1920s, in an age still marvelling at the tinny voice of the phonograph, the frenetic eccentricities of silent motion pictures and the new freedoms granted by the automobile. It was a heady time: the war was a fading memory, the "Spanish influenza" had run its course, airplanes were becoming a commonplace, Victorian morality was dying and, almost overnight, our homes were filled with the music and voices of the world.

I have lived through the entire radio era, and two of the most vivid memories of my childhood have to do with it:

I was sitting at home in Regina, a pair of heavy earphones on my head, delicately turning a dial while searching among the

beeps and howls and banshee squeals for an intelligible sound.
Then, as it grew dark outside, a distant spectral voice faintly
singing, the volume fading and then swelling . . .

> Oh, if I had the wings of an angel,
> Over these prison bars I would fly.
> I would fly to the arms of my darling
> And there I would peacefully die. . . .

And then, as the song ended, a sudden increase in the volume and
a voice dinning in the ears, shouting, "You are listening to KDKA,
Pittsburgh, Pennsylvania, the United States of America." The
thrill of it!

By 1927, we had a speaker-horn atop the new batteryless
radio. The entire family sat in a tense circle listening to a blow-by-
blow description of the second Dempsey-Tunney fight. I saw it
more vividly than I have seen any sports event since.

At its zenith, radio was more pervasive than television is
today. As did every boy, I built my own "crystal set" and listened to
it long after I was supposed to be asleep. I can recall walking down
Beaty Avenue in Toronto on a muggy spring evening in the late
1920s and not missing a phrase of Bing Crosby's song as the
sound emerged from the open windows of every house I passed.
Foster Hewitt's high-pitched and unmistakeable voice dominated
our Saturday nights as television's *Hockey Night in Canada* never
has.

Not long after the advent of television, Fred Allen, the radio
comedian, lamented that radio had forever missed its potential. In
radio drama, for instance, there was no need to construct an
expensive set or to create elaborate make-up and costumes; the
imagination of the listener did that free of charge, and did it
better. Let an announcer describe a human fly scaling a soaring
building, add some sound effects, and listeners will construct an
Empire State Building in their minds, mobilize a tension-ridden
crowd to stand at the base, and climb handhold by handhold with
the man as he claws his way to the top.

Fred Allen was right, of course — at least in part. Listening to
radio, you *saw* Amos and Andy and the Kingfish in their scruffy
taxi office. You *saw* Jack Benny and Mary Livingstone and Roches-
ter in Jack Benny's home. So real were these people that, when
finally you did see them on television, they had about them an air

of the imposter. ("Does he really look like *that*?") The sense of reality went far beyond the tacky settings and monochromatic images of early television.

Television did not, as was predicted, "kill" radio, but it did stunt its growth and limit its options. Whether radio would have continued to grow is a lively question. It is argued by its advocates that radio has prospered since television began, and it is true, but commercial radio has become in fact a poor relation. With barely a struggle, it has accepted a subsidiary role and seems content to make do with the leftovers.

It is certainly true that commercial radio has abandoned programming. There are no comedy shows or dramatic presentations. There are few outlets for artists who don't have a record contract. The broadcast day is filled with "block-programming." A block of time – usually two hours or more – is allocated to what used to be called a disc-jockey but is now known as a "host" or "radio personality." He or she fills the time mostly by playing records, inserting into the interstices bland chatter, syndicated ad-libs, "commercial messages," time checks, traffic reports, weather forecasts and sports results. On the hour or half hour he or she may break for a "news package." In the evenings, when the fickle listener has been seduced by television's blandishments, half-hearted attempts may be made to justify the station's licence by altering the pattern, but the effort is usually cautious, unimaginative and cheaply produced.

There are exceptions, of course. A few stations work hard and spend money to cover the news and to present features of special relevance. We have seen the advent of the all-news station. Western Canada makes much of open-line shows, and some of them do enlighten and do serve the community's interests. But most are interested in controversy and depend on a relatively small claque of garrulous regulars to keep things lively. FM stations provide a higher ratio of music to chatter, but many are indistinguishable from their AM competitors. Increasingly, individual stations specialize, playing an identifiable kind of music – rock, country and western, jazz, "semi classical" or classical.

The news on commercial radio varies little from station to station. Some depend on "rip and read," namely, the tearing of a piece of copy from the teleprinter, modifying it with a few strokes of a pencil and parroting it on the air. Few on the news staff are journalists with any experience as reporters; most of their skills have been picked up on the job. Investigative reporting is almost unknown. Nor do the owners of most radio stations care about the quality of the newscast; they want news-readers who, regardless of their knowledge or experience, sound "authoritative" or are distinctive enough to build an audience.

It must be added that there are private stations that do a commendable job of reporting and providing background to the news. Unfortunately, they are fewer than a dozen across the country.

Public radio – the Canadian Broadcasting Corporation – is, of course, an entirely different beast. It has a greater commitment at the upper-management levels and a relatively larger budget, and it is able to program without the interruption of commercials. It has access to the resources of other stations along the network and to the pooling of reports by correspondents in the field. The CBC's *Six O'Clock Report* may be the best newscast on radio *or* television in North America.

In other programming, public radio offers classical and popular music, comedy, drama, sports, variety, informed opinion and intelligent discussion, although sometimes its presentation has a self-conscious seriousness. Some of its local programs seem to exist to ventilate the opinions of minority groups of every stripe, and tend periodically to rehash the perennial civil-liberties causes. None the less, they provide a service not generally available elsewhere and are a legitimate part of the Fourth Estate.

I have always had a particular liking for radio. It is a relatively uncomplicated medium and it is certainly the most immediate of the news media. If a story breaks, there is no need to set it in type, clamp it on the presses and deliver it to its destination. Nor need you manipulate the cumbersome "one-ton pencil" that is television. All that is needed is a microphone, an engineer to throw a switch and you can tell the world your story. Unfortunately, because most radio does not take its mandate seriously (nor is it required to by the Canadian Radio-television and Communications Commission), it seldom breaks news, and thus its intrinsic advantage is nullified.

10

Inside Books

INSIDE BOOKS

I

From my earliest childhood in Saskatchewan I have been enamoured of words. I was encouraged to read by a father
who frowned at any vulgarism or slang expression. Nor was
encouragement needed: the principal indoor entertainment
was the contents of two large bookcases jammed with an eclectic
selection, and other books elsewhere in the house. My first interest in fiction – beyond the usual Horatio Alger and G.A. Henty
yarns – was fed by a series of classic novels in identical bindings,
merchandised as *Collier's Five Foot Shelf of Fiction* and kept in a glass-
faced bookcase in the entrance hallway. I began with inch one and
read through the entire five feet. Even the advent of radio didn't
dampen my interest in reading: as any parent knows, a child can
simultaneously read, listen to music, join in the conversation,
fondle the cat and keep in touch with everything else going on.

Except for brief periods, I have earned my living through the
spoken or written word. That has been a constant in a life that has
paused at many way-stations. Over the years I have been published in the *Saturday Evening Post* (in "Post Scripts"), the *Reader's
Digest* ("The Joy of Christmas") and elsewhere. In the late 1950s I
sold television plays to the CBC and the British Broadcasting
Corporation. During my years in the ministry, I wrote two books
which were published by Harper and Brothers (now Harper and
Row) in New York and Hodder and Stoughton in the United
Kingdom. The first was a book of sermons, *Life Looks Up,* which
sold more than thirty thousand copies in the United States. The
second was the publication of the Stone Lectures, a critical analysis of contemporary evangelism, which I delivered at Richmond
Theological Seminary in Virginia; it was published in 1957 under
the title *Evangelism For Tomorrow.*

I wrote only one news story in my years at the Toronto *Star.* In

1960, I indulged my passion for boxing by assigning myself to cover the second Floyd Patterson – Ingemar Johansson heavy-weight title fight in New York.

It was our custom when my children were young to have discussions at the dinner table. I would introduce a subject by asking a question, and beginning with the youngest, each of the four children, Deborah, Michael, Bradley and Tyrone, would be asked for an opinion. Each response was taken seriously, no matter how puerile. Minds were stretched, skills were acquired in verbalizing ideas and respect was engendered for the opinions of others.

In spring 1971, a zealous fundamentalist neighbour started an after-school Bible class in her home, and peer pressure was exerted on Bradley to attend. The children had never been sent to Sunday school and had only occasionally been taken to church, so their opinions about religion were ill-formed and tended to be disdainful. They were not yet born during my years in the ministry, and they were and are somewhat bemused by the fact that their father was once an evangelist.

Now the question came from Bradley, "How can people say that Jesus was God? He was a man, wasn't he? He died, didn't he?"

I didn't respond to the question but followed the pattern of eliciting the views of the others. Afterwards, thinking about the discussion, I rummaged about in a carton of dog-eared and dusty papers.

In 1948, I had spent the summer between my first and second years at Princeton living in a borrowed house in Long Beach, California, synthesizing the four gospels into one narrative. My object was to produce a book that would make it easy for a reader to learn the essential facts of Jesus' life. I thought it important to do this. I still do. As I wrote in the preface:

> Jesus Christ is undoubtedly the most influential figure in the history of western civilization. Willy-nilly, his life touches the life of every individual. Yet, most know little about him, and most of what they do know has been altered by myth and coloured by misconception. The man portrayed in the four Gospels is unlike the common conceptions of him. To many, including most Christians, Jesus is a hopelessly idealistic demi-deity, not at all like a real man. They forget that, according to the record, he was dirty after a journey and sweaty after effort; that he wept when he was saddened, felt fatigue at the

end of the day, was sometimes impatient and argumentative and often angry. Anyone expecting to find in the New Testament, "the gentle Jesus, meek and mild," is in for a surprise. Gentle he was; meek and mild he was not. He said of himself: "I came not to bring peace but a sword," and as a consequence, his life was passionate with conflict and noisy with controversy. Meek and mild? – he was in every sense of the word, a revolutionary. . . .

I had been moved to undertake the project by the realization that, even when one is determined to read the New Testament, the obstacles are forbidding. In some versions the language is archaic. To get the story one must read all four gospels. There is much repetition and many confusing variations in Matthew, Mark and Luke, and usually, by the time the reader gets to John – which is different from the others in both style and content – the initial enthusiasm has flagged.

I thought the project worthwhile, not because I was a Christian (for I wasn't; I had become an agnostic) but because I believe that it is not possible for people to understand what their civilization is (and therefore who they are) without an understanding of their roots. Our laws, our morals, our mores are predicated largely on the Judeo-Christian tradition. The standards and attitudes of our society have been profoundly influenced by the person and the life of Jesus. Regardless of one's attitude toward religion, a knowledge of what Jesus of Nazareth said and did is enormously enriching.

So, twenty-three years after that summer in California, I decided to complete the project. Working from the synthesis, I rendered it in a modern-English paraphrase, in language familiar to the contemporary reader. I also adopted the comfortable form of a modern novel, using indented paragraphs, direct quotations and the other familiar devices. Meticulous care was taken to include every event and every word spoken. Nothing was deleted but the repetitions; nothing was added. To ensure that I had been faithful to the text, I asked four expert biblical scholars to review the paraphrase and to consult on the finished manuscript.

Earlier, I had presented the concept of the book to publisher Jack McClelland. It was my first contact with him. He was interested

but said he would withhold judgement. With the finished manuscript in hand he decided to go ahead. Normally inventive in
promotion, he seemed unsure about how to publicize *Jesus,* as the
book was called, and finally decided, for want of a better idea, to
launch it with a press conference at the Park Plaza hotel in
Toronto.

A room was hired and some forty chairs set out. McClelland
and I arrived early and stood about fearing the worst. Indeed, only
three reporters turned up, plus an apparently confused man who
wandered in in hopes of a free drink. Kildare Dobbs, reporting for
the *Telegram,* wrote a witty report of the press conference, making
sport of the Scribe (me) and the Pharisee (Jack).

To everyone's surprise but mine, the book moved swiftly onto
the non-fiction bestseller list, settling in second position after that
immortal work, *Dr. Atkins Diet Revolution.* Subsequently, it was
distributed in paperback in Canada by General Publishing. In the
United States, Simon and Schuster purchased the hardcover
rights, with the paperback edition going to Pocket Books. Angus
and Robertson was the publisher in the British Commonwealth
and Gottmer/Haarlem in the Netherlands.

In the spring of 1973, I was one of a small group of Mississaugans
who formed a company and filed an application with the Canadian
Radio, Television and Communications Commission for a cable
licence for our city. I was certain we would be granted the franchise and had allocated the project a year of my time following the
date when the decision was due to be announced. A week early, I
received a telephone call from a friend in Ottawa informing me
off the record that our application had failed.

After dealing with the disappointment, I faced the fact that I
had time on my hands. A memory stirred. I went to a filing cabinet
and pulled out a manuscript. *The Hostage* was a thirty-two-page
outline for a screenplay and had to do with the kidnapping of the
president of the United States. I had written it as an exercise three
years earlier but had not submitted it anywhere. I read it, picked
up a telephone and called Berton.

"Pierre," I said, "I've written an outline for a screenplay. I'm
sending it over by taxi. Take a look at it and let me know if you
think that, purely as a thriller, the plot has possibilities."

He called back late that afternoon. "I've sent it off to my agent in New York," he said. "I like it. But look, the guy you should talk to is Art Hailey. He knows more about fiction than I do. Give him a call."

I had met Hailey some years earlier, and reached him at his home in Lyford Cay in the Bahamas. "Charles," he said, "the important thing isn't whether or not it's a good idea – that's only the beginning. The first question is, do you believe in it?"

"I think so."

"Then bet two years of your life on it. Sit down and write it as a novel. Forget the screenplay. Anyway, the money isn't in selling to a film company; it's in publishing a novel. And get back the outline Pierre sent to his agent. Don't let a copy of your plot get in anyone else's hands."

Before settling down to write, I had to solve two fundamental problems in the plot. I briefly considered having as the hostage a Canadian prime minister but rejected that possibility because there would be little suspense in it – it would be too easy to do. Kidnapping the Queen was dismissed as well. Obviously, the ideal subject for my purposes was the most carefully guarded individual in the world, the president of the United States. But what made him ideal created a problem: could I devise a credible plan? I puzzled over it for weeks and buried myself in research.

When the plot finally was drafted, I spoke to an old high school friend, Inspector Herbert Thurston of the Metropolitan Toronto police. Among other duties, he had served as Canada's representative on a number of international police organizations.

"Herb," I said, "I'm writing a novel. In it, the president of the United States is kidnapped by a group of South American radicals. I want to spell out to you how it's done and get your critical reaction."

"Don't waste your time," he said, smiling at me tolerantly. "It's not possible to kidnap the president. An assailant might manage to assassinate him – it's been done – but kidnap him? No way."

"Let me tell you the plan."

"Go ahead. But believe me, Chuck, you have no idea how complex the security system is."

I outlined the plot. There was an extended silence. "And you're going to put this in a book?"

"Yes."

"You realize what I'll have to do. I'll have to call some friends of mine in the Secret Service. Just to be certain they have defences against the method you've outlined."

"I'd like that," I said, grinning. "Wouldn't want to put anybody up to anything."

"What do you do after you kidnap him? It would be impossible to hide him. The entire country would be out looking – every cop, every kid and his dog, everyone."

"I realize that. That's why instead of hiding him in some remote spot, like the middle of the Mojave desert, I'm going to have him held hostage in the most public place in the world – in a booby-trapped Brinks armoured truck in Times Square."

He laughed as he rose to go. "You're out of your mind, you know. But good luck."

I used the opportunity to learn how to write a novel. I aspired to no more than a carefully crafted thriller and found that difficult enough. Working mornings, seven days a week, *The Hostage* took eighteen months. When it was finished, it had become *The Kidnapping of the President*. I sent it with great trepidation to Jack McClelland. He came to see me in my tiny office over the bank. "It works very well, Charles. A few solecisms but nothing that can't be fixed. We'd like to publish it."

The writer who inflicts his book on the public must pay a triple penance: the night sweats of self-doubt, the ordeal of "the author tour" and the verdict of the critics.

I will say little of the self-doubt except to note that it can cause extended periods of depression, change a normally equable disposition into waspish irritability and lie like a malevolent cloud over the most sunny day. Reworking a manuscript, there will be times when you will exult in a turn of phrase or the aptness of an alliteration. More often, your most cherished passages seem leaden and gauche, and you rue having begun the journey through this wilderness. But all writers are egotists – why else would we presume to address ourselves to our readers? – so you press on.

The promotion of a book begins, especially at McClelland and Stewart, with the not unwelcome embarrassment of the publication-day hoopla. There are few limits to the outrageous gimmickry, all designed to get a photograph or a mention in the press. The "launch" for *Kidnapping* was a relatively sedate one: bundles of books wrapped in gold paper were delivered to downtown Toronto bookstores by armed guards in a Brinks truck, while cameras clicked and bemused passersby frowned. So far as I know, no newspaper published the pictures.

I was now introduced to that incredible ritual known as "the author tour" – described more aptly in the trade as "flogging your book." Mostly an autumn phenomenon, with an eye toward Christmas sales, it is a form of cruelty that, if inflicted on animals, would lead to pickets before publishing houses and venomous letters to the editor. The system is based on the willingness – nay, the eagerness – of authors to submit to any indignity if it will induce people to buy their books. That some authors are able to exploit the media (while being exploited by the media) and thus stimulate sales is undoubtedly true. It is equally true that others – especially novelists who maunder on with stultifying seriousness about the intricacy of their characterizations and the overtones of their allusions – sometimes destroy whatever hope of sales they may have had.

All authors complain about the rigours of touring but most insist on it, prepared – in that particular strain of masochism to which writers are subject – to endure jet lag, nervous debility, rampant indigestion, fatuous interviewers and near-terminal fatigue. And a pox on the publisher who, in the name of common humanity or budgetary constraints, tries to say them nay.

You go from city to city – or more accurately, from airport to airport – interrupting your cross-Canada flight to race madly into town and ricochet from one television or radio station to another. Lunches are ordered but left to congeal while you try to impress newspaper reporters. Your chauffeur is a publisher's rep (bless 'em all!), usually a woman, who gossips with you about the world of books, the while filling you in on the difficulties she has endured with some of the writers who have preceded you on the assembly line. Example: the "name author" who, in his hotel suite, went to the bedroom "to change" and appeared in the doorway naked. "I hope my being nude doesn't bother you," he said. "No," the rep replied. "I never let little things distract me." Example: the author of a "coffee-table book" who debarked from a plane carrying two enormous metal suitcases he had somehow managed to get aboard. Setting them down on the tarmac, he strode off to the passenger lounge, barking to the hundred-pound rep as he passed, "Bring those." Later at the hotel, he summoned the manager and demanded to be moved immediately to the vice-regal suite.

You soon discover that many of the people who interview you haven't read your book. To gloss over this, they may question you on anything from the Crow rate to "What is Peter Newman *really* like?" Some are obsequious to the point of sycophancy. Others are arrogant and rude: having to take the time to interview you is obviously keeping them from Very Important Things. Others lead you into a dark, broom-closet studio to tape an interview, telling you that they'll do their best to "air it" some time in the next few weeks. But The Few are gifts from heaven: men and women who have read your book and ask tough and evocative questions about it. May their number increase.

You return from the junket ten pounds lighter (who says author tours are worthless?), your arms elongated to simian proportions from hauling your luggage through airports, addicted to Tums, worried about the bags on the bags under your eyes, lusting for a beach somewhere and certain you should call your publisher to alert him to what will surely be a run on your book.

But the full penance has not yet been paid. You must now stand before two terrifying tribunals: the judgement of the critics and the national bestseller list – the one having no necessary relationship to the other. Both are a form of literary criticism – the newspaper review being one reader's opinion, the bestseller list being the judgement of the hardover-book-reading public.

There is an incestuousness to the lists. Books appear because they are read and are read because they appear. Authors with books riding high are certain the list renders an accurate reading; those whose books are nowhere in sight assume the lists are rigged. (Booksellers, the allegation goes, report a run on overstocked books, hoping to move them out.) There can be little doubt that bestseller lists help the sale of books that appear on them. The lists are a form of peer pressure. In the same way that being *au courant* leads many to carry an advertisement for the manufacturer on the pockets of their clothes, the list announces, "This is what the in-crowd is reading, dummy. Get with it!" But for all the cavilling, seeing the title of your book at the top of the list gives the coolest head a rush.

The publication date ("pubdate," you learn to call it) for *Kidnapping* was also my birthday – I seized on it as a good augury. Knowing that I would sleep little the night before the verdict in the Saturday book pages, I went at 9:30 p.m. Friday to the *Globe*'s loading dock to get a first copy of the bulldog edition. In my car, with the map light on, I turned up the page – and immediately endured a kind of dying. The reviewer not only disliked the book, he used it as an object of fun, getting his disdainful jollies in large part by disregarding the facts. It is one thing to be criticized, it is another to be scorned. I drove home in despair. The following morning I addressed a letter to the editor of the *Globe*, listing the errors of fact in the review. The letter was printed under a heading running the full width of the op-ed page. It helped.

So did the arrival of the afternoon papers. Robert Fulford praised the book highly in the *Star*, and the *Telegram* was equally kind. The reviews from across the country were, with a few exceptions, laudatory. Within a month, *Kidnapping* went to the top of the bestseller list, hung in second place for a while and finally moved to first. It was a lovely Christmas.

In the meantime, I had travelled to New York City with three copies of the manuscript to see if I could interest an American publisher. I left one with Peter Schwed, then vice-president and now chairman of the board of Simon and Schuster (S and S had published my non-fiction book, *Jesus*). Another I left at Doubleday with Ken McCormick, a former Canadian and a man reputed to be a friend of Canadian authors. I took the third manuscript to literary agent John Cushman, to whom I had been referred by a friend in New York and by Jack McClelland.

Cushman fitted my romantic notion of what an agent should be like. He is a tall man, gregarious, balding, Brooks Brothers dressed. He has a Harvard accent and took me for a drink and lunch at the Harvard Club. His offices were in mid-town Manhattan in a not too prepossessing building. His private office was floor-to-ceiling books, with manuscripts and galley proofs heaped on the floor. The telephone interrupted every few minutes. I explained my mission and asked him if he would represent me.

"I don't know," he said. "I haven't read your book. I will read it, however. But so you won't be on tenterhooks, you should know now that I won't be able to get to it for perhaps six weeks."

I explained that I had left copies with two publishers.

He laughed. "No problem. It'll be more than six weeks before you hear from them."

That was a Thursday. The following Sunday evening I received a telephone call from Peter Schwed. "Charles," he said, "you've ruined my weekend. I had to finish your book. We'd like to publish it. Do you have an agent?"

"I don't know," I said. "I may have."

"Tell him to get in touch with me."

I told Cushman what had happened and asked him would he represent me. "I can't say, Charles," he responded. "I haven't yet read the book. But I will, and I'll call you Tuesday morning." On Tuesday he called to say he'd be pleased to handle me. "Not so much for this book, which I like very much, but for the books you will write."

We sold the paperback rights to Avon, the United Kingdom hardcover and paperback rights to Quartet Books. The Detective Book Club made it their March selection. We also sold Italian, Spanish, Portuguese and Japanese rights and newspaper syndication rights in the United Kingdom. Later, I sold the film rights to a Canadian company and wrote a screenplay.

Interestingly, some three months later, I heard from Doubleday. They expressed a wish to publish the book but wanted me to do some revisions and asked if I would be willing to work with a collaborator. "Irwin Shaw, Arthur Hailey and other eminently successful authors have done so with their first book," they said. I thanked them but informed them, a bit smugly, that *Kidnapping* would be published that spring by Simon and Schuster.

I was anxious to promote *Kidnapping* in the United States and reminded Simon and Schuster's promotion department that I was an experienced television performer. They resisted, arguing that they had a policy not to send novelists on tour – it was "counterproductive." When I was unable to budge them, I decided to take things into my own hands and called David Susskind.

I knew David through Joyce Davidson, whom he had married, and with whom I had worked on the CBC television shows *Close-up* and *Tabloid*. He invited me to New York to appear on his syndicated show. At the end of an hour of far-ranging conversation, he turned to the camera.

"You who watch this program regularly," he said, "know that, of the hundreds of guests who have appeared here, I have said to only four of them, 'Come back any time you can.' Those four are

Gore Vidal, Anthony Burgess, John Kenneth Galbraith and Henry Sloane Coffin Jr. (the former Yale chaplain) and I want to add a fifth to that list, my guest tonight." He turned to me. "Charles, you are now a member of a very select club. Come back any time you can."

The following morning, Susskind telephoned the producer of NBC's *The Today Show,* then undoubtedly the most influential of the morning network news programs. Within days an invitation came to appear on the show. The publisher flew me to New York, sent a limousine to meet me at the airport, reserved a suite at the Waldorf Astoria and arranged my transportation to the NBC studios at 6:30 the following morning. I was, of course, filled with apprehension; what I didn't know was that Jim Hartz, co-host on the program with Jane Pauley, would be as ill at ease as I.

In my final year in the ministry, I had delivered a series of lectures at Louisville Theological Seminary. Hartz's father was, as I recall it, a preacher in the Southern Methodist church. He had heard me preach in Nashville some years earlier, and, upon learning that I was to be at Louisville, his alma mater, arranged to spend the week there during my visit. To put it simply, Hartz' father was a fan of mine, and for years Hartz had heard about me from his father, whom he greatly admired. Consequently, when I was ushered onto the set during a commercial break, I found myself sitting opposite a man who was as intimidated by me as I was by him.

He asked me only a question or two about *Kidnapping,* and then, as if I were an oracle, said, "Mr. Templeton, I'm going to ask something unusual of you. As you know, we are a country in something approaching a state of shock. We have just emerged from the Watergate affair, during which we learned that our government, at the highest levels, was corrupt. Our president has just resigned before he could be impeached. We are a nation shamed and confused. For months we've been examining ourselves, questioning our system, wondering what's happening. Now, Mr. Templeton, I'm going to ask you to do something for us this morning: you're a journalist and a novelist, and for years you were in the ministry: tell us how we look from the outside."

It was an unsettling request, a challenge that demanded some presumptuousness on my part. But in the circumstances there seemed no way out. We talked for about ten minutes. Afterwards, when I met with the Simon and Schuster representative, she reminded me we hadn't once mentioned the title of the book.

After Pierre Berton and I completed *Dialogue* one morning and were chatting, I said, "Pierre, you've written – how many is it? – twenty-five books. All non-fiction. Why have you never tried your hand at a novel?"

"I have," he said.

"What happened to it?"

"I showed it to Jack McClelland. He told me to put it in a drawer, lock the drawer and lose the key. But, you know, my mother wanted to be a novelist. She had this marvellous idea: it was the story of a young Jesuit priest. He's sitting on the deck of a cruise-ship on the Mediterranean and falls into conversation with an archaeologist. The archaeologist confides that he has discovered the bones of Jesus of Nazareth, thus making the doctrine of the resurrection suspect. The Jesuit decides that he's got to kill the archaeologist before the word gets out."

The idea wouldn't leave me. For days it intruded on my thoughts. As the possibilities fermented in my imagination, I grew increasingly excited and finally could hardly sleep. One morning I said to Berton, "I've decided to write your mother's novel." Later, I would dedicate the book:

> To Laura Beatrice Berton
> who unwittingly sowed the seed

As I worked out the plot, the young Jesuit became the Cardinal Archbishop of the Archdiocese of New York, the archaeologist became his oldest friend, a classmate from college, the bones are discovered near Qumran where the Dead Sea Scrolls were found, the Pope is dying and there is a major political crisis at the Vatican. The story ends in tragedy: for the Cardinal, the archaeologist and all concerned. I gave it the title *Act of God*.

I began my research at St. Patrick's Cathedral and at the Palace of the Archbishops at 50th Street and Madison. On the telephone, Monsignor Eugene Clark of the chancery office agreed to help and suggested that we meet for drinks at the Pierre. I found him an erudite and cultivated man who had, to my good fortune, served for years as secretary to Cardinal Cushman, living during that time in the archbishops' palace. We talked for an hour or two about high churchmen and their ways and about the floor plan and furnishings of the Archbishops' residence.

Later, I flew to Israel where I spent ten exhausting days doing research. Still later, there was a week in Rome. There again I chanced to contact the right man – Paul Tremblay, then the Canadian ambassador to the Holy See. I explained that I needed to be able to describe Vatican headquarters and especially the interior of the papal apartment but had found these areas off limits. He had his car brought around and said, "Come with me."

With the Canadian flag fluttering on the front fender, our driver swept us down the Via della Conciliazione, turned right at St. Peter's Square and followed the wall of Vatican City to the entry gate. The Swiss Guard saluted the diplomatic licence plate and the car moved without slowing through the massive romanesque archway, plunging immediately into what seemed to be the gloomy, overarched street of a mediaeval city. A moment later we broke into sunlight, where there were more salutes, passed through another archway and suddenly came upon the Court of St. Damasus. We alighted and took an elevator to the fourth floor. A few steps along the *loggia,* and Tremblay pointed at an unimpressive door flanked by two guards.

"The papal apartment," he said softly. "I'll show you colour photographs of the interior when we get back to the embassy."

We walked the halls, coming upon a more imposing entrance where there was much coming and going. "The office of the Secretary of State," he said. "Next to the Holy Father, the most important man in the Vatican."

At the end of a deserted hallway, we came upon a set of stairs. "What's down there?" I asked.

"I have no idea. Let's find out."

We went down a broad, dark stairway to the floor below and entered a great, high-ceilinged room. It was deserted and our footsteps echoed hollowly on the tessellated marble floor. The walls and ceilings were rococo in style and covered with priceless tapestries, paintings and elaborate carving. Enormous crystal chandeliers hung from the ceiling. But there was no furniture, no sign of habitation. We pressed on to other great rooms, all of them empty, all of them abandoned.

"We'd better go back," Tremblay whispered. "I don't think we're supposed to be down here."

Back in Toronto at my typewriter, I peopled the empty rooms

and went with easy familiarity within the papal apartment to the bedside of a dying pope.

I had help from many sources, but none so useful or so freely given as that provided by Monsignor Clark of the chancery office in New York. In the months when I was writing the book, he forwarded suggestions about research sources and even sent photocopies of articles and pages from Catholic encyclopediae he thought might be helpful. His kindness troubled me, for although I had said nothing to suggest it, it was clear that he had the impression I was writing about St. Patrick's Cathedral or about the responsibilities of the cardinal of the archdiocese.

When the penultimate draft was finished, I sent him a copy with a note asking for an appointment. There was no reply. I was certain that, realizing I had been writing about the cardinal of the archdiocese being tempted to murder, he was not amused. When six weeks passed without word, I called the chancery office, informing Monsignor Clark's secretary that I would be in New York the following week and would very much like to see him. She relayed word that he would meet me at his office.

I went to the appointment suffering a mixture of guilt and trepidation. I needed his counsel but was sure he would be angry. He greeted me cordially and drew me into his office.

"Mr. Templeton," he said, "we've had a long discussion here about your book. You've done your homework. And it's obvious that you're not bent on attacking the Church." He paused and smiled shyly at me. "As for the cardinal being involved in murder, that doesn't trouble us – no good Catholic will believe it for one minute. Now," he continued, "we think it's an important book and we've decided to help you make it as accurate as you can. There are some points of Catholic theology where you go astray and some errors, if I may call them that, having to do with a cardinal's responsibilities, his attire and that kind of thing. I can be useful there."

We talked for the better part of an hour. As I left, we shook hands and he smiled at me. "It'll make a great movie," he said. "I'll look forward to it."

Over the next six weeks I received in the mail pages from my manuscript with notes and comments in the margins in a precise, minuscule hand. Months later, when I returned to New York on a tour to promote the book, I called him to ask if I might mention in press interviews his active cooperation. He laughed and said, "Of course. Tell it as it is, Charles."

Sixteen months and three rewrites later, the manuscript went off to Jack McClelland. A photocopy went to John Cushman. Within days a letter came from McClelland, predicting that the book would be sold around the world in millions of copies. Cushman telephoned to say that, rather than offer it to a single publisher, he planned to auction the rights.

However, Simon and Schuster had a right of first refusal. Cushman was reluctant to permit them the six weeks specified and pressed Peter Schwed for a response. In the interval, Jack McClelland had – a touch deviously, it may be said – forwarded a copy of the manuscript to Mark Jaffe, then editor-in-chief at Bantam Books. Jaffe read the manuscript overnight and called McClelland to say he wanted to buy it.

The morning Schwed was to respond, Cushman telephoned and told me to stay within range of my telephone. "Could be an interesting day," he said.

He called again just before noon. "Charles," he said, "Peter Schwed at Simon and Schuster is prepared to pay $150,000 for the U.S. rights. Jack McClelland just called to say that he's had an offer of $175,000 from Mark Jaffe. I told him I wasn't in a position to respond to Jaffe until Simon and Schuster has made a final bid. Now Charles," he said, "what do you want to do?"

I wanted to ring bells and jump over the wall. I said, "John, I don't know. You're the professional; what do you think?"

"Well," he said. "I think we should turn down Simon and Schuster and see what happens. It's their first offer."

He was back on the line an hour later. "Peter Schwed says he'll go to $175,000. I told him I didn't think you'd accept."

"But Bantam has already offered that much. Maybe they'll go higher. Have you talked to Jaffe?"

"Charles, you'll have to understand; I can't talk to Jaffe at this point."

I drew a deep breath. "Tell Simon and Schuster no."

An hour passed. "Charles, Peter says he doesn't want to be put in the position of making one offer after another. He said, 'Ask Charles what he wants. We've published two of his books and we think of him as one of our authors. Let's not play games; what does he want?'"

I was feeling some guilt about Peter. We had always talked to each other straightforwardly; now there was a marriage-broker. "I've never played this game before," I told Cushman. "Tell me what I should ask for."

"A quarter of a million dollars," he replied without hesitation. It was obvious John was enjoying himself.

I swallowed hard. "Yup," I said. "That's what I want."

Schwed responded by saying, "I'm afraid that's a bit too rich for our blood." Bantam agreed to $200,000 with the right to offer the hardcover rights in an auction. (Bantam was at the time solely a paperback house.) Little, Brown, Harper and Brothers, Harcourt Brace and Doubleday all submitted bids, with Little, Brown winning. When all was concluded, the advances, including the Canadian rights, totalled $300,000.

A reasonably good hardcover sale for a Canadian novel is three thousand copies. Jack McClelland believed so strongly in *Act of God* that he decided, in an unprecedented action, *to give away thirty-six hundred copies* of a pre-publication edition, his purpose being to create word-of-mouth publicity. From every quarter, the reaction to the book was enthusiastic. Little, Brown was convinced it had a bestseller. Michael Joseph, one of England's major publishers, purchased the hardcover rights for the United Kingdom, Corgi the paperback. Mondadori was the publisher in Italy, De Kern Bussum in the Netherlands, Circulo Delectors in Spain, Editorial Sudamerica in Argentina and Radha Krishna in India.

On the cover of the pre-publication give-away edition, McClelland wrote a personalized letter and offered a prize – a copy of every book published that year by M & S – to whoever guessed most accurately how many copies of *Act of God* would be sold in Canada that year. McClelland made his own broader prediction: "Ten million copies throughout the world in the next five years." As a means of creating attention it was ingenious promotion; to Canadian newspaper critics it was a flea in the ear.

The sniping began immediately. It was charged flatly that the figures were false. One journalist commented that, having read the advance copy, he was at a loss to understand what the fuss was about; the book was a total bore. Columnist Dennis Braithwaite, having found an imperfect grammatical construction in the opening paragraph of the uncorrected page proofs, dismissed the book and refused to read on. A blurb on the front page of the Toronto

Star groused that "Templeton is being paid one million dollars [sic] for a book that isn't even well written."

The Calgary *Herald* devoted a half page to such vitriol as "McClelland and Stewart and Templeton have pulled off a con-job. The book is an insult to its readers. . . . *Act of God* is a sham masquerading as a novel." The reviewer in the Vancouver *Province* wrote that reading the book left him "with the feeling that time had been wasted on a silly exercise." The *Catholic Register* concluded that "the author has foisted a callous deception upon his readers." An editorial cartoonist in the Maritimes drew a picture of me kneeling at the foot of the cross, a leer on my face and a sword in my hand on which were inscribed the words, "Act of God." Above, on a cross, was the figure of the dying Christ. From a wound in his side, dollar signs were falling into my upraised hand.

As the reviews came in from across the country it became clear that we had kindled a rage and that it had been stimulated in large part by the amount of money the book had earned. I was attacked, McClelland was attacked, the book was attacked. *Maclean's* carried a feature story by Barbara Amiel, deliberately distorted and riddled with factual errors. Elsewhere I was called "charlatan," "a profiteering religious defector," "a talentless scribbler," a "literary butterfly."

I was baffled by the virulence of the attack – and hurt. The reports from outside Canada had been favourable almost without exception. Why was I perceived differently by critics and reviewers in my own country? Moreover, the book was going into repeated printings, had moved immediately to the top of the bestseller list and was on its way to becoming one of the best-selling hardcover novels in Canadian history. At autographing sessions, the lines reached beyond the store into the mall or the street. One man reported receiving six copies as Christmas gifts.

I struggled against feelings of rancour and resentment.

From the United States the news was upbeat. There was no doubt among Little, Brown's senior people that they had a bestseller on their hands; the early reviews in the "trades" were raves. *Publisher's Weekly* called it "a smashing suspense story, and one that does not pander to the grosser tastes of our time." Advance orders from booksellers were pouring in. A first printing of seventeen thousand was bumped to twenty-five thousand, and on the eve of publication to thirty-five thousand – high for a novel, even by American standards.

Page proofs had been sent to, among others, a most extraordinary lady, Celia Summer, the manager of the Scribner's Book Store on Fifth Avenue in New York City. She is a diminutive woman with the quick precise energy of a bird and is something of a phenomenon among booksellers.

On publication day in the U.S. I was taken to meet her. She had two massive tables heaped with books at the entrance to the store. On one table was *The World According to Garp,* and on the other, *Act of God.* She greeted me as I entered the store by exclaiming, "There are two novels this season, *Garp* and *Act of God."*

A month before publication in the United States, Roger Donald, Little, Brown's senior editor, took me to dinner at a magnificent restaurant in midtown Manhattan. At dinner (uncharacteristically, according to his wife) he proposed a bet: "That *Act of God* will be on the New York *Times* bestseller list within three weeks of publication." Heady stuff. I went to my hotel room that night, shivering with excitement.

An author tour of the United States had been planned jointly by Bantam and Little, Brown. Before it was approved, Mark Jaffe decided, in effect, to examine the merchandise. In Toronto, he took me to dinner at the Westbury hotel. With us were Bantam's chief publicist, Esther Margolis, another Bantam official and Anna Porter, then head of Bantam-Seal.

It was an occasion. Jaffe was host and played the role in the grand manner. Learning that I particularly like white wine, he summoned the *somellier* and engaged him in an extended conversation. The result was a superb wine, chilling in a bucket beside my chair. The chef was called to the table and given detailed instructions. The food was extraordinary, the conversation was spirited and the wine flowed.

The desserts removed, Jaffe lighted a cigar, clinked his glass for attention and addressed himself to me. "Now Charles," he said, "I want you to tell us about yourself. Please do go on; that's why we're here."

I began awkwardly, saying that I felt like an actor taking a cue, and then, mostly responding to questions, filled them in on my background and talked about the book. Some time later, Jaffe turned to his publicist and said, "What do you think?" Without dropping their voices, they discussed me as though I wasn't there: my appearance, my ability to talk, my understanding of the media . . . The judgement: approved.

When the session finished, Porter and I walked out together. I said, "I feel like Miss North Dakota of 1977." She laughed and said, "Maybe that's not all bad."

A sudden discordant note intruded. In Roger Donald's office I was shown proofs of the proposed newspaper display ads. I flinched. "Roger," I said, "you're going to kill the book."

One of the proofs was of the quarter-page that would run on the New York *Times* Thursday book page on publication day. It would be a full page in the Sunday *Times* literary supplement the following weekend and in other newspapers across the country. It included a photograph of the wooden box in which the purported bones of Jesus had been placed after being excavated at Qumran. Above it, in bold type, was the headline:

IN THIS BOX IS A SECRET THAT COULD DESTROY YOUR FAITH!
DARE YOU OPEN IT?

I was shaken. "Don't you see what you're doing in this ad? It's as though you'd asked the best brains at your advertising agency to come up with a headline that will, in one stroke, alienate all your potential readers!"

"I don't follow," he said.

"The first line reads: 'In this box is a secret that could destroy your faith!' Obviously then, the book is intended for people who have faith. People who *don't* have faith are immediately turned off. There go your secular readers. But worse than that – read the headline again. 'In this box is a secret that could destroy your faith! *Dare you open it?*' The answer to that question by anyone who has faith is an immediate no. People are struggling to hold onto their faith. The last thing in the world they want to read is something that will destroy it. So now you've alienated your religious readers. As a deterrent to sales, it's a masterpiece."

"I have to agree," he said. "I don't like it either. I've said so. But it was written by our editorial chief. It's his baby and he thinks it's great."

"And look at the second ad," I said. It included my photograph, bearded as I was at the time, smiling and looking from the corners of my eyes with something not far from a leer. The headline read:

THIS MAN IS GOING TO DESTROY
THE LAST TABOO ON NATIONAL TV!

"What's *that* supposed to suggest?" I asked. "I get a mental picture of that dirty old man in the photograph opening his fly on the Johnny Carson show. And Roger, what in God's name does it have to do with the *book*?"

He promised to see what could be done about it but held out little hope. On the plane to Toronto I felt ill.

Two weeks later, I was back in Manhattan for an appearance on the *Today* show. Again, things went less than ideally.

I was scheduled for the 8:00-8:30 segment. As I waited to go on, I had observed intermittent spasms of frenetic activity, sudden runnings about and brief, ill-tempered conferences. Something was amiss. Suddenly, as I was gathering myself to go before the cameras, the door burst open and three black men were herded in, their topcoats being stripped from their backs even as they entered. A woman pressed an unwanted cup of coffee into my hands. "Some bubble-head," she explained, "overlooked the fact that it's the tenth anniversary of Martin Luther King Jr.'s assassination. There's going to be a change in plans." I would be moved to the 8:30-9:00 segment – did I mind? As she spoke, the three blacks were rushed by me out the door, straightening ties and patting hair as they went. A moment later I saw them on the monitor talking to Tom Brokaw about the dead hero.

I was scheduled to be interviewed by co-host Jane Pauley. It was the morning following the Academy Awards, and she had stayed up to watch the telecast, instead of doing her homework. As I was ushered onto the set during the commercial, she was flipping frantically through some notes and scanning the inside flap on the jacket of the book, too occupied to say hello. Suspended above our heads against the backdrop was an enormous blow-up of the wooden box in which the bones had been transported.

On cue, Pauley took the only way open to her and began the interview by saying, "Well now, Mr. . . . uh, Templeton, why don't you set the stage for us by telling us briefly the plot of your book . . . uh, *Act of God*?"

I did, but she seemed not to be listening, occupied as she was with surreptitious glances at her notes. We soon left the book. "I understand you're an atheist," she said.

I explained that, no, I wasn't an atheist but an agnostic, a very different thing. I really didn't want to get into it; we had only seven minutes and I wanted to promote the book. I'd come five hundred miles to do that.

"But you don't believe in God," she said, her face mirroring distaste.

"Nor do I disbelieve," I said. "I just don't know."

"But you were a preacher."

"Yes I was."

"Well then, let me ask you this: are you happy? How *can* you be?"

She was doing her twenty-four-karat-earnest bit, looking deeply into my eyes. I looked back into hers for a moment, irritated, tempted to say, "You silly girl – what in God's name has believing in God got to do with being happy?" I restrained myself and said the same thing in a more judicious way. She persisted nonetheless.

Quickly, the seven minutes were gone and, again on the *Today* show, I hadn't talked about my book. As I emerged from removing my make-up, a man, presumably the producer, was talking animatedly to Pauley. "And you never even referred to the blow-up of the goddamn box, for Chrissake!"

I toured most of the eastern United States, surprised at the number of fundamentalist Christians who interviewed me on all the news media. I was well treated, driven from place to place in chauffeured limousines and quartered in the best hotels. Then, on to the United Kingdom – London to Manchester, York, Leeds, Edinburgh, Glasgow and Dublin. By North American standards, their radio and television studios are antiquated and fusty, and some of the feigned upper-class accents get close to precious, but everything was accomplished in that oddly fumbling British way that is somehow marvellously efficient. My enjoyment was enhanced by the fact that the public-relations people at Michael Joseph quartered me in London at the Savoy hotel and that I was greeted by a quarter-page article in the *Times*.

In Canada I was interviewed mostly about myself. In the United States I was queried mostly about being an agnostic. In the

United Kingdom I was questioned on the book. As I recall it, not one interviewer in the UK raised the fact that I had left the ministry other than as a bit of biographical background – which may have been a lapse on their part but was welcomed by me. The reviews across the British Isles were excellent, with exceptions of course. I remember one especially that sounded almost plaintive. It ended, "Why, after all that Mother Church has endured in recent years, must she now suffer this; one of her princes painted as a murderer? One wishes that Mr. Templeton, with his vivid imagination and his evident familiarity with matters ecclesiastical, had put his pen to better use."

The Third Temptation followed. Of all my novels it was the least successful. I was dealing with subject matter close to me and thrashed about in the material for eighteen months, taking a dozen wrong directions. Three days after completing the final draft, I came apart, collapsing one morning on the living-room floor. There followed time in bed under sedation, and it was not until the end of the summer that I was entirely myself again.

Reviewers praised the book, but the public was not enthused. It made the bestseller list but only just and only for a week or two.

Undoubtedly, some of my motivations were wrong. Resentful after the hostile reception given to *Act of God* by Canadian reviewers, I was determined to demonstrate how well I could write. The book was crafted, not merely to tell a story and in the doing to cast light on human experience, but to enable me to say, "So there!" What a pointless and futile exercise when there are not half a dozen legitimate critics in all of Canada.

I had set out to produce the definitive novel about a mass evangelist, a subject about which I have some knowledge. It needed to be written but hadn't been. Sinclair Lewis' *Elmer Gantry,* the best of many books on the subject, presents a man who is an evangelist, but for all Lewis' extraordinarily detailed research and despite his undoubted skills, *Elmer Gantry* is essentially about a scoundrel who happens to be an evangelist. He could as easily have been a politician or a salesman. The smell and the feel of the fundamentalist faith Lewis describes is convincing only to the uninitiated.

There was only moderate interest in *The Third Temptation* by American publishers. William Morrow paid me an advance after

Harvey Ginsberg, a senior editor, insisted that it could be "an important book," but only if it underwent major revisions. Ginsberg had been Saul Bellow's editor, and the opportunity to work with him intrigued me. I spent a day with him at Morrow's New York offices. He is a wise editor and an enormously stimulating man, and I returned to Toronto keen to press forward. But I had cooled to the book and, after a number of false starts, decided to postpone the reworking until another day, returning the advance I'd been paid.

II

When it was widely publicized that the motion picture version of *The Kidnapping of the President* had been sold to NBC-TV for $2.4 million, there were congratulations from all sides and an occasional jealous gibe from friends. When I told them that not a penny of the revenue would accrue to me but would go to the producer, there was open incredulity. It was none the less true.

I was merely debunking one of the myths about the rewards to an author when his book is made into a motion picture. There are payments, of course, but usually the amounts involved are not large. More often than not — unless the film is a major production — they do not amount to a third of the royalties received from the book. Moreover, as the author soon learns, the sale to a motion-picture company does not necessarily mean that a film will be made. Or that, having been made, it will ever be released. Indeed, the likelihood is that it will not.

The late 1970s was a boom time in Canada for the sale of novels to the movies. Stimulated by the largesse available from the Canadian Film Development Corporation, many eager and often amateur film-makers bought options on "properties," all envisioning themselves as incipient Norman Jewisons or Claude Jutras.

The CFDC had been set up by the Liberal government to encourage the creation of a Canadian film industry through the provision of funds. Usually, the money was provided only after certain conditions were met. A Canadian film-maker was permitted to use certain American "stars" of varying magnitude (thus presumably helping the box office), but to ensure that home-grown talent was employed, points were credited for the use of Canadian producers, directors, actors, chief cameramen, art directors and so on. Despite the benefits that flowed from the system, it tended to encourage mediocrity and hypocrisy: the mediocre, whose films lacked the professionalism needed to attract a distributor; the hypocritical, who disguised their Canadian locations with such shoddy devices as the faking of street signs and settings to suggest exotic locales.

In the sale of a book to a film company the author sells not the rights but "an option to buy the film rights." If, when the option expires, the film is not underway, the purchaser must pay a specified sum to renew the option; otherwise the author gets his or her rights back and keeps the money. (An author may thus sell an option a number of times.) If, however, the film is going forward, two further payments are made: one on "the first day of principal shooting" and another on "the final day of principal shooting." Usually, that's the end of it.

Sometimes, the author negotiates a further agreement: to receive a small percentage of the "producer's net" – the surplus left when all the bills have been paid. The likelihood of receiving money from this source is, however, roughly equivalent to winning a lottery. Nine in ten Canadian films don't recover their "nut," as it is called, and many of those that do seem never to show a profit. In Hollywood, profits are commonly siphoned off to relatives or friends of the producer who, with a surplus in sight, adds them to the payroll. It has been said there is more creative thinking done in this area than in the making of most films.

Kidnapping had not yet been published when I received an offer from John Vidette of Dermet Productions Ltd., a Canadian company. I found myself immersed in the frenetic optimism and intermittent despair that seems to be the habitat of most independent film-makers. Vidette informed me that he had "connections" with many of the "big movers in the business," was known to "top people in the majors" and had access to "important money." It was all very exhilarating to a neophyte.

But somehow the deals never got signed, the hot prospects cooled, the money didn't materialize. Vidette seemed immobilized by an odd inertia that kept him from following up on lively opportunities in Hollywood and caused him to hold at arm's length offers of help. The year passed with nothing concrete happening and on the due date the option was renewed.

The second year was almost spent when there was sudden hope. A bona fide Hollywood producer with an impressive track record, Marty Rackin of Martin Rackin Productions, a subsidiary of Metro-Goldwyn-Mayer, read the book and was enthusiastic about its potential. He tried to negotiate an arrangement with Vidette but got only vague responses. Frustrated, he flew to Toronto to seek my intervention. I pressed the matter with Vidette. He had nothing tangible in prospect, but, with a strange obduracy, was unwilling to join forces with Rackin. It seemed that he saw *Kidnapping* as a chance to make a name for himself in the film business and was unwilling to share what he regarded as his prize. Rackin finally went off to other projects.

Over the next three years there were a number of approaches, none of which came to fruition. Finally, a young Toronto man, George Mendeluk, came to see me, wanting to purchase an option to *Act of God*. When I told him it had been sold, he took a one-year option on *Kidnapping*.

I was certain he would never produce the picture and viewed the transaction only as found money. I was agreeably surprised when he came up with a screenplay, found financial backing in Calgary and proceeded to cast the film. The lead players were all American with the exception of William Shatner – Hal Holbrook, Van Johnson and Ava Gardner. The locale of the kidnapping was changed from Times Square in New York to Nathan Phillips Square in Toronto, and the shooting was done in three locations, in Mexico, Los Angeles and Toronto. Equally important, a deal was struck with an international distributor guaranteeing exposure around the world. I was impressed.

Unfortunately, I didn't like the picture. The performances by Johnson and the aging Ava Gardner verged on the pathetic. The dialogue was unreal. The opening scenes pandered to the desire for violence now common in films and were positively grisly.

The film opened in New York City to mixed reviews and then came to Toronto. I was invited to a private screening but couldn't muster the courage to go. I feigned another engagement and sent Anna Porter in my place. Anna had been a great help to me in the preparation of my books, and I had confidence in her judgement. Moreover, she had a stake in the film as president of Bantam-Seal.

She had published a special paperback edition of *Kidnapping* to coincide with the release of the movie in Canada; she reported the following morning, a note of surprise in her voice, "Charles, it's not bad. Really. About six on a scale of one to ten."

I saw it at an advance screening and sat squirming in my seat at some of the scenes. A reception was held at Toronto City Hall prior to a première at the Sheraton Centre theatre, but I couldn't bear to watch it and slipped from the theatre with Madeleine to go to dinner. Nor have I watched any of the four performances on television.

For all that, I will confess to a sense of excitement at standing on Broadway in New York City looking up at the marquee advertising the film and at receiving reviews in various languages from around the world.

I sold options to *Act of God* five times. It has yet to be made into a film.

The first offer was from Jalor Productions, an independent American company headed by the legendary Fred Coe. In the early years of American television Coe was the producer of *Playhouse 90,* and he had gone on to produce films and Broadway plays.

Four of us gathered for lunch at the Harvard Club: Cushman, Fred Coe, Paul Jacobson, Coe's "money man," and I. It was a festive meal. As we talked about casting and about the problems of translating the story to film, my excitement mounted. Coe showed a sensitivity and an inventive imagination that guaranteed the movie would not be misbegotten. Champagne was ordered and toasts were made all around.

Within the month there was word from a dismayed Cushman. "They've backed out. Someone has convinced them that there will be a negative reaction from the Catholic church and it will hurt the box office. They're afraid that, after the theatre run, the networks won't pick it up. And these days, everybody counts on the television money. We can sue," he said, "we've got a signed deal letter, but I don't think we want to do that. . . ."

While we were negotiating with Coe, there had been persistent interest by a Canadian producer, Stephen Young, an actor who appeared to be in an association with Garth Drabinsky, the Toronto lawyer who was quickly becoming a successful theatre and film entrepreneur. Cushman began negotiations with Drabinsky and soon concluded a deal. A few weeks later I received a call from Cushman. "I've had a long wire from Drabinsky," he said, outrage in his voice. "He wants out."

"John," I said. "I can't believe this. Every detail has been agreed to. What's the problem?"

"He's asking us to indemnify him against any lawsuit that might eventuate."

It is standard practice for an author to protect a publisher or a film-maker against a lawsuit charging libel or an invasion of privacy, inasmuch as the publisher can't possibly know if the writer has modelled his or her characters on people who might recognize themselves, take umbrage and sue.

"But he wants more than the usual indemnification," John said. "He wants us to indemnify him against *any* lawsuit of *any* kind from any group who mightn't like the book."

"You mean, if some little holy-roller sect in the hills of Kentucky takes offence, or if a publicity-seeking television evangelist institutes a nuisance suit, I'd be responsible for the entire cost of the production or for any costs growing out of delays?"

"That's the thrust of it," Cushman said. "In all my years in the business I've never heard of such a thing. Nor have our people out on the coast. They think it's a device, for whatever their reasons, to back out."

I won't detail here the weird variety of my experiences in the wacky world of film-making. I know many men and women in that world and some of them are extraordinarily talented. But it has been my observation that the proportion of oddballs is greater there than in any profession I know of. It is a bizarre business, yes; it is also a genuine art form, and unlike any other.

Even as "a camel is a horse designed by a committee," a motion picture is the end product of the efforts of hundreds of people. That a director can fuse a coherent (and occasionally magnificent) entity from so many different parts, and that an actor can create and maintain a fully integrated person despite hundreds of brief "takes," is little short of astonishing. To know at first hand something of the incredibly complex process by which a book is translated into a motion picture is to learn respect for the film-maker. That there are dozens of pretenders to every artist – men and women who have learned the rudiments but are incapable of transcending them – only increases your admiration for the gifted individual who can comprehend human emotions and great ideas and, despite the difficulties, transfer them to film.

Etcetera Etcetera

ETCETERA ETCETERA

"**W**hich of your various jobs have you enjoyed most?" It's an inevitable question whenever I'm interviewed – and impossible to answer. I've enjoyed them all. (I feel about them somewhat as the mother did who was asked which of her children she loved most. She replied, "The one who's away until he's home. The one who's sick until she's well.") I have enjoyed whatever I was doing when I was doing it.

I stated in the foreword that this book would not occupy itself with a plumbing of my motives or a rummaging about in my psyche. None the less, it is almost mandatory that I speak briefly to what is perceived to be in me a lack of constancy, a tendency to be a vocational butterfly. As will be evident from the preceding pages, I changed jobs, not because I lost interest in what I was doing and needed another challenge; the changes resulted from my being presented with a larger opportunity. I do not, as it may appear, suffer from a vocational itch that requires frequent scratching. After all, I was in the ministry almost twenty years, appeared on *Dialogue* five days a week for eighteen years and have worked as a performer or producer in television for thirty years – longer, I think, than any other Canadian. As well, I have written eight books and am at work on another.

Preparing a response to the frequent question, I have settled on an analogy. My various "careers" are not like beads on a table, each separate and solitary; rather, they are like beads on a string, the common thread being that I am essentially a communicator. Whether at the drawing board or on a platform, whether in the electronic or print media, whether before the cameras or behind them, I have continually sought to communicate ideas and viewpoints that have seemed important to me. If I have a compulsion, it is the need, being caught up in an idea, to communicate it to others by such means as are available.

There have been two principal wellsprings from which my convictions have flowed: a religious philosophy informed by, among others, Jesus of Nazareth, Albert Schweitzer and Mohandas Gandhi; and a political disposition toward traditional liberalism, a philosophy that sees society as in need of reform and seeks to effect the necessary changes through law – as few laws as possible but as many as necessary.

Do I sometimes, in retrospect, wish I had stayed with one of my interests, had persevered, say, in politics or as a print journalist? Yes, sometimes. But were I to do it again, I would probably follow the paths by which I have gone. I recognize the value of an unswerving commitment; some goals are achieved only by a long-term dedication to them. But single-mindedness has its disadvantages, too. Its very intensity makes forfeit other options.

Rightly or wrongly, I am convinced that, had I remained active in politics, I would have become premier of Ontario. But would that have been better than what did happen? Do I prefer Bill Davis' life to the one I live? The answer is an unhesitant no. (Put the question to Bill Davis and I have no doubt that his answer would be the same as mine.) I don't argue that one way or the other is better, I contend merely that the path I have chosen has yielded a rich, full and happy life, a life that has been eventful and rewarding, and most of the time, exciting. It has kept my eyes on tomorrow and has made retirement, not a goal to be looked forward to, but a time to be postponed indefinitely.

I admire the man or woman who perseveres, but it has been my observation that many continue in what they do mostly because they are afraid or don't know how to change direction. They feel trapped. They are captives of their fear, and intimidated by a concern for security; so they spend their lives at jobs that bore and diminish them. It is folly to spend your working life toiling at something you dislike or resent. Men and women who dislike what they do should quiet their fears and seek out a vocation that will satisfy as well as reward them. I don't say this glibly. Having changed directions many times, and having suffered trepidation in the doing of it, I can assert from experience that the difficulties are never so great as imagined.

Do I have regrets? Of course. Many. Most of them are in the realm of personal relationships, but they are not what this book is about. I have often been so immersed in what I am doing that I have neglected friendships, sometimes even my family. If I have been successful in what I have done it has usually been because all my energies have gone into the work at hand. I know nothing about "hours of business" — for me they have been all my waking hours. As does everyone in the news media, I receive dozens of invitations to what may loosely be described as social functions; I rarely accept. Madeleine and I seldom go to parties and, other than for our children, seldom give them. Undoubtedly we miss much in so doing, but we prefer it the way it is. Indeed, we rejoice in it.

I have sometimes wondered why I work with such single-mindedness. It is not for the financial rewards — I have never been much interested in the accumulation of money — nor is it primarily for notoriety. There is a paradox here: I have lived much of my life in the limelight but I am uncomfortable in public and almost reclusive in daily life. I have never sought power, except in politics, where power is the name of the game. In business I have not set my sights on the top job and then manoeuvred to get it. I have given myself to the task at hand and the rest has fallen into place. If there has been one dominant drive it has been a deep need for approval. For a while I considered calling this book *Hey Dad, look at me!*

What will I do next? I am by no means sure. I will certainly continue to broadcast. I will maintain an active interest in politics. It is, I think, the most interesting activity in which people engage, and probably, despite the trivializing of it by small men and the exploiting of it by the strong, the most important. I will continue to work as an amateur inventor. It is more than a hobby with me — it is akin to exploring. It is the seeking out of places where no other mind has been and it yields all the excitement of a discovery. I will continue to draw, and intend to return to sculpting, something I have neglected for twenty years. The only activity I will not return to is the Christian ministry; I remain a reverent agnostic.

I will surely continue to write. It is the most rewarding and the most difficult of the tasks I have put my hand to. The writer never achieves the summit, never lacks for a challenge and is surrounded by opportunity. The condition of the writer is one of discontented contentment; the personal satisfactions are profound; the discouragements are abyssal. With seven books behind me (eight, including a novel, *Mr. Nobody,* that no one wished to publish), I am beginning to learn to write. I may yet write a good novel; I shall certainly try.